American Council on the Teaching of Foreign Languages

The Integrated Performance Assessment: Twenty Years and Counting

Francis John Troyan, Ph.D., The Ohio State University

Bonnie Adair-Hauck, Ph.D., World Language Consultant

Eileen W. Glisan, Ph.D., Professor Emerita, Indiana University of Pennsylvania

The American Council on the Teaching of Foreign Languages
1001 North Fairfax Street, Suite 200
Alexandria, VA 22314

Graphic Design by Paintbox Creative, LLC

ISBN: 978-1-9425448-6-9

Acknowledgements

We would like to thank the American Council on the Teaching of Foreign Languages, under the leadership of Howie Berman, Executive Director, as well as Joe Vallina, Director of Marketing and Membership, and Dr. Meg Malone, Director of Assessment, for supporting this third edition of the IPA manual. We thank Dr. Jason Martel, Middlebury Institute of International Studies at Monterey, for his insightful and supportive preface to this edition. We are also grateful to Deborah Kennedy of Key Words for copyediting support and Emily Christenson of Paintbox Creative for design and layout. We are deeply indebted to the original Standards Assessment Design Project Task Force, who designed the IPA:

Elvira Swender, ACTFL, Project Director
S. Paul Sandrock, ACTFL (formerly Wisconsin Department of Instruction), Project Coordinator
Bonnie Adair-Hauck, University of Pittsburgh (PA)
Eileen W. Glisan, Indiana University of Pennsylvania
Keiko Koda, Carnegie Mellon University, Pittsburgh, PA
Michael Stewart, Standard & Poor's, New York, NY

We acknowledge the contributions of Everett Kline of the Center on Learning, Assessment, and School Structure [CLASS] (Pennington, NJ), and Greg Duncan, InterPrep, Inc., Marietta, GA, who helped shape the original IPA design.

The following individuals played a pivotal role in the field testing of the early versions of the IPA:

Pilot Site Coordinators
Martha G. Abbott, Fairfax County Public Schools, VA
Peggy Boyles, Putnam City Schools, OK
Donna Clementi, Appleton West High School, WI
Deborah Lindsay, Greater Albany School District, OR
Frank Mulhern, Wallingford-Swarthmore School District, PA
Kathleen Riordan, Springfield Public Schools, MA

Teachers/Assessment Fellows at Pilot Sites
Rosa Alvaro-Alves, Springfield Public Schools, MA
Linda Bahr, Greater Albany School District, OR
Carolyn Carroll, Fairfax County Public Schools, VA
Christine Carroll, Putnam City Schools, OK
Kathy Ceman, Butte des Morts Elementary, WI
Donna Clementi, Appleton West High School, WI
Karin Cochran, Jesuit High School, OR
Michele de Cruz-Sainz, Wallingford-Swarthmore School District, PA
Margaret Draheim, Appleton East High School, WI

Cathy Etheridge, Appleton East High School, WI
Carmen Felix-Fournier, Springfield Public Schools, MA
Catherine Field, Greater Albany School District, OR
Stephen Flesher, Beaverton Public Schools, OR
Nancy Gadbois, Springfield Public Schools, MA
Frederic Gautzsch, Wallingford-Swarthmore School District, PA
Susana Gorski, Nicolet Elementary School, WI
Susan Harding, Putnam City Schools, OK
Heidi Helmich, Madison Middle School, WI
Mei-Ju Hwang, Springfield Public Schools, MA
Betty Ivich, Putnam City Schools, OK
Michael Kraus, Putnam City Schools, OK
Irmgard Langacker, Wallingford-Swarthmore School District, PA
Dorothy Lavigne, Wallingford-Swarthmore School District, PA
Deborah Lindsay, Greater Albany School District, PA
Conrad Lower, Wallingford-Swarthmore School District, PA
Linda S. Meyer, Appleton North High School, WI
Paula J. Meyer, Appleton North High School, WI
Linda Moore, Putnam City Schools, OK
Frank Mulhern, Wallingford-Swarthmore School District, PA
Rita Oleksak, Springfield Public Schools, MA
Frances Pettigrew, Fairfax County Public Schools, VA
Rebecca Rowton, Rollingwood Elementary School, OK
Ann Smith, Jesuit High School, OR
Dee Dee Stafford, Putnam City Schools, OK
Adam Stryker, Fairfax County Public Schools, VA
Catherine Thurber, Tigard High School, OR
Ghislaine Tulou, Fairfax County Public Schools, VA
Carter Vaden, Fairfax County Public Schools, VA
Sally Ziebell, Putnam City Schools, OK

Students of
Albany High School, Albany, OR
Appleton Area Public Schools, WI
Beaverton Public Schools, OR
Casco Bay High School, Portland, ME
Fairfax County Public Schools, VA
Franklin Regional High School, Murrysville, PA
Putnam City Public Schools, OK
Public Schools of Springfield, MA
Wallington-Swarthmore Schools, PA

This edition would not have been possible without the contributions of the following individuals:

Dr. Myriam Abdel-Malek

Mary Jo Adams

Naysa Altmeyer

Dr. Mark A. Darhower

Daniel S. Ferguson

Na Lu-Hogan

Dr. Elizabeth Kautz

Elizabeth Lake

Tammy Lyons

Lauren Miranda

Nicole Naditz

Iya Nemastil

Margaret Newcomb

José Pan

Sarah Peceny

Dr. Eva Rodrigues-González

Dr. Helena Ruf

Dr. Michele Schreiner

Dr. Tracy Seiler

Kathleen Shelton

Dr. Dawn Smith-Sherwood

Ryan Wertz

We would like to extend a special thanks to Jesse Carnevali, World Language Coordinator at Franklin Regional High School, Murrysville, PA, for the enormous effort and contribution that he made to Chapter 4, Linking IPA and Instruction: A Transformative Tool for Backward Design and Formative Instructional Practices.

Finally, we are grateful to the following professionals who reviewed earlier versions of this book and provided many valuable suggestions and insights:

Dr. Peter Swanson, United States Air Force Academy

Dr. Gabriela Zapata, University of Nottingham, UK

Dr. Isabel Espino de Valdivia, retired Spanish teacher, Pittsburgh Public Schools

Table of Contents

Preface

Jason Martel, Ph.D.
Associate Professor and Program Chair, TESOL/TFL
Middlebury Institute of International Studies at Monterey

When it was launched 20 years ago, ACTFL's Integrated Performance Assessment (IPA) project had three primary goals: (1) "to develop an assessment instrument that would measure students' progress towards the [standards];" (2) "to conduct preliminary research on the effectiveness of this assessment instrument in measuring students' progress towards achieving the standards and the feasibility of implementing this type of assessment in a typical classroom situation;" and (3) "to use the assessment prototype as a catalyst for curricular and pedagogical reform" (Adair-Hauck et al., 2006, p. 363). I think it's evident that these goals have been successfully met. The IPA's design specifications have been clearly established and continue to undergo refinement. Public examples of effective IPAs across a range of languages and levels abound, such as those available on the Virtual Assessment Center website maintained by the Center for Advanced Research on Second Language Acquisition (CARLA) at the University of Minnesota (see https://carla. umn.edu/assessment/vac/CreateUnit/unit_examples.html). There is also a steady stream of scholarship on the IPA that explores its effectiveness through a variety of lenses, including student, teacher, and teacher educator voices. I have conducted some of this research myself (for example, Martel, 2018, 2019; Martel & Bailey, 2016), motivated by my deep interest in the IPA. In addition, the IPA continues to serve as a tool for helping teachers refine their understanding of standards-based curriculum design. As Wiggins wisely said, "Assessment reform is, I think, the key to long-lasting school reform; what we assess is what people pay attention to" (Annenberg Learner, n.d.). In my own experience as a language program administrator, implementing the IPA helped me ensure the central role of communication in my program's curriculum and establish a common vocabulary for discussing effective teaching strategies with my colleagues. The present manual is thus a testament to the IPA project's important achievements, as well as a springboard for renewed interest in this cutting-edge curriculum design and assessment framework.

The IPA's staying power can be attributed to several key features. First, as noted above, it puts communication front and center in language education. It reminds us that our primary goal as language teachers is to help our students make sense of culture-rich texts, engage in dynamic conversations with others, and deliver audience-aware messages in authentic genres. As such, the IPA helps us push against one of the core problems that has consistently plagued language education, namely the treatment of language as an object of study rather than a subject for meaningful exchange (Tedick & Walker, 1994). Second, the IPA is not simply a test; rather, it represents a global framework for language curriculum design. Indeed, when we say "the IPA," we're often referring to its clustered summative version, administered at the end of a thematic unit. However, the IPA represents much more: As a framework, it facilitates a backward design approach to curriculum creation and alignment, meaning that the curriculum leading up to a test robustly prepares students for success on that test (Sultana, 2018; Wiggins & McTighe, 2005). Third, the IPA provides space for foreign language teachers to exert agency within a common framework. As Gadbois said, "The IPA is not etched in stone, and that's one of the attractions of it; it gives me freedom to take what's suggested in the model but then improvise on my own" (Annenberg Learner, n.d.). To give a couple of examples, teachers get to choose their own authentic texts based on their unit themes and decide how much time students have to prepare presentational tasks. Such flexibility is pivotal, as it means that the IPA is localizable into myriad teaching contexts. Benefitting from this flexibility, I experimented myself with a five-task version of the IPA; that is, one that includes interpretive reading, interpretive listening, interpersonal speaking, presentational reading, and presentational writing (Martel & Bailey, 2016). Fourth, the IPA aligns with innovative approaches to language curriculum design, such as content-based instruction (CBI), which is defined as "a curricular and instructional approach in which nonlinguistic content is taught to students through the medium of a language that they are learning as a second, heritage, indigenous, or foreign language" (Tedick & Cammarata, 2012, p. S28). Recently, I argued that there are four benefits to implementing CBI in foreign language education: (1) it facilitates proficiency development; (2) it has the potential to foster improved language learning outcomes; (3) it allows for incorporating critical thinking; and (4) it provides opportunities for addressing social justice issues (Martel, 2022). The IPA fits seamlessly into content-based thematic unit planning and supports these four categories in exciting ways; in fact, there is no IPA without engaging, thoughtful content.

Building on these characteristics, the authors of this manual have introduced a slate of exciting improvements to the IPA. The changes are listed in detail in subsequent pages, so here I'll highlight a few that stand out to me. For starters, I admire the authors' commitment to integrating diversity, equity, and inclusion into the framework. It's exciting to see sample IPAs on themes ranging from "social media and bullying" to "language and racial ideologies." In truth, I don't see how it's possible these days to address any theme in a language class without exploring underlying social inequities (Ennser-Kananen, 2016). Next, I appreciate the authors' multimodal approach to updating the comprehension guides and rubrics. According to Paesani, Allen, and Dupuy (2016), "modern communication practices, particularly those that are technologically enhanced, combine text with image, movement, hypertext, or sound" and "the study of multimodality involves looking at [a text's] components and how they

interact to convey meaning" (p. 14). To this end, there is a new comprehension guide devoted specifically to viewing, and the construct "impact of multimodal presentations" has been added to the presentational communication rubric. Lastly, I am thrilled about the new chapter on using the IPA in upper-level language courses, which is aimed at erasing the entrenched language/literature divide (Paesani & Allen, 2012). This chapter is powerful in that it helps us understand that no matter what level or content area we teach, we are all language teachers (Zwiers, 2013). As a proponent of CBI, I appreciate the guiding principle from scholars at Georgetown University that reads "content from the beginning, language to the end" (Eigler, 2001). The IPA can help us realize this aspiration to balance at both ends of the spectrum by providing a meaningful context to beginning-level learners and highlighting form-meaning connections with Advanced-level learners.

In conclusion, I am thrilled about this updated manual, *The Integrated Performance Assessment: Twenty Years and Counting*, on multiple levels. As a practicing language teacher, I use the IPA to inform my curriculum design on a day-to-day basis because it helps me implement standards-based instruction. I will look to this new manual for inspiration when creating classroom activities and unit-concluding summative assessments. As a language teacher educator, I will continue to employ the IPA as a key feature of my practice-based methods courses (Glisan & Donato, 2017, 2021; Troyan et al, 2013). One of my favorite things to do is to introduce teacher candidates across a variety of contexts to the IPA; it is a tool that any language teacher can use to improve their curriculum, whether they're teaching German in Wisconsin or English in Japan. I am grateful to the authors of this manual and the engineers of the IPA project for their efforts, and I am excited to witness the continued success of the IPA in the next ten years and beyond.

What's New in the Third Edition of the Integrated Performance Assessment Manual?

The third edition of the IPA Manual, *The Integrated Performance Assessment: Twenty Years and Counting*, builds upon the original framework presented to guide instructors in designing and implementing this cutting-edge assessment into their world language classrooms. As in the second edition, the revised manual provides a thorough description of the Integrated Performance Assessment (IPA) with step-by-step procedures for implementing the assessment, including strategies for modeling and providing feedback to learners. The need for the IPA is explained using support from a research base that has grown considerably over the past decade.

Since its inception in 1997, the IPA has been embraced by instructors at various levels of instruction as well as by foreign language education researchers. The interest in the IPA has grown from the initial pilot group of teachers in 1999 to its current use in elementary, secondary, and post-secondary settings as well as in several states as a state-level assessment (see Chapter 8). Since the publication of the second edition, interest in the IPA has increased even more, not only from instructors at all levels, including those at the post-secondary level, but also from researchers who have conducted many investigations into this assessment (see Chapter 3). Given the current expanded scope of the IPA and the volume of research on it, the impetus for producing a third edition of the manual arose from a need to disseminate findings from research conducted on the IPA since 2013; the potential of the IPA as a vehicle for enacting instruction and assessment for diversity, equity, and inclusion in the world language classroom; the role that the IPA has to play at the post-secondary level in bridging the traditional divide between language and literature; a new set of model IPAs created by instructors who have implemented the assessment across proficiency levels and languages; an expanded interpretive mode comprehension guide to address more specifically the assessment of interpretive viewing and listening; revised rubrics with tools to assist instructors in more easily rating learner performance across the three modes of communication; and ways in which the IPA continues to have an impact on teacher perceptions, classroom instruction, and learning.

The reader will find the following new elements in the third edition:

1. Discussion of how the IPA can serve as a vehicle for instruction and assessment for diversity, equity, and inclusion in the world language classroom

2. Expansion of the Interpretive Mode Comprehension Guide Template into three separate templates, each of which addresses one modality: viewing, listening, reading (Chapter 2 and Appendices D-1, D-2, and D-3)

3. Presentation of formative instructional practices (FIP) and their connection to the IPA, specifically highlighting the central role that feedback plays in the IPA framework and the focus on learners with special needs (Chapters 4 and 5)

4. A new chapter on transforming the post-secondary literature class with the IPA, including voices of college-level learners who have experienced the IPA (Chapter 7)

5. In the interpersonal rubrics, the addition of the criterion *intercultural communication: interact* to assess learners' ability to interact with others using appropriate cultural norms (Chapter 2 and Appendix F-2)

6. In the presentational rubrics, division of *impact* into the categories *impact of written/oral presentations* and *impact of multimodal presentations* to provide greater flexibility in the types of presentations learners may be asked to design (Chapter 2 and Appendix F-3)

7. Rubric conversion tables to accompany each set of rubrics as a tool to assist instructors in converting raw rubric scores to percentages that can be used to assign grades for the IPA (Chapter 2 and Appendices F-1, F-2, and F-3)

8. New model IPAs in Arabic, Chinese, French, German, Japanese, and Spanish, with a series of IPAs at the Novice,

Intermediate, Intermediate-High, and Advanced levels in Spanish (Chapter 6)

The following elements of the second edition have been significantly expanded:

1. Justification of the need for the IPA into the future to promote learner progress in the goal areas of the World-Readiness Standards for Language Learning (National Standards Collaborative Board, 2015) and across the proficiency continuum while connecting instruction and assessment seamlessly (Chapter 1)

2. Presentation and discussion of the wealth of research that has been conducted on the IPA over the past decade (Chapter 3)

3. Discussion of how to prepare learners for IPA interpretive, interpersonal, and presentational tasks and how to link instruction and assessment (Chapter 4)

4. Discussion of strategies for offering modeling and feedback to learners on their performance (Chapter 5)

5. Description of the impact that the IPA continues to have on instructor perceptions, classroom instruction, and learning (Chapter 8)

The Integrated Performance Assessment: Twenty Years and Counting is designed for K-16 world language instructors who are interested in learning how to implement the IPA in their classrooms, as well as K-16 world language instructors who *already* implement the IPA in their classrooms and want to learn more. In-service teachers might use this manual for purposes of professional development, particularly along with an IPA workshop, or for teacher study groups such as lesson study. In addition, methods instructors can use it to introduce the IPA to their K-12 world language teacher candidates and/or post-secondary teaching assistants, including as a tool in a field experience where teacher candidates are learning to conduct performance assessments. Undoubtedly, the third edition can be effectively used in concert with other language education volumes such as *Enacting the Work of Language Instruction: High-Leverage Teaching Practices, vols. 1 and 2* (Glisan & Donato, 2017, 2021); *Words and Actions: Teaching Languages Through the Lens of Social Justice* (Glynn et al., 2018); and *Common Ground: Second Language Acquisition Theory Goes to the Classroom* (Henshaw & Hawkins, 2022). The manual might also be used by faculty who wish to use the IPA as a tool for planning curriculum and/or for establishing the IPA as a district- or state-wide assessment. Researchers will find many ideas in this edition for conducting further research on the assessment. Further, the IPA can be integrated within K-16 programs seeking to develop, implement, and promote multilingualism by supporting learners in attaining the Seal of Biliteracy (Davin & Heineke, 2022). In sum, this third edition will be a valuable resource to all world language educators who are in search of an innovative strategy for blending instruction and assessment in a seamless fashion.

Chapter 1

The Need for the Integrated Performance Assessment Into the Future

Since the original Integrated Performance Assessment (IPA) project (1999-2003), the subsequent publication of the first IPA Manual (Glisan et al., 2003) and report of the IPA pilot study (Adair-Hauck et al., 2006), the extensive implementation of the IPA has prompted a body of classroom-based research and materials development. The second edition, *Implementing Integrated Performance Assessment* (Adair-Hauck, Glisan, & Troyan, 2013), provided an update based on the first ten years of IPA research and practice and introduced a detailed account of the role of modeling and feedback in the IPA together with sample IPAs from the field at proficiency levels from Novice to Advanced. Given the growing interest in the use of the IPA, the research that has been conducted since the 2013 edition, and the increased attention to diversity, equity, and inclusion in world language education, this third edition, *The Integrated Performance Assessment: Twenty Years and Counting*, is intended to take the work of the IPA through the next ten years and beyond.

This chapter outlines the ongoing need for the IPA, the history of its initial development, and its relationship to the World-Readiness Standards for Language Learning (National Standards Collaborative Board, 2015), the ACTFL Proficiency Guidelines (ACTFL, 2012b), the ACTFL Performance Descriptors for Language Learners (ACTFL, 2012a), the NCSSFL-ACTFL Can-Do Statements (ACTFL, 2017), and high-leverage teaching practices (Glisan & Donato, 2017, 2021). Further, the chapter explores the potential of the IPA as a vehicle for enacting instruction and assessment for diversity, equity, and inclusion in the world language classroom. Finally, through a focus on formative instructional practices (FIP), it integrates concepts from Special Education to build a bridge between fields.

The World-Readiness Standards for Learning Languages (Standards), first developed through the National Standards in Foreign Language Education Project in 1996 and expanded in 1999 and 2006, provide a vision for language learning based on assumptions regarding the role of linguistic and cultural competence in the global community, the circumstances under which learners can be successful in acquiring this competence, and the place of language and culture education within the core curriculum (National Standards Collaborative Board, 2015). To this end, the Standards offer:

- A vision for the future of language and culture education;
- A rationale for the inclusion of all learners in language study;
- Realistic expectations for learner performance over an extended sequence of language study and at benchmark points (grades 4, 8, 12, 16);
- A framework for development of state and local standards; and
- Innovative ways of implementing instructional resources.

The Standards (See Appendix A) feature five goal areas, known as the Five Cs of Language Education, which provide a rationale for language education: Communication, Cultures, Connections, Comparisons, and Communities. Each goal area delineates one to three content standards that describe the knowledge and skills that learners should demonstrate as a result of their language study. The Standards re-conceptualized several traditional aspects of language study by

1. Broadening of the definition of the content of the language curriculum to include not only the language system and cultural knowledge but also other subject areas, critical thinking skills, learning strategies, communication strategies, and technology

2. Depicting communication in terms of three modes—interpersonal, interpretive, presentational—that place primary emphasis on the context and purpose of meaningful communication

3. Presenting an anthropological view of culture based on the relationships between and among cultural products,

cultural practices, and cultural perspectives or attitudes and values.

The initial development of the IPA occurred as a result of the call for an assessment that could be used to assess learners' progress in meeting the Standards across the five goal areas.

The concern about assessing the functional speaking ability of learners who complete second language programs goes back to the late 1970s, when U.S. President Jimmy Carter's Commission on Foreign Language and International Studies recommended that the profession develop language proficiency tests (President's Commission, 1979). As a result of an international project to adapt the proficiency scale and oral interview procedure developed earlier by the Foreign Service Institute (FSI) of the U.S. Department of State, the ACTFL Provisional Proficiency Guidelines were published in 1982, together with the ACTFL Oral Proficiency Interview (OPI) (Liskin-Gasparro, 1984). The Guidelines described "what individuals can do with language in terms of speaking, writing, listening, and reading" at levels of performance labeled Novice, Intermediate, Advanced, Superior, and Distinguished (ACTFL, 2012b, p. 3). The Proficiency Guidelines and the OPI heralded a shift in instructional focus from *what* was taught (that is, the contents of a textbook) to the *outcomes* learners could accomplish as assessed through the OPI and proficiency-based assessments. Since the 1980s, the Proficiency Guidelines, expanded in 2012, have continued to have a pivotal impact on instruction and assessment (ACTFL, 2012b; Liskin-Gasparro, 2003). Further, current research in the field is pointing to the importance of longitudinal assessment to track the development of proficiency over time in extended sequences of language instruction (see, for example, Davin et al., 2014; Donato & Tucker, 2010; Watzinger-Tharp et al., 2021). Based on this proficiency framework, ACTFL has developed and made available a number of valid and reliable summative assessments (such as the ACTFL OPI, OPIc, RPT, LPT, AAPPL and ALIRA); the IPA allows for articulation between such tests and classroom-based formative and summative assessment.

While the ACTFL Proficiency Guidelines continue to describe language proficiency in the four skills, their connection to the Communication goal area of the World-Readiness Standards is obvious. However, to delineate the specific performance of language learners at the various K-12

benchmarks of learning and development, ACTFL published its ACTFL Performance Guidelines for K-12 Learners in 1998 and revised and renamed them the ACTFL Performance Descriptors for Language Learners in 2012. The Performance Descriptors describe the levels learners attain in different instructional settings at various points along the language learning continuum from Novice to Intermediate to Advanced levels. These descriptors define performance outcomes in terms of language functions, contexts/content, text types, language control, vocabulary use, communication strategies, and cultural awareness.

Expanding the focus on performance in the language classroom, the National Council of State Supervisors for Languages (NCSSFL) and ACTFL collaborated to create Can-Do statements that were influenced by the European Can-Do statements for classroom-based learner self-assessment aligned with the Common European Framework of Reference (Council of Europe, 2001, 2020). The NCSSFL-ACTFL Can-Do Statements (ACTFL, 2017) provide world language instructors and learners with a set of learning goals across the Novice, Intermediate, Advanced, Superior, and Distinguished levels. In addition to the language-focused goals, the NCSSFL-ACTFL Can-Do Statements provide intercultural can-do statements to guide instructors and learners in developing intercultural communicative competence (ICC) as they learn about and engage with others through world language.

Many states and local districts have aligned their K-12 world language curricula with the Standards to continue the impetus toward teaching for real-world competence in the goal areas of Communication, Culture, Connections, Comparisons, and Communities (see, for example, California State Board of Education, 2019; New York State Education Department, 2021; Ohio Department of Education, 2020). In addition, an increasing number of post-secondary world language programs have revised their curricula to reflect standards-based outcomes. The ACTFL Proficiency Guidelines have provided the field with a common yardstick for assessing functional proficiency in real-world situations in spontaneous and non-rehearsed contexts, while the ACTFL Performance Descriptors for Language Learners and the NCSSFL-ACTFL Can-Do Statements provide roadmaps for teaching and learning and assist instructors in setting expectations for formative and summative assessments of performance. However, these frameworks do not provide practical approaches to support measuring learner progress toward those benchmarks within a proficiency-based instructional context. Thus, the IPA provides a means for answering questions that K-16 world-language instructors are asking, such as

- Am I assessing performance using real-world tasks that are meaningful to learners?
- Am I assessing in the same way that learners are learning in my classroom?
- How can I more effectively assess the abilities of my learners in the three modes of communication as they relate to the ACTFL Performance Descriptors for Learners?
- Are my learners developing intercultural communicative competence as they learn to communicate in the world language?
- Are my learners making progress toward the Intermediate or Advanced proficiency levels as defined in the ACTFL Proficiency Guidelines?
- How can I develop and manage classroom discourse so that it reflects the spirit of interpersonal communication and the characteristics of conversation that occurs in the world beyond the classroom?
- What kind of feedback will improve learner performance?
- Are my learners becoming the kind of independent, life-long language learners that they will need to be to improve and maintain their language skills to meet the demands of the 21st century?

The ACTFL IPA was designed to address the national need for assessing learner progress in meeting the content areas of the World-Readiness Standards, in demonstrating performance as depicted in the ACTFL Performance Descriptors, and in illustrating progress toward specific proficiency levels in the ACTFL Proficiency Guidelines. Accounting for the interconnected nature of communication, the IPA enables learners to demonstrate their ability to communicate within specific goal areas of the Standards across the interpretive, interpersonal, and presentational modes of communication. Further, the IPA can serve as a vehicle for instruction and assessment for diversity, equity, and inclusion in the world language classroom. That is, through

the selection of the themes, texts, and tasks of the IPA, instructors can enact instruction and assessment that center social justice, equity, and inclusion in the work of the world language classroom (see, for example, Anya & Randolph, 2019; Glynn et al., 2018; Miranda & Troyan, 2022; Wassell & Glynn, 2022). In short, the IPA has filled the previously existing void for an assessment that could determine the level at which learners interpret authentic texts, interact with others in oral and written form, and present oral, printed, and multimodal messages to audiences of listeners, readers, and viewers, all using the world language. In fact, over the years since its development, the IPA has had a notable impact on world language teaching at all levels, as well as a central role in world language teacher preparation.

In addition to its connection to the proficiency-based frameworks discussed above, the IPA is also interwoven into the profession's high-leverage teaching practices (HLTPs), which are the current focus of teacher preparation and practice. HLTPs are the "tasks and activities that are essential for skillful beginning teachers to understand, take responsibility for, and be prepared to carry out in order to enact their core instructional responsibilities" (Ball & Forzani, 2009, p. 504). In a two-volume series recently published by ACTFL, Glisan and Donato (2017, 2021) present a set of ten practices that provide the greatest leverage for teachers in bringing about high levels of learning in the world language classroom. Each practice is deconstructed into instructional moves that can then be planned, rehearsed, coached, enacted with learners, and assessed. In short, these ten HLTPs represent the field's professional core of knowledge. The IPA builds upon the high-leverage teaching practices for language instruction in that the IPA

- Is couched in meaningful and purposeful contexts for communication;
- Is created using a backward design approach that begins with the end goals in mind;
- Addresses the development of interpersonal speaking;
- Is based upon learners' ability to interpret authentic texts;
- Features attention to cultural products, practices, and perspectives as well as intercultural communicative competence;
- Engages learners in purposeful presentational communication;
- Addresses differences among learners and supports equity in learning;

- Articulates with and provides a classroom-based connection between ACTFL's official tests and learner progress on the ACTFL Proficiency Guidelines; and
- Is used to assess language use with the use of performance rubrics and feedback to improve learner performance.

Analyzed through the lens of the broader educational field beyond the language learning setting, the IPA builds upon foundational research on assessment and approaches to instructional planning. According to Wiggins (1998), *educative* tests (that is, those that improve the performance of both learner and teacher) must feature *authentic* tasks, or those that mirror the tasks and challenges encountered by individuals in the real world. As an authentic activity, Wiggins (1993) traced the word *assessment* to its Latin root *assidere*, meaning "to sit with," and he contends that assessment is something we should do *with* learners rather than *to* them (as cited in Phillips, 2006, p. 83). An assessment task, such as those featured in the IPA, is authentic if it

- Is realistic in that it tests the learner's knowledge and abilities in real-world situations
- Requires judgment and innovation
- Asks the learner to "do" the [academic] subject rather than reciting information so that the learner carries out a task using the language in a meaningful way
- Replicates or simulates the contexts in which adults are "tested" in the workplace, in civic life, and in personal life so that learners address an actual audience, not just their teacher
- Assesses the learner's ability to use a repertoire of knowledge and skill efficiently and effectively to negotiate a complex task
- Allows appropriate opportunities to rehearse, practice, consult resources, get feedback, and refine performances and products (Wiggins & McTighe, 2005, p. 154)

In recent years, the key role of assessment in improving learner performance and informing instruction continues to be both acknowledged by and valued in K-16 settings. Wiggins (1993) emphasizes that assessment is something that learners and teachers should work on together; current research from language learning contexts around the world calls for assessment practices whose primary purpose is to inform teaching and learning (see also Bachman, 2007; Lee & Butler, 2020; Leung et al., 2018; Malone, 2013; McNamara, 2001; Muñoz & Alvarez, 2010; Wiggins & McTighe, 2005).

As will be explored in detail later in this manual, the IPA is predicated on an Understanding by Design (UbD) approach in which learners understand the criteria and standards for the tasks they are striving to master before they are asked to perform (Wiggins & McTighe, 2005). This model features a cyclical approach to second language learning and development, in which learners perform, practice, and receive feedback before, during, and after the IPA. Figure 1.1 below illustrates the three stages of backward design, in which the teacher first identifies the desired end results of instruction, then determines the evidence that will verify that the end results have been achieved, and finally plans learning experiences that will enable learners to demonstrate the end results. What is striking about this type of approach is that it combines instruction and assessment seamlessly while contrasting sharply with the traditional approach of planning instructional activities (often from a textbook) first and designing assessments later in the instructional process. According to Wiggins and McTighe, educators who use backward design think first like assessors, then like curriculum designers, and finally like activity designers. The advantage of the IPA within a backward design approach is that the target for performance is always in focus, and consequently both learners and instructors understand what the goal is and how instruction and assessment work as one system to enable learners to reach that goal. Learning activities

Figure 1.1 Stages of Backward Design

| 1 Identify desired results | 2 Determine acceptable evidence | 3 Plan learning experiences and instruction |

Source: Wiggins & McTighe, 2005, p. 18.

and assessments are designed to develop learners' abilities to think critically, question, and examine issues through intentional investigation of the content.

In addition to promoting critical thinking skills in the world language classroom, the IPA also enables a feedback loop, the Co-Constructive Approach to feedback on performance (Adair-Hauck & Troyan, 2013). As Chapter 5 describes in detail, the Co-Constructive Approach offers the learner systematic feedback on performance that is guided by IPA rubrics. This rubric-based conversation between the instructor and the learner is clearly focused on the learner's current level of performance and on planning with the learner for ongoing development of proficiency.

The Co-Constructive Approach enables instructors to enact inclusive assessment and instruction for learners with disabilities through the use of Formative Instructional Practices (FIP). Because of testing requirements and other historical practices (see, for example, Wight, 2015), learners with disabilities have had fewer opportunities to participate in world language learning. FIP, a framework from special education, guides teachers in enacting inclusive education in any content area by focusing on a set of key practices:

- Articulate clear learning targets based on standards
- Collect and document evidence of learning
- Provide effective feedback
- Plan for learner involvement (Graham-Day et al., 2014; Graham-Day et al., 2020).

As Table 1.1 below outlines, FIP tenets have been central to the IPA from its inception; in other words, the IPA is a means for enabling instructional equity in world language education (Graham-Day et al., 2020). For instance, the Co-Constructive Approach to providing feedback related to the IPA, along with the other components of FIP, can support teachers in their efforts to include learners with disabilities in world language classrooms.

Finally, the IPA is aligned with new developments in language use in context and multimodality in language learning. Recently, pedagogies and scholarship have focused on the role of the purpose of communication in context, guiding learners in developing the ability to interpret and create texts that fulfill the purpose of the communication (see, for example, Abdel-Malek, 2019, 2020; Crane & Malloy, 2021; Glisan & Donato, 2021; Herazo, 2020; Ryshina-Pankova, 2016; Troyan, 2021). This work has contributed to updates in this edition of the IPA manual that guide world language teachers in developing learners' abilities to consider the impact of their messages in the presentational mode of communication. In terms of the multimodal nature of interpreting and composing, recent innovations in visual literacy and multimodal composing (for example, Gironzetti & Lacorte, 2023; Hafner, Yee, & Ho, 2020; Paesani et al., 2016; Shin, Cimasko, & Yi, 2020; Warner & Dupuy, 2018; Zapata, 2018a, 2018b; Zapata & Lacorte, 2018) have led to updates in the interpretive guide that account for distinct features

Table 1.1 Formative Instructional Practices in the IPA

FORMATIVE INSTRUCTIONAL PRACTICES	INTEGRATED PERFORMANCE ASSESSMENT
Clear learning targets based on standards	Clear learning targets are identified in the standards and through the backward design process.
Evidence of learning	IPA tasks and performance rubrics provide evidence of language development over time and across the three modes of communication.
Effective feedback	Use of the Co-Constructive Approach for Feedback in the IPA allows for rich interaction between teachers and learners that is focused on performance.
Learner involvement	The learner is central throughout IPA tasks and the feedback loop.

of interpretive reading, listening, and viewing through provision of a separate interpretive guide for each of the three. The enhancements in this edition will help to ensure that world language instructors are equipped to address the World-Readiness Standards through assessment and instruction that reflect the multimodal nature of language use that learners will encounter throughout their lives.

In sum, over the past 20 years, the IPA has filled the need for a classroom and course-based tool that assesses learners' progress in meeting the national Standards and attaining proficiency levels on the continuum of the ACTFL Proficiency Guidelines. Further, it fits well within current research-based educational paradigms that stress the importance of modeling and feedback for improving learner performance, and the development of language use in context and multimodality. Finally, it represents a visionary approach for integrating teaching, learning, and assessment in a seamless and inclusive manner so that these elements work in concert to foster classroom learning.

Chapter 2

Description and Design Features of the Integrated Performance Assessment

Model of the IPA

Taking into account the interconnectedness of communication, the IPA prototype is a multi-task or cluster assessment featuring three tasks, each of which reflects one of the three modes of communication—interpretive, interpersonal, presentational—as outlined in the World-Readiness Standards for Learning Languages (Standards) (National Standards Collaborative Board, 2015).

Interpretive   The appropriate interpretation of meanings, including cultural, that occur in written and spoken form where there is no recourse to the active negotiation of meaning with the writer or speaker.

Interpersonal   The active negotiation of meaning among individuals. Participants observe and monitor one another to see how their intentions and meanings are being communicated. Adjustments and clarifications can be made accordingly. Participants need to initiate, maintain, and at some levels sustain the conversation.

Presentational   The creation of oral, written, and multimodal messages in a manner that facilitates interpretation by an audience of listeners, readers, or viewers where no direct opportunity for the active negotiation of meaning exists.

Each task provides the information and elicits the linguistic interaction that is necessary for learners to complete the subsequent one. The tasks thus are interrelated and build upon one another. Meaningful content and culture are at the heart of the IPA inasmuch as all three tasks are aligned within a single overarching theme or content area (for example, Social Media and Bullying, Latin America, Ecology) that should be of interest to learners and complement the curriculum. Through the selection of the themes, texts, and tasks of the IPA, instructors can enact instruction and assessment that center social justice, equity, and inclusion in the work of the world language classroom (see, for example, Anya & Randolph, 2019; Glynn, Wesely, & Wassell, 2018; Miranda & Troyan, 2022; Wassell & Glynn, 2022).

In focusing on real-world use of language as reflected in the Standards, the interpretive phase of the IPA uses authentic texts—"those written and oral communications produced by members of a language and culture group for members of the same language and culture group" (Galloway, 1998, p. 133). (From this point forward, when the term *text* or *authentic text* is used, it refers to any written/print, video, audio, or multimodal text.) By using authentic texts, instructors can interweave the Cultures goal area seamlessly into the fabric of an IPA. Further, it is critical that these texts connect with learners' lived experiences in their own worlds and communities (Gironzetti & Lacorte, 2023; Zapata, 2018a, 2018b; Zapata & Lacorte, 2018). To this end, depending on the theme and task design for the different modes, IPAs should connect with at least one other goal area: Cultures, Connections, Comparisons, or Communities. Note how the texts featured in the sample IPAs in Chapter 6 address the various goal areas as well as learner experiences.

This multi-task or integrative assessment approach reflects the manner in which learners naturally acquire and use language in the classroom and in the world beyond the classroom (Glisan et al., 2003). In real life, listening and reading are often catalysts for speaking and writing; to provide an assessment experience that mirrors this, therefore, an IPA should begin with the interpretive task. Using the theme of Finding an Apartment in Germany, for example, learners would first read an apartment listing or view a video listing about the available apartments and then talk to one another about their living preferences. In other words, the interpretive mode affords learners the opportunity to gain critical content or knowledge regarding the IPA theme. This gives them some content with which to interact interpersonally (for example, discussing pro/cons of visiting an apartment or sending email messages to a potential flat mate to inquire about their background and preferences as they prepare to share an apartment). Finally, the presentational mode enables learners to share their thoughts and ideas through presentational speaking, writing, or multimedia (for example, designing a public service announcement about recycling; creating an online ad to find a flat mate in Germany). By incorporating the three modes of communication, the IPA becomes a multi-dimensional, multimodal, cyclical, and integrative assessment. Figure 2.1 captures the cyclical nature and the framework of the IPA.

IPAs are designed for learners at four levels of proficiency, aligned to the ACTFL Proficiency Guidelines and the three major levels and one sublevel of the ACTFL Performance Descriptors for Language Learners: Novice, Intermediate, Intermediate-High, and Advanced. IPAs aligned to these descriptors are presented throughout this manual

to offer instructors tools for capturing the range of performance that is likely to occur in K-16 instructional settings.

Structure of the IPA

Overview

An IPA begins with a general introduction or overview that describes for the learner the context and purpose of the series of authentic tasks. This introduction provides a framework for the assessment and illustrates how each task is integrated into the next and leads up to the culminating task, which results in an oral, written, or multimodal presentational product. The overview may also be shared at the beginning of the instructional sequence (unit, semester, or year) leading to the IPA. Moreover, the overview, when presented at the beginning of the instructional sequence, can be paired with exemplars of student performance from previous years, providing an essential model for learners (see Chapter 5 for an example and further discussion on modeling).

The following is an example of the overview section of an Intermediate-level IPA. The IPA was designed by Jesse Carnevali and is titled Social Media and Bullying.

Figure 2.1 Integrated Performance Assessment: A Cyclical Approach

I. Interpretive Communication Phase
Students listen to or read an authentic text (e.g., newspaper article, radio broadcast, etc.) and answer information as well as interpretive questions to assess comprehension. Teacher provides students with feedback on performance.

II. Interpersonal Communication Phase
After receiving feedback regarding Interpretive Phase, students engage in interpersonal oral communication about a particular topic which relates to the interpretive text. This phase should be either audio- or videotaped.

III. Presentational Communication Phase
Students engage in presentational communication by sharing their research/ideas/opinions. Sample presentational formats: speeches, drama skits, radio broadcasts, posters, brochures, essays, websites, etc.

Source: Glisan, Adair-Hauck, Koda, Sandrock, and Swender, 2003, p.18.

> **Overview of Tasks**
> **Intermediate Level**
> *"Social Media and Bullying"*
> You have decided to join a new anti-bullying club that just formed in your school district to advocate for the social health and well-being of the students in the district. The club is looking to gain as many Spanish-speaking members as possible and therefore needs help with promoting their goals and mission. In order to contribute as a new member, you will first observe a meeting and watch a video to get a better understanding of the club's goals. You will then interview an exchange student in the district to identify their own beliefs, needs, ideas and experiences with bullying and anti-bullying. Finally, you will create a flyer to hang in the school promoting the new anti-bullying club to help gain more members and promote positive behavior in the school district.

This IPA is fully presented in Chapter 4, where it is the focus of the discussion and description of backward design informed by the IPA. Additional IPAs in various other languages appear in Chapter 6.

The Interpretive Tasks

The interpretive mode involves activities such as listening to a broadcast or radio commercial; reading an article in a magazine, a short story, or a letter; or viewing a film or video segment. This mode involves not only *literal comprehension* of a text but also *interpretation*, which includes making inferences ("reading between the lines"), identifying cultural perspectives, and offering personal opinions and points of view (Shrum & Glisan, 2016). In each IPA, learners read, listen to, or view an authentic text related to the theme of the IPA. The interpretive mode as represented in the IPA reflects the current view of how the interpretive process unfolds: the listener/reader/viewer constructs meaning from a text by using both bottom-up and top-down processing (Bernhardt, 1991; Swaffar et al., 1991; Shrum & Glisan, 2016). In bottom-up processing, the learner arrives at meaning by analyzing language parts in a sequential manner (sounds/letters to form words, then words to form phrases, clauses, and sentences), while in top-down processing, the learner derives meaning "through the use of contextual clues and activation of personal background knowledge about the content of the text" (Shrum & Glisan, 2016, p. 178). In sum, the learner uses both types of processing to understand and interpret a text. To this end, Bernhardt (2005) has explained reading as a "juggling or switching process" in which learners compensate for lack of knowledge in one area by relying on knowledge from another; for example, when confronted with an unknown word or phrase, learners implement a compensatory strategy such as guessing meaning from context (p. 140).

This meaning-making process can also be applied to listening and viewing in the interpretive mode. Key components that learners use in the interpretive process are the knowledge and experiences that they bring to the text to derive meaning, including new insights gained in discussing texts with others (Bernhardt, 1991; Schmitt et al., 2011; see Chapter 6 of Shrum & Glisan [2016] for a more in-depth review of this research). Further, in making meaning from texts, learners also analyze the interplay between the language as heard or read and the visual elements provided, such as photos, drawings, infographics, and video images (see for example Shin et al., 2020; Zapata, 2018a, 2018b; Zapata & Lacorte, 2018).

Learners complete the interpretive task using a comprehension guide that supports them in obtaining information. The information acquired in the interpretive task is necessary for learners to be able to complete the interpersonal task. New in this third edition is the inclusion of three different comprehension guides—one each for interpretive reading, interpretive listening, and interpretive viewing. Based on research and practice in multimodal interpretation and composing (for example, Gironzetti & Lacorte, 2023; Kress & van Leeuwen, 2021; Paesani et al., 2016; Zapata & Lacorte, 2018), having comprehension guides specific to each modality will provide greater assistance to instructors as they design the interpretive tasks for the authentic text, be it in printed, audio, or video form. (See Appendix D for the IPA Interpretive Comprehension Guide Templates, and Appendix E for the Comprehension Guide for "Social Media and Bullying" as well as links to the authentic video that was the focus of this IPA.)

Following are the instructions for the interpretive task from Jesse Carnevali's Social Media and Bullying IPA.

Interpretive Task
Intermediate Level
"Social Media and Bullying"
We have been studying the themes of social media, cyberbullying, and bullying over the past three weeks. You just joined the new anti-bullying club at school and were invited to view a special introductory video from *El País* with the Spanish-speaking students. View the video and complete the accompanying comprehension guide.

The Comprehension Guide Analysis, shown in Figure 2.2 below, depicts the performance for learners on a continuum from literal comprehension to interpretation of the text. Notice that interpretive skills such as key word recognition, main idea detection, and supporting detail detection are considered *literal comprehension tasks*, since they involve surface-level meaning. For these interpretive skills, learners will most likely all have the same or similar "literal" responses. On the other hand, the *interpretive tasks* require learners to interpret, draw conclusions, and infer deeper meanings from the text, that is, read/listen/view between the lines. Identifying organizational features of the text, guessing meaning from the context, making inferences, and gleaning author/cultural perspectives are interpretive tasks that require inferencing skills. Inferencing has been defined as "a thinking process that involves reasoning a step beyond the text, using generalization, synthesis, and/or explanation" (Hammadou Sullivan, 2002, p. 219). Wiggins (1998) observes that it may be impossible to assess learners' understanding of a text unless one discovers the extent to which learners recognize the author's intent and, by extension, understand the cultural nuances underlying the text.

Like previous editions, this third edition represents interpretive tasks at each level as engaging learners in both literal comprehension and interpretation. This approach to the interpretive tasks is informed by much research on text-based and multimodal literacy development (Gironzetti & Lacorte, 2023; Kress & van Leeuwen, 2021; Paesani et al., 2016; Zapata & Lacorte, 2018). In this view, literacy development is not linear, but rather is emergent, dynamic, and ever shifting based on a variety of local factors. As such, the interpretive task in the IPA allows instructors to observe learners'

use of the available semiotic resources to communicate their understanding of texts (Kress & van Leeuwen, 2001).

For these reasons, the specific task and text types that instructors use for the design of the interpretive task will vary according to the ages, backgrounds, and literacy experiences of learners. For example, inferencing for a third grader might consist of anticipating what will happen next in a story, while for a secondary or post-secondary learner it might consist of gleaning the author's viewpoint on an abstract topic or identifying possible sociocultural perspectives that may be represented in the text. To this end, the format used for the inferencing task may also be tailored to the level and the background of the learner, as indicated in the templates that appear in Appendix D. See the description of the interpretive rubric in Figure 2.2 for a more detailed discussion of the IPA assessment criteria for the interpretive mode of communication. Chapter 4 presents a detailed discussion of how this view of the interpretive mode influences decisions regarding selection of authentic texts.

Several points about conducting the interpretive phase of the IPA should be kept in mind. First, as illustrated in the comprehension guide templates, the use of English is suggested (or given as an option) in several of the interpretive tasks. A body of research has shown that learners tend to perform better when assessed in their first/strongest language and that using the new language in interpretive tasks may limit learners' ability to show the meaning they glean from a text (Mahoney, 2017; Martin-Jones & Jones, 2021; Shrum & Glisan, 2016). A further complication is that use of the new language can promote use of the "look-back-and-lift-off" approach to reading, in which students match the wording of comprehension questions to language found in the text without necessarily understanding either the questions or the text (Lee & VanPatten, 1995).

However, the use of English to check comprehension should not be confused with translating from one language to the other, which is *not* advocated in the IPA, since translation does not demonstrate one's ability to glean meaning from a text. Since the purpose of the interpretive tasks is to assess learners' ability to deal with language that may be new for them in an authentic text, glossing or translating new words and expressions should be avoided. Similarly, the use of translation from the target language to the first or strongest language(s) should be avoided, since this activity does not demonstrate ability to interpret a text and can lead to

Figure 2.2 IPA Comprehension Guide Analysis: Performance Expectations

Criteria	What is Involved?
LITERAL COMPREHENSION OF TEXT	
Key word recognition	Learners identify key words in the text that provide clues to the overall meaning of the text.
Main idea detection	Learners identify the main idea(s) of the text.
Supporting detail detection	Learners identify important details that further explain the main idea(s), including details that are gleaned from images and/or other visual support.
INTERPRETATION OF TEXT	
Organizational features	Learners identify the ways in which the text is organized and the purpose of organizing the information in that manner.
Guessing meaning from context	Learners use contextual clues and knowledge of language and text structure to infer the meaning of new words and phrases.
Inferences (reading/listening/viewing between the lines)	Learners interpret the overall meanings contained in the text by combining knowledge of key vocabulary, important details, text features, and their own background knowledge.
Author's perspective	Learners identify the author's perspective and provide a justification.
Cultural perspectives	Learners identify cultural perspectives/norms by making connections with practices/products referenced in the text.

both frustration and boredom on the part of language learners. Even in the first task of the template, in which learners are asked to identify key words and figure out their meaning, they are not engaged in rote translation but rather must use the context of the text, which includes the key words, to make meaning. However, the decision of which language to use is always left up to individual instructors based on the levels of their learners and their specific instructional contexts.

As a final point regarding conducting the interpretive phase, when the instructor discusses the text with the class (both as a whole group and individually) in the feedback phase after the interpretive tasks have been done, learners should be given an opportunity to analyze how accurate their contextual guessing was. This type of analysis will give learners helpful information regarding how successful their own contextual guessing is and how they might use this strategy more effectively.

The Interpersonal Tasks

Interpersonal tasks are spontaneous, two-way, interactive activities such as those that occur face-to-face, in telephone conversations, or in a virtual format such as a chat room or conferencing platform such as Zoom. Interpersonal communication can also occur in written form through text messaging, email, and exchanges that occur on social media platforms. The information gathered during the interpersonal task is necessary to complete the presentational task that follows.

In oral interpersonal communication, such as that featured in the IPA, learners communicate in a spontaneous manner and do not use a printed script. They exchange information and express feelings, emotions, and opinions about the theme. Each of the two speakers comes to the task with information that the other person may not have, thereby creating a real need for them to provide and obtain information through the active negotiation of meaning. Further, the instructor may design some interpersonal tasks that engage learners in interacting with member(s) of the target culture, thus providing a means of assessing intercultural communication, that is, the extent to which learners are able to interact with others using appropriate cultural norms.

Following are the instructions for the interpersonal task from Jesse Carnevali's Social Media and Bullying IPA.

> **Interpersonal Task**
> **Intermediate Level**
> *"Social Media and Bullying"*
> After viewing the video and acquiring different perspectives from the students around the topic of bullying, you will have the opportunity to interview one of the Spanish-speaking exchange students in the club to gather their viewpoints, experiences, and perspectives. During the interview, try to gather as much information from the student as possible related to the topic and the club.
>
> *(Note: Students do not read any written notes during the interpersonal task. The interpersonal task is a spontaneous two-way interaction.)*

The Presentational Task

Presentational tasks are generally formal speaking or writing activities involving one-way communication to an audience of listeners, readers, or viewers, such as giving a speech or report, preparing an informative report or story, producing a newscast or video, or posting messages/videos to social media. In the IPA, learners prepare a written, oral, or multimodal presentation based on the topic and information obtained in the interpretive and interpersonal tasks. The written or spoken presentational task reflects what the learners would do in the world outside the classroom and provides an opportunity for them to investigate cultural products, practices, and perspectives. Thus, in the presentational mode, learners illustrate their intercultural compe-

tence in terms of investigating aspects of the target cultures. The intended audience should ideally include someone other than the instructor so that the task avoids being merely an opportunity to display language for the instructor and the impact of the presentation can be more realistically assessed. The presentational task is the culminating activity that results in the creation of a written, spoken, or multimodal product.

Following are the instructions for the presentational task from Jesse Carnevali's Social Media and Bullying IPA.

> **Presentational Task**
> **Intermediate Level**
> *"Social Media and Bullying"*
> Based on what you have learned from the video, your interview, and this unit in general, you are now ready to create the flyer to promote the new anti-bullying club. The flyer should include important information about the purpose of the group, including the club's goals. Additionally, you should give some basic information to start promoting positive behavior within the school district. Remember, the goal of a club flyer is to gain interest and also provide a variety of information to help those who are interested make an appropriate decision regarding bullying and anti-bullying!

A perusal of the thematically-based IPA tasks for the Social Media and Bullying theme illustrates that the IPA mirrors tasks encountered in the world and thus encourages learners to use a repertoire of linguistic skills and knowledge across the three modes of communication. Indeed, to perform the tasks cited above, learners will not be able to simply recite verb conjugations or memorized vocabulary lists. On the contrary, they will need to use and create in the language with divergent and creative responses. Furthermore, learners will take risks and use language learning strategies, as well as critical thinking skills, as they conceptualize, analyze, synthesize, interpret, make inferences, share opinions, or exchange different points of view in the language. In this way, the IPA is an integrative and dynamic form of assessment.

In addition, using an authentic document to launch the interpretive stage of the IPA enables the instructor to interweave the cultural practices, products, and perspectives of the Cultures goal area. This particular IPA addresses the Cultures Standard, Relating Cultural Practices to Perspectives. Through interpretation of the video from *El País* on bullying in the academic setting, the *cultural practices* of how individuals typically engage in bullying at school (such as social exclusion, verbal aggression, direct/indirect aggression) are revealed. Moreover, learners in the discussion group portrayed in the video share ideas about how others might intervene when witnessing episodes of bullying. In uncovering these practices, students learn the *cultural perspectives* of students in a region in Spain through the expression of their attitudes and brainstorming of possible solutions to the problem of bullying. Besides the Communication and Cultures standards, this IPA can also address Connections (health, psychology, issues of diversity and inclusion) and Cultural Comparisons (comparing problems with bullying in Spain and the U.S.). Furthermore, since learners will interact with Spanish speakers in the interpersonal task and create and display anti-bullying posters at their schools for the presentational task, this particular IPA addresses the Communities standard by engaging learners in using the language to interact and collaborate in their school community and possibly beyond.

Selection of IPA Level for Use in the Classroom

Instructors will need to decide which level of the IPA would be most appropriate for their learners. There is not a strict one-to-one match-up between the IPA level and the level of instruction of learners; for example, an Advanced Spanish class may need to be given an Intermediate-level IPA. This determination should be based on the abilities of learners according to the IPA rubrics and the nature of classroom instruction and experiences, since the IPA is designed to form a seamless connection with instruction. Since the Novice-level IPA requires learners to create with the language, it is advisable for learners to be approaching Novice-High proficiency so that they experience success with the IPA; that is, they should be moving from using only memorized language to combining and recombining language elements on their own. A particular IPA level may be used for an entire year or even longer before progressing to a higher-level IPA, depending on the progress learners make.

Preparing Learners for IPA Tasks

Each stage of the IPA requires instructors to consider particular skills, knowledge, and performances as they design instruction that prepares learners for the performance tasks in the IPA. The IPA rubrics and companion materials can support this process. For instance, the IPA interpretive guides provide roadmaps for teaching learners to interpret spoken, printed, and multimodal texts in the target language. Using authentic texts throughout the curriculum, instructors can guide learners in a systematic approach to meaning making by teaching the interpretive skills featured in each part of the guides. Instructors might also design interpretive activities that include pair and group work or provide opportunities for learners to select their own authentic texts of interest and demonstrate their comprehension and interpretation of them. Through the process of preparing and participating in the interpretive task, learners develop their skills as interpreters of texts.

To prepare for the interpersonal mode, learners need to know and be able to use conversational gambits for negotiating meaning (*Could you repeat that?*). While learners may use scripts to plan for and practice an interpersonal task, it is important to wean learners gradually from the use of scripts in oral communication. During practice tasks leading up to an IPA, learners can also be allowed to create vocabulary lists that are specific to their particular communicative needs within the context in which they are learning to speak. The key for instruction in the interpersonal mode is to provide learners with sufficient practice in a variety of speaking tasks that are similar to the IPA speaking task. As much as possible, learners should also have opportunities to rate their own performance using the rubric.

In planning and enacting instruction and assessment aligned with the IPA, it is important to consider that the IPA measures *performance*. In other words, the IPA involves the learner in hands-on practice and use of language. It is possible, and advisable, for learners to practice, rehearse, and study for an IPA—they cannot cram for it. There is no replacement for in-class and out-of-class practice, preparation, and engagement with the language.

Integrated Performance Assessment Rubrics

Appendix F contains the revised IPA rubrics for use in scoring the tasks across the three modes of communication. As defined by Wiggins, a rubric is "a set of scoring guidelines for evaluating students' work." Rubrics answer the following questions:

- By what criteria should performance be judged?
- Where should we look and what should we look for to judge performance success?
- What does the range in the quality of performance look like?
- How do we determine validity, reliability, and fairly judge what score should be given and what that score means?
- How should the different levels of quality be described and distinguished from one another? (Wiggins, 1998, p 154)

The three sets of IPA rubrics all contain *descriptors* for each level of performance (see later discussion of how instructors might assign points for each level of performance in assigning a score on a continuum of quality). These rubrics are *generic* in nature—that is, they describe characteristics of language performance without specifying particular content or task details. Also, they are *analytic* inasmuch as each one includes a set of criteria for performance with a range of descriptions for each criterion (Center for Advanced Research in Language Acquisition [CARLA], 2021). In an IPA, the rubrics serve the following purposes:

1. To inform learners of how they will be assessed prior to the assessment—that is, what the performance expectations are. Instructors are encouraged to share models or exemplars of student work with learners, together with the performance rubrics in preparation for the IPA.

2. To provide descriptive feedback to learners along the continuum of performance so that they understand their current level of performance and what they need to do to improve.

3. To illustrate to learners how they might exceed or go beyond task expectations and therefore challenge themselves to improve (note that each rubric includes in the range of performance an "Exceeds Expectations" level).

4. To provide educators with a model for adjusting performance expectations in light of learner exemplars.

The format of each ready-to-use IPA rubric includes space for the instructor to provide a description of the learner's evidence of strengths, areas in which improvement is needed, and any other comments that might assist the learner in making progress. A brief description of the rubrics for each mode follows and includes a discussion of how learners might demonstrate progress in interpretive, interpersonal, and presentational communication through their performance across multiple IPAs over time.

IPA Interpretive Rubric

This edition of the IPA manual maintains the approach to the interpretive mode that was introduced in the second edition, in that it embraces current research indicating that interpretive skills do not develop in a linear manner as speaking and writing do, but rather involve the use of top-down and bottom-up processing in concert. For this reason, the IPA interpretive rubric does not reflect the proficiency-based orientation of the rubrics for the interpersonal and presentational modes. Instead, it enacts the view that the interpretive mode can be assessed along a continuum of performance that includes both literal and interpretive comprehension, and that this continuum is the same regardless of the linguistic level or age of the learner.

The IPA interpretive rubric assesses the following aspects of performance:

Literal Comprehension of Text
- Key word recognition
- Main idea detection
- Supporting detail detection

Interpretation of Text
- Organizational features
- Guessing meaning from context
- Inferences (reading/listening/viewing between the lines)
- Author's perspective
- Cultural perspectives

This approach reflects the conceptualization of the interpretive process that is presented in reading/language arts research (Deane, 2020; Moje et al., 2020). Further, since the publication of the second edition of this manual, the IPA interpretive rubric has been proposed in the literature on language teaching and assessment as an example of a tool that can be used to give learners helpful feedback as they work toward developing greater interpretive abilities (see, for example, Center for Advanced Research on Language Acquisition [CARLA], 2021 and Shrum & Glisan, 2016).

The IPA rubric for the interpretive mode describes performance across a four-part continuum: Exceeds Expectations-Accomplished; Meets Expectations-Strong; Meets Expectations-Minimal; Does Not Meet Expectations-Limited. At each level for which the IPA is designed (Novice, Intermediate, and so on), learners demonstrate progress in the interpretive mode as they move from meeting expectations to exceeding expectations over the course of a series of IPAs. It may take a year or two working at one IPA level to see consistent progress across the rubric categories. When learners advance to higher level IPA tasks, at first, they may exhibit stronger performance on the literal tasks than on the interpretive ones, but as they gain experience in interpreting authentic texts at the new level, their interpretive skills should also improve. Use of this continuum over time will thus illustrate learners' progress in developing both literal and interpretive comprehension with a variety of texts and within a variety of contexts.

IPA Interpersonal Rubrics

The rubrics designed to assess the IPA interpersonal tasks rate the following aspects of performance:

1. **Language Functions:** Language tasks the learner is able to handle in a consistent, comfortable, sustained, and spontaneous manner; e.g., posing questions to a restaurant server to make a decision regarding what food to order.

2. **Text Type:** Quantity and organization of language discourse, on a continuum from words to phrases to sentences to connected sentences to paragraphs to extended discourse.

3. **Communication Strategies:** Quality of engagement and interactivity in the conversation; how the learner participates in the conversation and advances it; how the learner uses strategies for negotiating meaning in the face of communication breakdown.

4. **Comprehensibility:** Types of listeners who can understand the learner's language, on a continuum from sympathetic listeners used to the speech of language learners to target language speakers unaccustomed to such speech.

5. **Language Control:** Degree of grammatical accuracy, appropriate vocabulary use, and fluency.

6. **Intercultural Communication: Interact:** Degree and quality of use of cultural norms appropriate for interpersonal interaction.

The criteria presented in the interpersonal rubrics are aligned with both the assessment criteria in the ACTFL Proficiency Guidelines (ACTFL, 2012b) and the performance indicators in the ACTFL Performance Descriptors for Language Learners (ACTFL, 2012a). In this third edition of the IPA Manual, a new criterion has been added to the interpersonal rubrics—Intercultural Communication: Interact—to reflect the current dialogue in the field regarding the inseparable roles of language and culture in communication. In the most recent version of the NCSSFL-ACTFL Can-Do Statements (ACTFL, 2017), intercultural communication is defined as "the ability to interact effectively and appropriately with people from other language and cultural backgrounds." In the rubric, the definition for this criterion has been changed to *interaction with others* to make it more inclusive and address intercultural communication in all interactions.

The interpersonal rubrics describe a range of performance across a four-part continuum: Exceeds Expectations; Meets Expectations-Strong; Meets Expectations-Minimal; Does Not Meet Expectations. The performance descriptors reflect progress according to the abilities described in the ACTFL Proficiency Guidelines (ACTFL, 2012b); that is, the rubric at each IPA level (Novice, Intermediate, and so on) features overall performance that corresponds to the ACTFL Guidelines. In this third edition, the target proficiency level has been included at the top of each rubric column to indicate correspondence with the performance descriptor it represents. However, instructors should remember that, while they can relate a learner's performance on an IPA to a particular proficiency level, the learner's overall level of oral proficiency cannot be determined on the basis of IPA tasks;

it can only be determined by an official Oral Proficiency Interview (OPI). Learners show progress within a particular IPA level in the interpersonal mode when their performance moves across the rubric from Meets Expectations-Minimal to Exceeds Expectations. They demonstrate ability to perform at a particular IPA level when they can do so consistently across the criteria at the Meets Expectations-Strong point over the course of a series of IPAs, which may take a whole year or longer! Both progress within a level and consistent performance at a level may take significant time and multiple IPA experiences to achieve.

IPA Presentational Rubrics

The presentational rubrics are similar, although not identical to, the interpersonal rubrics. Both sets of rubrics feature the criteria of language functions, text type, comprehensibility, and language control, all of which are described across a proficiency-based continuum. As with the interpersonal rubrics, these criteria are aligned with both the assessment criteria in the ACTFL Proficiency Guidelines (ACTFL, 2012b) and the performance indicators in the ACTFL Performance Descriptors for Language Learners (ACTFL, 2012a). However, the presentational rubrics also include two criteria that do not relate to language proficiency. New to this third edition is an intercultural communication criterion, Intercultural Communication: Present, that focuses on learners' ability to identify products and practices and make the appropriate connections to cultural perspectives as a part of what they present. This addition reflects the way in which intercultural communication is defined in the current version of the NCSSFL-ACTFL Can-Do Statements (ACTFL, 2017). The second criterion unique to presentational communication is Impact of Written/Oral Communication, which addresses the way in which learners engage in one-way communication with an audience whose interest they need to maintain. Wiggins (1998) describes impact as characteristic of a performance that brings about a response from the audience of listeners/readers/viewers and/or holds their interest; this means that, in assessing impact, one might ask whether the performance is "powerful, memorable, provocative, or moving" (p. 67). While traditionally oral and written tasks have been evaluated primarily on linguistic accuracy, performances of authentic tasks such as those found on an IPA must be assessed on the impact that they would have on a real-world audience beyond the classroom.

In the third edition, the criterion of Impact has been expanded to reflect the two different presentation types that are typically assigned in an IPA: Written or oral presentations that are usually completed spontaneously by individual learners but could also be the result of collaborative small group work, as in creating a written product or giving a short impromptu talk; and multimodal presentations that include the use of media such as video, pictures, objects, graphs, diagrams, or tables, prepared either by individual learners or collaboratively in small groups. The criterion Impact of Written/Oral Presentation gives the instructor the option of substituting the new criterion Impact of Multimodal Presentation for presentations that include multimodal elements. This new feature will provide increased flexibility for instructors while addressing the increasing use of multimedia in the presentational mode.

The rubrics designed to assess the IPA presentational tasks rate six aspects of performance divided into two parts: Language proficiency/performance criteria and intercultural communication and impact criteria.

Language Proficiency/Performance Criteria
1. **Language Functions:** Language tasks the speaker/ writer is able to handle in a consistent, comfortable, sustained, and spontaneous manner.
2. **Text Type:** Quantity and organization of language discourse, on a continuum from words to phrases to sentences to connected sentences to paragraphs to extended discourse.
3. **Comprehensibility:** Types of listeners/readers who can understand the learner's language, on a continuum from sympathetic interlocutors accustomed to the speech/writing of language learners to target language speakers unaccustomed to the speaking/ writing of such learners.
4. **Language Control:** Degree of grammatical accuracy, appropriate vocabulary use, and fluency.

Intercultural Communication and Impact Criteria
5. **Intercultural Communication: Present:** Learner's ability to identify products and practices and connect them to cultural perspectives appropriately in a presentation.

6a. **Impact of Written/Oral Presentation:** Clarity, organization, and depth of the written/oral presentation and the degree to which the presentation maintains the audience's attention and interest.

6b. **Impact of Multimodal Presentation:** Clarity, organization, and depth of the presentation; the degree to which the presentation maintains the audience's attention and interest; and the use of multimodal design (such as video, pictures, objects, graphs, diagrams, tables).

The presentational rubrics describe a range of performance across a four-part continuum: Exceeds Expectations; Meets Expectations-Strong; Meets Expectations-Minimal; Does Not Meet Expectations. The performance descriptors for the four language proficiency/performance criteria reflect progress according to the speaking and writing abilities described in the ACTFL Proficiency Guidelines (ACTFL, 2012b); that is, the rubric at each IPA level features overall performance that corresponds to the ACTFL Guidelines for both speaking and writing, since the presentations may include either speaking or writing tasks. For these criteria, as for the interpersonal rubrics, the targeted ACTFL proficiency level has been added at the top of each performance column to correspond with the performance descriptor it represents. However, instructors should remember that, while they can relate a learner's performance on an IPA to a particular proficiency level, a learner's specific level of proficiency in presentational speaking or writing cannot be determined on the basis of IPA tasks; as with the interpersonal mode, proficiency level can only be determined by an official ACTFL Oral Proficiency Interview (OPI) for speaking and by an official ACTFL Writing Proficiency Test (WPT) for writing.

In the lower section, containing the criteria of Intercultural Communication: Present, Impact of Written/Oral Presentation, and Impact of Multimodal Presentation, the descriptors correspond only to the Exceeds, Meets, Does Not Meet Expectations continuum and not to an ACTFL proficiency level. Therefore, the descriptors across the performance continuum for these criteria are the same regardless of the IPA level.

Learners show progress at a particular IPA level in the presentational mode when their performance moves across the rubric from Meets Expectations-Minimal to Exceeds Expectations, and they demonstrate ability to perform at a particular IPA level when they can do so consistently across the criteria at the Meets Expectations-Strong point, which may take a whole year or longer! Both progress within a level and consistent performance at a level may take significant time and multiple IPA experiences to achieve.

Adapting the IPA Rubrics for Specific Learning Contexts
As indicated above, the IPA rubrics across the modes are generic. Instructors may find it advantageous to adapt the rubrics for the following two purposes:

1. To make them more specific to the performance expected in particular IPA tasks.

2. To make them more learner friendly and appropriate to the age and linguistic level of learners. For example, elementary school learners may need rubrics that use simpler language that they can more easily understand, as shown by Davin, Troyan, Donato, and Hellmann (2011a), who found it necessary to revise the language of the IPA rubrics to make them clearer and more meaningful to younger learners.

However, instructors are cautioned to make every effort to maintain the integrity of the original IPA rubrics while making adaptations that are deemed necessary.

Using the IPA Rubrics to Evaluate or Assign Grades
Although rubrics are best used for purposes of communicating expectations to learners, describing learner progress, and giving learners meaningful feedback, the reality of the educational system is that the use of rubrics must somehow result in scores or grades. It is likely that individual school districts and university language departments have their own systems of converting rubric results to grades. However, in the absence of such systems, instructors may find it helpful to assign a point value to each column on the four-part continuum of performance on the rubric. In this third edition of the IPA Manual, points have been added on each rubric to make it easier for instructors to compute a score: The Exceeds Expectations performance level is assigned 4 points, the Meets Expectations—Strong level is assigned 3 points, the Meets Expectations—Minimal level is assigned 2 points, and the Does Not Meet level is assigned 1 point. In an analytic rubric that includes an Exceeds Expec-

tations level of performance, a special conversion formula is typically used to assign percentages or points to the final score. It is essential for instructors to remember that raw scores on these rubrics cannot be converted directly to percentages, which would, for example, result in assigning low grades to students who have met expectations on the task. As an example, if a learner earned 3 points in each criterion of the Interpersonal rubric, the total raw score would be 18 out of 24. If straight percentage is used to assign a grade, the result would be a 75%, although the learner met expectations at the strong level. Many school districts have developed a system for converting rubric scores to grades. Because it is not possible for learners to score a zero on a rubric provided that they completed the assessment task, instructors must decide what the minimum passing score would be (for example, 60%); as explained by Shrum and Glisan, "a mathematical equation then converts the rubric points to a range of percentages between the highest possible—100%—and the lowest possible—e.g., 60%" (2016, p. 386). Using this type of system, the following rubric formula could be used to assign a percentage: (Total points x 52)/24 + 48 = _____%.

In the example provided above, a total raw score of 18 out of 24 would result in 87%, which is typically a high B. Instructors may also consult a Web site called Roobrix (http://www.roobrix.com), which calculates the score based on the number of criteria and the lowest passing grade entered by the instructor. Post-secondary institutions such as Indiana University of Pennsylvania have also adopted this system for converting rubric scores to grade percentages: see https://www.iup.edu/foreignlanguages/undergrad/spanish/additional-information/spanish-course-assessment-site.html

This edition of the IPA Manual adds a table after each rubric to assist instructors in converting rubric points to percentages, which can then be used to assign letter grades if desired. Note that these tables use 60% as the lowest passing score; instructors may choose to use the Roobrix website mentioned above if they wish to use a different lowest passing score as consistent with their own grading principles or the guidelines their institution has established. Also, note that a zero (0) for a given criterion would be given only if the learner had no performance that corresponded to that criterion; for example, on the interpretive task, a learner who did not answer the question regarding author's perspective would receive a 0 for that criterion because a response could not be rated.

Instructors will find it helpful, if not necessary, to explain to their learners how rubrics work, particularly if the rubrics are used to assign scores or grades. Teachers should also explain that learners do not need to reach the Exceeds Expectations level in each criterion to earn a grade of A, because this rating represents performance that is beyond what is expected on the IPA. The Exceeds Expectations column shows learners what they need to do to improve their performance beyond what is expected on the task. Anecdotal reports from instructors who begin to use this type of rubric have revealed that many of their learners work diligently because they want to exceed expectations once they see the criteria described on the rubric.

IPA Performance and Co-Constructive Feedback: Enacting Formative Instructional Practices

Feedback is an integral part of IPA assessment, since the main purpose or function of the assessment is to improve language performance across the modes of communication. In their book *Visible Learning: Feedback*, Hattie and Clarke (2019) note that:

> Feedback can have many functions: reinforcing success, correcting errors, helping to unravel misconceptions, suggesting specific improvement, giving improvements, advice for the future, praising, punishing or rewarding, all with different levels of effectiveness. Who gives the feedback, whether it is task or ego related, and *how and whether it is received and acted upon* are all factors in its effectiveness. This last point is particularly pertinent: more attention needs to be given to whether and how students receive and act upon feedback, as there seems [to be] little point in maximizing the amount and nature of feedback given if it is not received or understood. This is why [...] we emphasize the interpretations that are made by the receiver about the feedback, and how it helps them to answer questions 'Where to next?' or 'How could this be improved?' (p. 5).

Wiggins (1998) recommends that learners receive feedback as soon as possible after their performances. Effective feedback assists learners in developing knowledge about their performance and strategies for improving over time. Further, feedback is an integral component of Formative Instructional Practices (FIP), a framework that guides instructors in enacting inclusive education through focusing on a set of key practices, which includes "providing effective feedback to students" (Graham-Day et al., 2014). Graham-Day, Kaplan, Irish, and Troyan (2020) linked this framework for effective instruction to the IPA and, specifically, the central role that feedback plays in the IPA framework.

Finally, citing numerous research studies, Bellon, Bellon, and Blank (1992) stress that "Academic feedback is more strongly and consistently related to achievement than any other teaching behavior….This relationship is consistent regardless of grade, socioeconomic status, race or school setting" (p. 227). In this regard and considering the principles and practices of FIP, the IPA provides a framework for equity in world language education because it makes visible to all students what their current level of performance is across the modes of communication and provides descriptive feedback to assist them in moving to the next level of performance. To accomplish this, the IPA framework provides for a great deal of individual feedback and dialogue between the instructor and learner, which separates it from other types of assessment inasmuch as it attends more to the needs of each learner.

With this understanding of the important role of feedback in the IPA, Adair-Hauck and Troyan (2013) outlined the Co-Constructive Approach to IPA feedback, which can be characterized as an interactive, instructional dialogue between the learner (apprentice) and the instructor (expert). Co-constructive IPA feedback encourages learners to take an active role in self-reflection, self-assessment, and peer assessment.

Summary: Unique Features of the ACTFL Integrated Performance Assessment

1. All three modes of communication (interpretive, interpersonal, and presentational) are evaluated as an integrated unit of assessment, maintaining the same meaningful (content-based/sociocultural) theme throughout the tasks.

2. IPAs are performance based, providing learners with opportunities to perform meaningful, purposeful, motivating, age-appropriate tasks.

3. IPAs are authentic assessments because they reflect real-world tasks.

4. IPAs are developmental in nature, supporting cognitive and language development, as illustrated by the four levels of tasks in the interpersonal and presentational modes, including intercultural communication and impact, and the various levels of interpretive abilities in the interpretive mode.

5. The IPA framework supports a seamless connection between instruction and assessment.

6. Modeling of learner performance is an integral part of the IPA framework.

7. Co-constructive feedback that encourages learners to self-reflect and self-assess is a critical feature of IPA assessment.

Implementing the IPA: Resources and Recommendations

Instructors implementing the IPA for the first time will benefit from collaboration with others and from accessing professional resources. Instructors can form communities of practice with their colleagues in which they learn about the IPA together and then collaborate in the development and implementation of IPAs. These communities can form within a school district, university language department, or within a local professional organization such as a language collaborative. Sharing of ideas and resources can go a long way to support and encourage instructors as they develop skill in incorporating IPAs into their curricula.

Professional Resources

Becoming a member of a professional organization such as ACTFL connects the instructor with a wealth of resources such as *The Language Educator* magazine, which features topic-specific issues that include a variety of resources used by teachers in language classrooms. A second publication available on the ACTFL website is the academic journal *Foreign Language Annals*, which contains many scholarly articles dealing with the implementation and impact of the IPA. Further, the ACTFL website provides access to the professional documents mentioned throughout this manual, such as the ACTFL Proficiency Guidelines (ACTFL, 2012b),

ACTFL Performance Descriptors for Language Learners (2012a), NCSSFL-ACTFL Can-Do Statements (ACTFL, 2017), and the World-Readiness Standards for Language Learning (National Standards Collaborative Board, 2015).

State-Level Resources

Many states, such as New Jersey and Ohio, are increasingly using the IPA at all levels of instruction. In New Jersey, a consortium of four school districts has received numerous grants for teacher training in Integrated Performance Assessment. This work began in 2003 when the four districts were awarded a Foreign Language Assistance Program (FLAP) grant to create assessment tasks modeled after the IPA. Through the FLAP grant, teachers from the four districts received extensive training in standards-based teaching and assessment. Other world language educators in New Jersey were invited to attend trainings. In subsequent years, Foreign Language Educators of New Jersey (FLENJ), the state professional organization for world language educators, also offered several sessions on developing IPAs, open to all world language educators in the state. As capacity was developed for teachers to create and implement IPAs, districts began to incorporate IPAs as a way to assess learner performance at the ends of thematic units and as all or part of the midterm and final exam assessments. Through a separate FLAP grant to support a longitudinal study of learner proficiency growth in ten New Jersey pilot districts, additional training was provided to teachers to support the development of assessments aligned to the New Jersey Standards for World Languages. During Summer 2011, more than 50 world language educators from New Jersey attended a three-day session on designing three-mode assessments. Teachers from the pilot districts as well as teachers from other districts worked collaboratively to create IPAs targeting various proficiency levels.

In Ohio, the IPA has become a key performance measure for world language education across the state. In 2013, the Ohio Department of Education implemented the Ohio Teacher Evaluation System (OTES), an annual review process for teachers that included a combination of student growth measures and classroom observation of teaching. The original framework determined a final summative rating for each teacher that included goal setting at the beginning the year, a mid-year review, and a final review and conference at the end of the year. To determine a teacher's rating on a scale with four levels of performance—Ineffective, De-

veloping, Skilled, and Accomplished—50% of the data came from observational data and 50% was based on the results of a learner growth measure. The IPA was identified as the state-wide assessment that all world language teachers would use for the learner growth measure. As a result of this OTES initiative, teachers across the state began to use the IPA. This initiative led the Ohio Foreign Language Association to create an Integrated Performance Assessment Center that provided teachers with IPA guidance, a forum to support their work with IPA design, and model IPAs (Ohio Department of Education, 2021).

Resources for Design and Implementation

Twenty years ago, when teachers first started designing IPAs, locating authentic texts was indeed challenging. Fortunately, advances in technology have made resources much more available and this part of IPA design much less daunting. For example, banks of resources aligned to proficiency levels and themes have been curated and made available online. Kissau and Adams (2016) recommend the Center for Open Educational Resources and Language Learning (COERLL, www.coerll.utexas.edu) at the University of Texas at Austin for free authentic listening texts in Arabic, Chinese, French, German, Spanish and many other languages. Additionally, the websites of organizations such as Peace Corps and UNESCO provide access to authentic texts such as radio broadcasts and magazine articles, as well as instructor-created lessons in over 101 languages.

Finally, advances in technology over the past twenty years have supported innovation in the design and implementation of the IPA by enabling easy access to authentic materials. Loyola (2014) outlined a range of resources to support each mode of communication. For the interpretive mode, some examples include watching the news online, listening to online radio, and accessing videos on YouTube. For the interpersonal mode, possible activities include using Flipgrid.com to facilitate discussion. For the presentational mode, learners can use iMovie to create a film or presentation software to create stories and presentations. Further, the internet and mobile apps provide a plethora of possibilities for publication of learner-created texts.

Beyond identifying authentic texts and creating possibilities for engagement, the COVID-19 pandemic has pushed instructors to explore new and innovative ways to implement IPAs. Russell and Murphy-Judy (2020) provide guidance for embedding the IPA into online language teaching. For hybrid instructional settings, Abraham and Williams (2009) examined the use of discussion tools in online learning platforms to enhance the interpretive and interpersonal IPA tasks. Finally, focusing on instruction and assessment tasks in the interpretive mode of communication, Martel (2021) described his experiences as he sought to build his repertoire for conducting interpretive activities asynchronously and create a virtual experience that was user friendly, using his university's Canvas platform with his Spring 2020 Intermediate-Low French class on food. Based on his experience, he suggested using the Canvas quiz tool for literal comprehension and the Canvas discussion tools for figurative or interpretive comprehension. Finally, he outlined a range of practices to consider for facilitating interpretive communication in an asynchronous course.

Chapter 3

Twenty Years of Research on the Integrated Performance Assessment

IPA History: Initial Research and Development

The IPA was originally designed in 1997 as the result of a U.S. Department of Education International Research and Studies grant awarded to ACTFL. The grant-funded project had three goals:

1. To develop an assessment prototype that would measure learners' progress in meeting the Standards for Foreign Language Learning in the 21st Century (NSFLEP, 1996; 1999, 2006)

2. To conduct research on the effectiveness of the assessment in measuring learners' progress toward the Standards

3. To use the assessment to prompt curricular and instructional reform (Adair-Hauck et al., 2006).

During the three-year grant, a team of world language educators and assessment specialists designed the assessment prototype and delivered professional development on the IPA to participating language instructors at six pilot sites located in Massachusetts, Pennsylvania, Virginia, Oklahoma, Wisconsin, and Oregon. In addition, the instructors received training on the Oral Proficiency Interview (OPI) or the Modified Oral Proficiency Interview (MOPI). The IPA was subsequently piloted by 30 foreign language instructors and with approximately 1,000 learners of Chinese, French, German, Italian, and Spanish across grade levels 3-12. After each of three rounds of field testing the IPA for purposes of researching its effectiveness as an assessment, revisions were made to the assessment and rubrics, performance data were compiled, and both instructors and learners responded to questionnaires to share their perceptions of the IPA in terms of its usefulness and feasibility. This research and development led to the publication of the results of the IPA pilot study (Adair-Hauck et al., 2006) and the first edition of the *ACTFL Integrated Performance Assessment Manual*

(Glisan et al., 2003), as well as scholarly publications, teacher preparation materials that addressed the IPA (such as Shrum & Glisan, 2016), and a video segment in the popular Annenberg/CPB video library, *Teaching Foreign Languages K-12: A Library of Classroom Practices* (Annenberg Learner, n.d).

The results of the initial IPA project illustrated that the IPA had a washback effect on instruction—that is, it prompted instructors to modify their classroom practices to enhance their learners' performance (Adair-Hauck et al., 2006). More specifically, instructors indicated that the IPA

> served as a catalyst to make them more aware of the need to integrate the three modes of communication into their lessons on a regular basis, design standards-based interpretive tasks using authentic documents, integrate more interpersonal speaking tasks, use more open-ended speaking tasks, and use more standards-based rubrics to help the students improve their language performance. (Adair-Hauck et al., 2006, p. 373)

Of interest is that instructors reported that the challenges of implementing this type of performance-based assessment included the lack of age-appropriate authentic texts and the difficulty of preparing learners for oral interpersonal tasks in which they would have to be spontaneous rather than read from a prepared text.

The First Decade of IPA Research

After the pilot study, the early research on the IPA examined its implementation in post-secondary and elementary school contexts. A study conducted at the U.S. Air Force Academy with cadets in an advanced Spanish course on Latin American Culture and Civilization explored learner performance across the three modes of communication to determine the extent to which secondary and post-secondary language study influenced learners' IPA outcomes (Glisan et al., 2007). This study marked the first instance of a video text being used in the interpretive mode, in contrast to the IPA pilot study, in which only printed texts were used. In terms of the modes of communication, this investigation provided five key findings. First, learners performed best on the presentational task, presumably because this mode had historically been the focus of instruction in world language classrooms. Second, the interpretive mode was the only mode in which some cadets did not meet expectations, perhaps due to the fact that their secondary language classes did not expose them to listening strategies, according to their post-IPA surveys. Third, learners did not perform as well on the interpersonal task as on the presentational task, which confirmed the findings of the pilot project regarding the challenge of teaching spontaneous face-to-face communication. Fourth, survey data revealed that cadets who had studied language in middle school performed better on the interpersonal task. Finally, there was a negative correlation between years of language study in high school and performance across the three modes of communication, possibly pointing to learners' traditional grammar-based courses and their lack of focus on meaningful communication (Glisan et al., 2007). In addition to demonstrating the potential of the IPA at the post-secondary level, the results of this study pointed to the continuing need to strengthen K-12 world language programs in terms of their abilities to deliver high quality instruction aligned with the Standards and, more specifically, the three modes of communication.

To explore the feasibility of using the IPA with elementary school learners, Davin et al. (2011) studied the implementation of the IPA in a class of learners in Grades 4 and 5 who had studied Spanish for four years. In a comparison of performance across the three modes, data revealed that learners received the lowest ratings on the interpretive task, which paralleled the findings reported by Glisan et al. (2007). The authors hypothesized that these results might have been a consequence of a lack of learner exposure to authentic spoken texts and the presence of a large amount of unfamiliar vocabulary in the video segment (Davin et al., 2011). Another similarity between these two studies was that learners in both contexts responded quite positively to the IPA on a follow-up survey, and both groups reported that they enjoyed the opportunity to interact orally with their classmates in the interpersonal task. Finally, this elementary school study revealed a positive washback effect on instruction, which corroborated the findings of the IPA pilot study

(Adair-Hauck et al., 2006).

The Davin et al. (2011) study also led to several insights for use of the IPA with elementary school learners. First, it showed that the IPA promoted learners' metacognitive awareness inasmuch as they were able to assess their own abilities on the interpretive and presentational tasks of the IPA, and they perceived a connection between classroom activities and the IPA as an assessment. Further, they recognized the types of knowledge and experiences that they needed to have in order to progress and perform at a higher level. Second, the study indicated that learners who spoke languages in addition to English might have had an advantage on the IPA, as demonstrated in the interpersonal task performance, suggesting that, while completing the IPA, multilingual learners drew upon their well-developed strategies and metalinguistic awareness (Anya, 2017; García, 2009; Sapienza et al., 2006).

Two themes from this study helped to shape the second edition of the ACTFL IPA Manual. First, Davin et al. (2011) revealed a significant correlation between the interpersonal and presentational Novice-level tasks of the IPA; that is, there was consistency between performance in these modes. In contrast, the authors described a "discontinuity between the interpretive task and other two tasks of this IPA," illustrating that the integrated use of the three modes of communication in this assessment does not imply that performance across the modes is parallel (Davin et al., 2011, p. 613). Second, the authors revised the language of the IPA rubrics to make them clearer and more meaningful to younger learners.

To better understand the dynamics of the feedback loop of the IPA, Adair-Hauck and Troyan (2013) presented a descriptive and co-constructed approach to IPA feedback. Their study examined the interactions in the teacher-to-learner feedback on performance on the interpersonal mode task and highlighted the ways in which discourse features of effective co-constructed IPA feedback encouraged learner self-reflection and self-regulation. Based on their study, Adair-Hauck and Troyan described the characteristics of effective feedback in the form of guidelines for teachers implementing the IPA in their classrooms. These guidelines provide insight on ways to carry out this type of feedback interaction with learners. See Chapter 5 for more complete details on this type of descriptive and co-constructed feedback.

During the first decade of the IPA, research at the elementary, secondary, and post-secondary levels provided a number of insights pertaining to learner performance, the washback effect, and the potential of the feedback loop to enhance learners' performance. This research served to inform the second edition and the subsequent research studies, which will be outlined in the following section.

The Second Edition of the IPA Manual: A Catalyst for New Research

Since the publication of the second edition, research has examined a wider range of topics and issues related to the IPA, providing a deeper understanding of the assessment and its impact on instruction, learning, and learner experiences. This work has focused on learners' and instructors' perceptions of the IPA (Altstaedter & Krosl, 2018; Darhower & Smith-Sherwood, 2021; Eddy & Bustamante, 2020; Kang, 2022; Zapata, 2016), instructor attitudes toward IPA implementation (Martel, 2018; Martel & Bailey, 2016), and the washback effect of the IPA on teaching and learning from elementary school through post-secondary language learners (Martel, 2019). Other research has expanded the IPA knowledge base by investigating the balance among the modes of communication in the IPA (Kissau & Adams, 2016), the impact of IPA-informed instruction on interpersonal speaking skills (Darhower & Smith-Sherwood, 2021), and the role of the IPA in pre-service and in-service teacher education (Eddy & Bustamante, 2020; Swanson & Goulette, 2018). The next section reports on the research insights from IPA implementation since 2013 according to the following themes in the research: Learner perceptions of the IPA, instructor perceptions of the IPA, assessment of the three modes of communication with the IPA, bridging the language and literature divide through the IPA, and the IPA in world language teacher preparation.

Learner Perceptions of the IPA

Research on the perceptions of learners regarding their experiences with the IPA in their world language learning programs has been conducted in a range of program types. In most cases, the research was part of comprehensive program initiatives that focused on IPA implementation, as well as understanding of the World-Readiness Standards for Language Learning (National Standards Collaborative Board, 2015) and proficiency development (see, for example,

Kang, 2022; Martel, 2018; Martel & Bailey, 2016; Sedor, 2020; Zapata, 2016). Zapata (2016) reported on the perceptions of 1,236 Novice (Level 1), Intermediate-Low (Level 2), and Intermediate-Mid (Level 3) learners of the IPA and the classroom instruction associated with it. In this study, 19 full-time instructors across language departments were required to participate in ACTFL Oral Proficiency Interview (OPI) tester/rater training and Writing Proficiency Test (WPT) rater training. In addition, the instructors participated in a two-day orientation workshop that shared World-Readiness Standards curriculum and methodology and tips for IPA implementation. In a similar vein, Martel and Bailey's project (Martel, 2018; Martel & Bailey, 2016) was embedded in an eight-week intensive language program that followed a communicative and content-based curriculum. IPAs were incorporated as the final exams for the 117 learners enrolled in the intensive programs in Arabic, Chinese, French, Russian, and Spanish. In contrast, Altstaedter and Krosl's (2018) research investigated learners' perceptions of the IPA in a single class of 20 beginning-level Spanish learners in a large southeastern public university. For this research project, learners took the two traditional tests focused on grammar and vocabulary, and a midterm "Study Abroad" IPA in place of the typical reading, writing, and oral assessments. Finally, Sedor (2020) conducted a longitudinal study of the IPA over three semesters in university-level beginning Spanish classrooms. Data sources included interviews, stimulated recalls, and classroom observations.

The studies that focused on learner perceptions of the IPA (Altstaedter & Krosl, 2018; Kang, 2022; Martel, 2018; Sedor, 2020; Zapata, 2016) found that learners appreciated that the IPA, unlike traditional tests, afforded them the opportunity to experience the target world language in ways that reflect real-life situations. Learners in Altstaedter and Krosl's study highlighted the IPA's format and ease of use as positive features, and those in Sedor's study viewed the IPA as contributing positively to their proficiency development in Spanish. In addition, learners in both studies were able to see a connection between class content and IPA tasks, and they developed metacognitive awareness in the IPA process because it encouraged them to reflect on their learning and language development, echoing the findings of Davin et al. (2011). Research on learner perceptions of the IPA in Korean language learning revealed that the IPA was highly feasible and viewed positively by learners (Kang, 2022). In this research, learners noted that IPAs were very challenging at the beginning, but activities such as classroom debates, short essay writings, and oral presentations helped them do better the second time. Two learners even commented that IPA tasks seemed more realistic than many other classroom activities (p. 527).

In addition to these positive perceptions, some negative perceptions were reported as well. For instance, some learners expressed a preference for traditional discrete-point tests because they perceived them as being easier (due to memorization) than the IPA (Zapata, 2016); moreover, some learners in the Martel and Bailey (2016) study found IPA assessment unfair because it did not contain a grammar section, while others found that the presentational task did not quite approximate what they would need to do with language outside of the classroom. Some of the Novice-level learners (Levels 1 and 2) in Zapata's study expressed an unfavorable opinion toward the IPA interpretive tasks; that is, they struggled with comprehension of authentic texts, and they stressed a lack of listening activities to prepare them for the IPA. This research supports two previous studies (Davin et al., 2011; Glisan et al., 2007) which demonstrated that for some learners, interpretive listening was the most challenging because it was not addressed adequately during instruction. Finally, some learners in the Martel and Bailey study perceived the IPA as an assessment for which they could not study and, therefore, they felt that they were at a disadvantage.

Instructor Perceptions of the IPA

Martel and Bailey's (2016) research provided important insights on instructor perceptions of the IPA. Many instructors reported that the IPA provided a common vocabulary across the language program to describe learner language proficiency and believed that the IPA aligned with their communicative and content-based approach to language learning. Despite this overall positive view of the IPA, the instructors expressed four concerns about their IPA implementation. First, a number of instructors were hesitant to use learners' first language (in this case English) to assess learners' comprehension in the interpretive tasks, which Adair-Hauck et al. (2013) recommend to allow for a full representation of what the learners interpreted. Martel (2016) explained that these instructors experienced difficulty with this premise. Since there was disagreement on this issue, the program agreed that the interpretive tasks could be carried out in

either learners' first language or the target language. Second, instructor attitudes toward using rubrics for grading were generally negative, with some instructors believing that the rubrics were not rigorous enough and caused grade inflation. Some instructors believed there should be more constructive feedback than what was offered on the rubrics. It is important to note, however, that this study did not include the IPA feedback loop and co-constructive feedback phase as recommended in the IPA literature (Adair-Hauck et al., 2006; Adair-Hauck et al., 2013; Glisan et al., 2003). Third, half of the instructors believed that IPA should not be used for true beginners or Novice-level learners, and that the IPA is more appropriate starting at the Novice-High level, that is, once learners have acquired a sufficient amount of vocabulary and grammar to carry out IPA tasks. The instructors' views on this point aligned with the recommendations in Adair-Hauck et al. (2013). Fourth, many of the instructors mentioned the difficulty of finding appropriate authentic materials, confirming the findings of previous IPA research (Adair-Hauck et al., 2006; Davin et al., 2011; Kissau & Adams, 2012). Fifth, the instructors felt that a database of summative IPAs with themes and content appropriate for college-level learners was needed to ease the burden of IPA design.

Assessment of the Three Modes of Communication with the IPA

Kissau and Adams (2016) researched the balance of the three modes of communication in IPAs in a K-12 setting. This mixed-methods investigation was conducted in a private K-12 school in the southeastern United States and explored how often Level I and Level II learners' performance in each of the modes of communication was assessed, along with teachers' reflections on their decision-making processes about the assessment of the modes. Six teachers in Grades 6-9—representing Chinese, French, German, and Spanish—and seven of their learners participated in the study. The world language teachers had adopted a proficiency-based approach to language learning to replace a traditional grammar-based curriculum that emphasized reading and writing. After participating in professional development on oral proficiency assessment, backward design, performance-based instruction, and the IPA, the teachers designed a new curriculum that included both IPAs and formative assessments linked to them. Results from this study showed that all of the teachers had implemented at least one theme-based IPA targeting interpretive listening and reading, interpersonal speaking, and presentational writing and speaking skills. However, an analysis of the formative and summative assessments revealed that the modes were not being assessed equally. For the interpretive mode, only 19 percent of all assessments targeted interpretive listening in both Levels I and II, with 26 percent of the assessments focused on interpretive reading in Level I and 37 percent in Level II. For the interpersonal mode, interpersonal speaking represented 13 percent of the assessments in Levels I and II. The presentational assessments differed between levels, with presentational writing targeted 31 percent of the time in Level I and 23 percent in Level II. Presentational speaking represented 13 percent of the assessments in Level I and 8 percent in Level II. See Figure 3.1 for the table from Kissau and Adams that summarizes all of the findings by language and level. These results demonstrated an imbalance across the modes of communication with an emphasis on reading and presentational writing.

Teacher interviews and faculty discussions highlighted teachers' shared beliefs that introductory world language classes should focus on interpretive listening and interpersonal speaking. However, even though many of the teachers expressed that presentational writing represented the great-

est challenge for beginning learners, data revealed that this mode was highly targeted. This study underscored a disconnect between the teachers' beliefs and their actual practice. Teachers cited both a lack of authentic materials for listening assessments for beginning-level learners, and a lack of time, space, and knowledge on how to collect speaking samples for interpersonal assessments. For this reason, they reported needing more professional development on how to assess the interpretive and interpersonal modes. While this study explored the teachers' first attempts at IPA implementation, it also served as a consciousness-raising tool to assist them in reflecting on their beliefs regarding language learning, assessment, and actual instructional practices.

Bridging the Language and Literature Divide through the IPA

Recent groundbreaking research at the post-secondary level has highlighted the potential of IPA implementation in a literature course. Motivated by over two decades of scholarship that has scrutinized the role of interpersonal speaking skills in literature courses (Donato & Brooks, 2004; Mantero, 2002; Paesani & Allen, 2012; Thoms, 2012), Darhower and Smith-Sherwood (2021) sought to bridge the language-literature divide by integrating IPA assessment into an introduc-

Figure 3.1 Modes of Communication Assessed in Kissau and Adams (2016)

Table 1					
Modes of Communication Assessed					
	Interpretive Listening	Interpretive Reading	Interpersonal Speaking	Presentational Writing	Presentational Speaking
French I	21%	24%	12%	24%	19%
French I	18%	45%	9%	14%	14%
Spanish I	15%	18%	13%	36%	18%
Spanish I	16%	23%	3%	55%	3%
Chinese I	26%	15%	15%	22%	22%
German I	16%	31%	14%	37%	2%
Level 1 Average	19%	26%	13%	31%	13%
French II	27%	42%	15%	8%	8%
Spanish II	26%	10%	15%	41%	8%
German II	3%	60%	10%	20%	7%
Level II Average	19%	37%	13%	23%	8%

tory literature course while also focusing on literary analysis. Specifically, the researchers sought to measure improvement of 15 learners' oral proficiency over the course of the semester and to capture their perceptions regarding an interpersonal listening/speaking component of the IPA-informed literature course.

This study revealed four key insights for the IPA in a post-secondary literature course. First, it demonstrated how the IPA can be a beneficial pedagogical tool in an undergraduate literature course through its focus on the three modes of communication, while integrating authentic literary texts. Second, nearly all learners in the study measurably improved their interpersonal speaking performance in one semester. Notably, interpersonal speaking gains were measured in language structures, communicative functions, and negotiation of meaning and vocabulary, whereas fewer gains were seen in comprehensibility and text type. Third, nearly all learners perceived that IPA-informed instruction had a positive impact on their interpersonal speaking development. Fourth, almost all learners found the co-constructed feedback important for developing their interpersonal language, due to its interactive nature and because it made the learners aware of their areas of strength and areas that needed developmental improvement. Chapter 7 provides an in-depth presentation and discussion of Smith-Sherwood and Darhower's work in implementing IPA for post-secondary literature classes.

The IPA in World Language Teacher Preparation

Eddy and Bustamante (2020) underscored the knowledge gap between student teachers (STs) and cooperating teachers (CTs) with respect to assessing the World-Readiness Standards (National Standards Collaborative Board, 2015). This case study included nine STs at two universities in New York, seven CTs, and one university field supervisor (UFS). Prior to and at the time of publication (2020), the New York State Learning Standards did not require or recommend the adoption of the Five Cs of Language Education from the World-Readiness Standards, nor did they recommend the need to plan, teach, and assess for the three modes of communication. However, in 2013 New York adopted the World Languages edTPA (https://edtpa.org/about), which required student teachers to design, teach, and assess in at least two modes of communication (interpretive, which is a required mode, and either the interpersonal or presentational mode),

and highly recommended integrating the three modes of communication with feedback into their portfolio artifacts. The dilemma for the two university world language departments participating in this study was their need to train STs on how to implement the IPA with CTs who had little experience in IPA implementation.

The results revealed that, in general, the CTs were unfamiliar with the IPA, the three modes of communication, and the need to maximize target language use in the world language classroom. The authors pointed out that the absence of the three modes of communication and the use of authentic documents from the New York World Language Learning Standards had contributed to this disparity between the knowledge and practice of STs and their CTs. (Note: Since the publication of this study, New York State has revised the Learning Standards to integrate the three modes of communication and other aspects of the World-Readiness Standards.) The study also highlighted that the few STs whose CTs were familiar with the IPA expressed no major issues regarding IPA implementation and that the majority of the CTs liked the effectiveness of the IPA format for lesson planning. Finally, a number of CTs stated that a challenge for IPA implementation was selecting age-appropriate authentic documents.

To better understand teacher candidates' patterns on a performance assessment for teaching, Swanson and Goulette (2018) conducted a research project to ascertain how teacher candidates from a large urban teacher preparation program performed on the performance assessment; what factors accounted for the differences between high scorers and lower scorers; and how the assessment practices used by high-scoring teacher candidates compared with those used by lower-scoring candidates. Twenty-two teaching performance assessment portfolios were selected and ranked. While all of the teacher candidates scored above the designated cutoff score for the performance assessment of teaching, only the five highest-scoring portfolios and the five lowest-scoring portfolios were examined.

The results revealed that all five candidates who received the highest scores incorporated the IPA to assess for learner communicative proficiency and grounded their assessments in a meaningful cultural context. In contrast, the five candidates who received the lowest scores used traditional assessment practices such as focus-on-form tests or structured and memorized dialogues that lacked meaningful cultural contexts. Together, the findings of the research in world language teacher preparation provide further evidence of the importance of developing world language teachers' professional repertoires for enacting the IPA and other practices that are critical to effective standards-based instruction (see, for example, Glisan & Donato, 2017, 2021).

The IPA in Online Language Teaching

With the transition to online language teaching since the inception of the IPA twenty years ago, research and practice have explored the use of the IPA in online contexts as well. In their book *Teaching Language Online: A Guide to Designing, Developing, and Delivering Online, Blended, and Flipped Language Courses*, Russell and Murphy-Judy (2020) outline principles and practices for integrating the IPA into online language teaching. Likewise, Gacs, Goertler, and Spasova (2020) advocated the IPA as a way for online language instructors to take advantage of the digital teaching and learning context in ways that traditional language testing does not allow. Early research by Abraham and Williams (2009) examined the use of discussion tools in online learning platforms to enhance the IPA. The findings of this research documented the affordances of online discussion tools in a unit of instruction that was constructed around IPA tasks focused on the theme of ecology. The authors proposed ways that discussion tools could enhance the discourse and opportunities for interaction in interpretive and interpersonal tasks.

In a qualitative study, Zhang (under review) examined the motivation of two Chinese as a Foreign Language (CFL) learners in online learning in an IPA-informed CFL curriculum. The learners, Miki and Fred, whose first languages were Japanese and Spanish respectively, were both 20 years old at the time of the study; they were enrolled in an intermediate CFL course at a Sino-American university in China during the 2021-2022 academic year. Miki experienced the online IPA tasks and related instructional activities "as a scaffolding gateway to real-life communication" with speakers of the language (p. 23). By contrast, Fred experienced low motivation in the course due to external factors as well as a lack of contact with speakers of Chinese because he was enrolled in the course from outside of China. Fred's official OPI ratings reflected the findings related to his motivation, as he was rated at Intermediate-Low both at the beginning and at the end of the year. Overall, this study demonstrated the feasibility of the IPA for remote online language learning and, at the same time, pointed to considerations that instructors need to make to maximize learners' motivation and engagement, such as raising their awareness of strategies for engaging with speakers of the target language outside of class (either virtually or in person) and making explicit connections to learners' interests and backgrounds.

Key Lessons From 20 Years of IPA Research

Building upon the IPA pilot study and the first ten years of IPA implementation, research over the past two decades has solidly positioned the IPA as a highly effective standards-based performance assessment and a professional development reform tool for the profession. The research results on learner and instructor perceptions of the IPA from both large- and small-scale studies has also reported positive perceptions of the IPA in terms of its ease of use, format, and inclusion of tasks that reflect real-world target language use. This research has also reiterated the potential of the IPA to develop learners' awareness of their growing abilities to use the target language.

While the IPA has generally been positively received, some of the research findings show that additional professional development is still needed. Some of the findings on learner perceptions highlighted negative perceptions of the IPA because, for example, learners still had preferences for traditional testing and struggled with certain task types, such as spontaneous interpersonal speaking tasks. In some cases, the research findings related to instructor practices revealed tensions in the implementation of the IPA. Specifically, instructors sometimes struggled with using the rubrics, integrating authentic texts, and preparing learners for IPA tasks. In addition, a key challenge was shown to be the balancing of formative and summative assessments across the three modes. This research has highlighted the challenges in implementing innovation and reform, as well as the long-term commitment that is required to carry out the shift toward standards-based assessment and instruction.

The research on world language teacher preparation highlights the central role of the IPA in preparing teacher candidates to enact effective instruction in the world language classroom. For post-secondary programs, the IPA can help bridge the language-literature divide and more fully position interpersonal language use at the center of literature courses. In all cases, making the shift toward the IPA has involved ongoing support for and reflection on implementation of the IPA. Such professional development not only supports the work of designing and implementing IPAs, but also promotes use of a full range of practices for effective world language instruction.

Finally, research on the use of the IPA in online language learning contexts has demonstrated its feasibility in both hybrid and fully online courses. In hybrid contexts, digital tools can enhance interaction and dialogue related to IPA tasks. In fully online settings, the IPA can serve as a vehicle for implementing authentic world language learning and assessment through backward design (Russell & Murphy-Judy, 2020; Zhang, under review). Moving forward, additional research is needed to understand how to maximize language proficiency development in online programs connected to the IPA.

This third edition of the IPA Manual has been developed largely on the basis of the research that has been con-

ducted since the second edition was published. As described in the introductory section What's New in the Third Edition of the Integrated Performance Assessment Manual, new features—such as expanded rubrics, guidance for using rubrics to assign grades, new comprehension guide templates for viewing and listening, and more in-depth discussions of how to prepare learners for the IPA—address specific recommendations that have emanated from research studies. Further, this edition sets the stage for continued dialogue on important research-based issues such as the connection between formative instructional practices and the IPA, the use of the IPA to transform the literature class in post-secondary classrooms, the use of the IPA in online instructional settings, and the potential of the IPA as a vehicle for instruction and assessment that centers diversity, equity, and inclusion in the world language classroom.

Chapter 4

Linking the IPA and Instruction: A Transformative Tool for Backward Design and Formative Instructional Practices

The twenty years of research on the IPA discussed in Chapter 3 present a clear case for the role of the IPA as a transformative tool in terms of its ability to establish the link between assessment and instruction. The research studies highlight the need for instructional design to reflect the tasks and performances of the IPA; in other words, the IPA is only as good as the instruction that leads to it.

This chapter uses an example of the IPA from a high school Spanish classroom to illustrate the formative instructional practices of the IPA in action, presenting the IPA as a tool for backward planning according to *Understanding by Design* (UbD; Wiggins & McTighe, 2005). In the first section of the chapter, the IPA "Social Media and Bullying" is integrated into a unit of instruction following the UbD planning template. Each step of the UbD process is briefly discussed to demonstrate how instructors can plan authentic learning activities that prepare learners for the performance tasks of a summative IPA. The second section of the chapter addresses the design of learning activities that prepare learners for each type of task in the IPA. This section also offers guidance to instructors as they begin to plan and implement the type of instruction that is called for in a UbD approach that integrates the IPA. Included in this section are updated guidelines for selecting authentic texts to assist instructors in identifying appropriate printed, audio, and video texts for interpretive mode tasks in IPAs and in instructional activities.

Understanding by Design: A Framework for Planning the IPA

Since the publication of *Understanding by Design* (Wiggins & McTighe, 2005), backward design has been promoted in the profession; see for example Glisan, 2010; Glisan & Donato, 2021; Glisan et al., 2003; Martel, 2022; Sandrock, 2010; Shrum & Glisan, 2016; Troyan, 2021; and Zapata, 2018a. Furthermore, the IPA was conceived as a tool for backward

design of assessment and instruction (Adair-Hauck et al., 2013; Glisan et al., 2003) and has been implemented as such (see for example Davin et al., 2011a, 2011b; Martel, 2019; Troyan, 2008). Backward design provides a framework for the planning and implementation of instruction that is linked to the Standards and the authentic performance tasks of the IPA. Using backward design also allows instructors to design IPAs that center social justice, equity, and inclusion in the work of the world language classroom (see for example Anya & Randolph, 2019; Glynn et al., 2018; Miranda & Troyan, 2022; Wassell & Glynn, 2022). Finally, backward design is a central feature of the Formative Instructional Practices (FIP) identified by scholars in special education to promote equitable access to world language instruction to all learners (Graham-Day et al., 2014; Graham-Day et al., 2020).

To assist instructors in implementing an approach to instructional planning that is informed by and explicitly linked to performance assessment and outcomes, Wiggins and McTighe provide a template that guides instructors through three stages: Desired results, assessment evidence, and learning plan. Figure 4.1 presents a version of the UbD template that incorporates the three tasks of the IPA to guide foreign language instructors in identifying these stages in relation to language teaching and learning:

- Stage 1, Desired Results: The Standards addressed, the essential questions answered, the understandings uncovered, and the language, content, and performances developed.
- Stage 2, Assessment Evidence: The formative and summative assessment tasks aligned with the desired results.
- Stage 3, Learning Plan: The activities that are linked to the assessments in the sequence of instruction.

Note that in implementing backward design, a "unit" may be considered the traditional unit of instruction, a semester, or a year-long sequence of instruction (Glisan, 2010).

Figure 4.1 Unit Planning Template Adapted for IPA

Stage 1—Desired Results	
Established Goal(s)—Standards Addressed:	
Essential Question(s):	**Understanding(s):** *Learners will understand that...*
Learners will know...	*Learners will be able to...*

Stage 2—Assessment Evidence	
Summative Integrated Performance Assessment (IPA) *Note: The statements below later become IPA task overviews.* Interpretive Mode: Interpersonal Mode: Presentational Mode:	**Formative Assessment Evidence** Interpretive Mode: Interpersonal Mode: Presentational Mode: Other evidence:
Stage 3—Learning Plan	

Source: Wiggins & McTighe, 2005. *Template adapted with permission from Association for Supervision and Curriculum Development (ASCD).*

The following example depicts the planning process of Jesse Carnevali, a high school Spanish teacher, to illustrate his design of an IPA and its link to the UbD planning template. Mr. Carnevali implemented this IPA with two sections of Spanish 4 learners. The learners had completed Level 1 in middle school across three different years (one trimester in 6th Grade, a half year in 7th Grade, and a full year in 8th Grade). They then had taken Spanish 2 as freshmen and Spanish 3 as sophomores; they were taking Spanish 4 as juniors. The IPA and the corresponding instruction were designed to answer the following essential questions over the course of a 7-week unit:

- Why do people use social media?
- How do social media and cell phone dependence affect daily life?
- How does cyberbullying differ from bullying?
- Why does bullying exist and what can be done to reduce it?
- What cultural products, practices, and perspectives influence the use of social media and the act of bullying?

IPA Overview
Intermediate Level
"Social Media and Bullying"

You have decided to join a new anti-bullying club that just formed in your school district to advocate for the social health and well-being of the students in the district. The club is looking to gain as many Spanish-speaking members as possible and therefore needs help with promoting their goals and mission. In order to contribute as a new member, you will first observe a meeting and watch a video to get a better understanding of the club's goals. You will then interview an exchange student in the district to identify their own beliefs, needs, ideas and experiences with bullying and anti-bullying. Finally, you will create a flyer to hang in the school promoting the new anti-bullying club to help gain more members and promote positive behavior in the school district.

Example: Using the UbD Template for IPA Design and Lesson Planning

Instructor: Jesse Carnevali
School: Franklin Regional Sr. High School, Murrysville, PA

Languages and
levels taught: Spanish 2, 4, and 5

IPA theme: Social Media and Bullying
Language: Spanish
IPA level: Intermediate
Class level/size: 2 sections of Spanish 4 / 20 & 25 Students

Standards addressed:
    Communication (interpersonal, interpretive, presentational)
    Cultures (relating cultural practices to perspectives)
    Connections (acquiring information and diverse perspectives)
    Comparisons (cultural comparisons)
    Communities (school and global communities)

Who Is Jesse Carnevali?

Jesse Carnevali graduated from Indiana University of Pennsylvania in 2013 with a B.S. Ed Spanish Education (K-12) and a B.A. in Spanish. He is currently teaching High School Spanish levels II, IV, and V at Franklin Regional School District in Murrysville, PA, where he also serves as the World Language Curriculum Coordinator and Teacher Leader. Jesse received his master's degree in Spanish Education from the University of Nebraska at Kearney in 2016. He also completed MOPI and OPI training workshops which led to his MOPI certification. Jesse is currently working with a textbook publishing company to create thirteen IPAs as a supplement to their new Spanish program.

Figure 4.2 shows how Mr. Carnevali used the UbD template to plan the IPA and the corresponding instructional activities. Note that he engages learners in comparing and contrasting and circumlocution using intermediate-level language. These functions may seem like higher-level

Figure 4.2 Unit Planning Template: IPA Example

Stage 1—Desired Results
Established Goal(s)—Standards Addressed: Communication (interpersonal, interpretive, presentational) Cultures (relating cultural practices to perspectives) Connections (acquiring information and diverse perspectives) Comparisons (cultural comparisons) Communities (school and global communities)

Essential Question(s):	**Understanding(s)**
Why do people use social media? How do social media and cell phone dependence affect daily life? How does cyberbullying differ from bullying? Why does bullying exist and what can be done to reduce it? What cultural products, practices, and perspectives influence the use of social media and the act of bullying?	Learners will understand that... Social media is used for a variety of purposes and differs among age groups. Cell phone addiction contributes to a dependence on technology and increases the pressures of social life. All types of bullying are intentional and can be reduced with an active voice. The use of and dependence upon technology for social media, cyberbullying, and daily life represents various cultural products, practices, and perspectives among different cultures.
Learners will know...(Key Cultural and Linguistic Knowledge)	**Learners will be able to...** (Key Language Functions and Communication Strategies)
· the most popular social media pages among adolescents and adults · the similarities and differences of the usage of social media among the age groups · the similarities and differences of cyberbullying and bullying · key vocabulary, expressions, and grammar to engage in interpretive, interpersonal, and presentational tasks related to social media and bullying · the formation and use of a variety of questions to function at the intermediate level of proficiency during interpersonal interviews · the basics of affirmative and negative commands in the context of the unit (promoting anti-bullying behavior in the school district)	· compare and contrast the various usages of social media among various age groups · demonstrate an understanding of and interpret various authentic texts related to social media and bullying · interview their classmates and other speakers of Spanish to gain useful information and diverse perspectives about their experiences with social media and bullying · describe some ways to reduce bullying within the school community and online

Stage 2—Assessment Evidence	
Summary Integrated Performance Assessment (IPA) The statements below are IPA task overviews.	**Formative Assessment Evidence**
Interpretive Mode	*Interpretive Mode*
We have been studying the themes of social media, cyberbullying, and bullying over the past three weeks. You just joined the new anti-bullying club at school and were invited to view a special introductory video from El país with the Spanish-speaking students. View the video and complete the accompanying Comprehension Guide.	• completion of a social media survey (Appendix G) • listening task connected to the song Hawái by Maluma • completion of a comprehension guide while reading a news article about "nomofobia" [fear of not having a phone] and signs of technology addiction (Link to text: https://theconversation.com/como-se-si-padezco-nomofobia-miedo-irracional-a-no-tener-el-movil-ni-whatsapp-168028)
Interpersonal Mode	*Interpersonal Mode*
After viewing the video and acquiring different perspectives from the students around the topic of bullying, you will have the opportunity to interview one of the Spanish-speaking exchange students to gather their viewpoints, experiences, and perspectives. During the interview, try to gather as much information from the student as possible related to the topic and the club.	• interview activity to assess the social media habits of a classmate • information-gap activities for vocabulary in context focused on the ability to create language, practice circumlocution, and function at the intermediate level • role play activities within the context of the unit
Presentational Mode	*Presentational Mode*
Based on what you have learned from the video, your interview, and this unit in general, you are now ready to create the flyer to promote the new anti-bullying club. The flyer should include important information about the purpose of the group, including the club's goals. Additionally, you should give some basic information to start promoting positive behavior within the school district. Remember, the goal of a club flyer is to gain interest and also provide a variety of information to help those who are interested make an appropriate decision regarding bullying and anti-bullying!	• brief class presentations describing the technological habits of the class • jigsaw activity group presentations of the pros/cons of technology **Other Evidence:** • reading/skimming daily discussion board posts relating to important unit concepts • contextualized quiz for vocabulary comprehension and production • student-generated google form survey of questions related to the unit • contextualized assessment of affirmative and negative commands

Stage 3—Learning Plan
• Learners will complete a survey about the amount of time they spend using their cell phone and will discuss the results as a whole class.
• Learners will circumlocute the vocabulary from the unit in meaningful, context-rich situations with their classmates and teacher.
• Learners will create their own survey on Google Forms to gather information about the technological habits of one of their classmates.
• Learners will listen to a song related to social media relationships and how that relates to their own experiences.
• Learners will interact in small groups in which they:
◦ discuss the pros/cons of technology and social media
◦ compare/contrast their online habits
◦ talk about the differences and signs of bullying and cyberbullying

language ones. However, Mr. Carnevali's students are using intermediate-level language, including complex sentences, present tense, descriptions, and questioning, which will be a springboard enabling them to perform these functions using higher-level language later on.

Stage One—Identify Desired Results

In the first stage, the instructor identifies the standards, the essential questions, and the overall objectives that the unit will address. These components comprise the targets or "desired results" of instruction. The process begins with the identification of the relevant established goals or, as this example illustrates, the *Standards addressed* in the unit of instruction. In his completed planning template (Figure 4.2), Mr. Carnevali identified the interpersonal, interpretive, and presentational modes of the Communication goal area; "relating cultural practices to perspectives" from the Cultures goal area; "acquiring information and diverse perspectives" from the Connections goal area; "cultural comparisons" from the Comparisons goal area; and "school and global communities" from the Communities goal area.

After the established goals have been articulated in the form of the World Readiness Standards, the instructor unpacks the goals by identifying essential questions and the corresponding understandings. To determine the essential questions for the unit, the instructor identifies the principles, laws, theories, or concepts that need to be uncovered in the unit (Wiggins & McTighe, 2005). Each understanding is phrased to complete the sentence starter "Learners will

understand that…" For example, among the understandings that Mr. Carnevali wanted his learners to develop in this unit of instruction was the understanding that "Cell phone addiction contributes to a dependence on technology and increases the pressures of social life." To arrive at this understanding, learners will investigate the essential question "How do social media and cell phone dependence affect daily life?" Throughout the learning activities and performance assessments, learners will examine the many ways in which youth, in particular, have become dependent on social media.

Based on the goals, questions, and understandings identified, Mr. Carnevali completes the final component of Stage One by identifying what learners will know and be able to do. To this end, Mr. Carnevali lists the important cultural knowledge (such as the most popular social media pages among adolescents and adults) and key linguistic features (for example, the key vocabulary, expressions, and grammar needed to engage in interpretive, interpersonal, and presentational tasks related to social media and bullying). Note that the "knowledge" identified in this section is bound to the content and contexts described in the essential questions and understandings sections. In particular, the linguistic knowledge identified here should be linked to the descriptions in the next column of what learners will be able to do with language.

To the right of what learners will know on the template, the instructor lists the language functions and communicative strategies that learners will be asked to perform. A *language function* reflects how speakers use language to realize a meaningful, communicative goal, such as comparing and contrasting uses of social media or interviewing others about their experiences with social media and bullying. In each case, the statements in this column should be linked back to the statements of what learners will know in the previous column. Linking the information in the two columns in this way ensures that language learning is embedded in a meaningful context (Shrum & Glisan, 2016).

Stage Two—Determine Acceptable Evidence

The second stage involves determining the type of evidence that will verify that learners have achieved the desired outcomes or results, through the design of summative and formative assessments, a central feature of both UbD and Formative Instructional Practices (FIP). In this part of the UbD template, Mr. Carnevali describes the two types of assessment he will use in the unit. The first type, summative assessment, consists of the performance tasks of the IPA that learners will complete at the end of the unit. The second type, formative assessment, includes assessments that serve as checkpoints throughout the unit of instruction. The formative assessments serve two purposes. First, they provide critical data for the instructor, who uses them to inform and modify instruction (Black & Wiliam, 1998; Halverson et al., 2007; Supovitz & Klein, 2003) by "uncovering the learners' *understandings and misunderstandings* all along the way" (Wiggins & McTighe, 2005, p. 247, italics in original). As Graham-Day et al. (2020) describe in their guide for integrating IPA and FIP, "to prepare for a summative IPA, a world language educator employs several formative assessment strategies where s/he collects evidence of student learning in relation to the standard and the final assessment for the learning segment" (p. 143).

In another respect, some of the formative assessment tasks are intentionally designed to mirror the performance in the summative IPA, thereby providing a critical opportunity for modeling and practicing of performance (Adair-Hauck & Troyan, 2013; Tharp & Gallimore, 1988; Wiggins, 1998). This layering of assessment types throughout the unit of instruction ensures that learners understand "the important attributes of a skilled performance" (Graham-Day et al., 2020, p. 144). In his example UbD template, Mr. Carnevali identifies the summative performance tasks in one column, and the formative performance tasks and other types of evidence (such as a social media survey, listening task, com-

prehension guide, information-gap activity, jigsaw activity) in another. Notice that the description of the summative performance tasks by mode of communication corresponds to the IPA task overviews that learners will receive before they complete each task. The formative assessments may include a range of assessment types; however, it is critical that some of the assessments in this column model the type of performance that will be required in the summative IPA. In other words, in addition to providing the instructor with data for instructional decisions, formative assessments allow learners to engage in performance tasks that are analogous to the summative IPA tasks.

Stage Three—Plan Learning Activities

Only after the goals for the unit have been established and the assessments designed can the instructor begin to plan instruction. In effect, this approach is the opposite of the traditional approach to instructional planning in which an instructor would, as Wiggins says, "teach, test and hope for the best" (Annenberg Learner, n.d.). By contrast, the learning activities that evolve in the UbD process are planned "with the end in mind" (Annenberg Learner, n.d). Notice that the activities described engage learners in meaningful communication that prepares them for the formative and summative performance assessment tasks. For example, Mr. Carnevali designed an ongoing learning activity to give learners practice and rehearsal for the summative interactive interviewing performance task that will be required during the IPA. The ongoing interview-based learning activity functions as a formative assessment and an opportunity for learners to self-assess their performance, as well as serving as preparation for an authentic interview that learners will later conduct with a Spanish-speaking exchange student.

Through one sample IPA, this section has traced the stages of UbD, beginning with the articulation of goals as expressed in the Standards, continuing in the depiction of assessments in the unit, and culminating in a description of learning activities linked to the goals and assessments. As noted above, the IPA will only be as effective as the instruction that leads to it. The UbD approach can support instructors, districts, and programs in using the IPA to align assessment, instruction, and learning with the Standards because UbD offers a framework for planning that is aligned with the design features of the IPA (Glisan et al., 2003, p. 24).

Considerations in the Preparation of Learning Activities

To expand on the discussion of planning for instruction and assessment, this section outlines guidelines for instructors in planning IPAs, formative assessments, and the instructional activities linked to the IPA in the UbD approach. It begins with a discussion of differentiated instruction that is informed by Formative Instructional Practices (FIP), which are intended to provide equitable access to world language instruction to all learners (Graham-Day et al., 2014; Graham-Day et al., 2020).

Differentiation of Tasks Across Three Modes Within a Unit

In order to promote equitable access to world language instruction for all learners during a unit based on an IPA, differentiation of instruction informed by the tenets of Formative Instructional Practices (FIP) can be integrated at various points. For example, one of the tasks in Mr. Carnevale's unit requires learners to complete a social media survey. When completing this survey, differentiation can occur in multiple ways informed by the FIP principle and practices for clear learning targets based on standards. First, with the learning targets in mind, the instructor can assist learners to interpret the questions within the survey by embedding images directly with them. That is, if a question involves a new or unfamiliar vocabulary word, an image can be used to help learners visualize what is being asked. A second method of differentiation can occur by using multiple surveys with similar questions but with different possibilities for responses. For example, a learner with lower functional language ability may be asked a question and then given three or four completed responses from which to choose. On the other hand, the same question can be used with open-ended responses for learners who are ready to create and produce their own thoughts and language. If needed, there can be a mixture of multiple choice and open-ended response options within the survey. Either way, the results of the survey should still be representative of the original intent.

Another example of differentiation that appears in Mr. Carnevali's unit is where learners are asked to work in small groups as they circumlocute various vocabulary words that pertain to the unit context. Because language at the Intermediate level means most learners have limited vocabulary,

circumlocution at this level may result in frustration on the part of some speakers. Instructors can help their learners circumlocute by letting them describe the word or phrase they mean instead of searching for a specific term.

Intermediate-level tasks that engage learners in circumlocution enable them to experience an Advanced-level skill while offering another effective opportunity to differentiate instruction based on the FIP principle and practices of learner involvement. In Mr. Carnevale's lesson, learners are placed in groups of four, and each receives a list of five vocabulary words from the unit. Their task is to use their ability to circumlocute the words so that the other group members can identify the word being described. One opportunity for differentiation is to adjust the difficulty levels of the lists. For example, Learner A could have a list of very basic vocabulary while Learner B's list has a few challenging words. Learners C and D could then receive lists with more challenging vocabulary. When planning out the groups, the teacher would determine which learners receive which lists. Another differentiation opportunity would be to reduce the number of words that certain learners or groups have on their lists so they can focus their attention on a smaller set.

One additional example of differentiation that involves the FIP principle of learner involvement can be implemented during the presentational task where learners analyze and summarize the results of the survey on their classmates' technology habits. A choice board of how these results can be explained and presented can work well to accommodate learners' needs and functional language ability levels. Choices may include meeting with the instructor in a one-on-one presentation; presenting findings in writing by taking screenshots of the results and graphs of the survey and explaining the interpretations of those results; or presenting the visual findings to the class or a group of their classmates. Learners can also work in small groups to compare the results of their surveys and present those findings and interpretations to the class. The instructor can decide what choices to offer and how small groups should be populated based on the individual and group needs of the class. Throughout the unit of instruction, focusing on the principles and practices of FIP allows the instructor to more effectively differentiate instruction for learners performing at a variety of levels.

Learning Activities to Prepare Learners for the Interpretive Task

Chapter 2 presented a detailed discussion of the IPA interpretive tasks and the comprehension guide that learners complete to illustrate their level of comprehension and interpretation. The tasks progress across levels from those that require *literal comprehension*—detection of key words, main ideas, and supporting details—to more *interpretive comprehension*—identification of organizational features, guessing meaning from context, gleaning inferences, and identifying author and cultural perspectives. Learners need a great deal of experience in exploring authentic texts and acquiring strategies for how to derive meaning from them. They must also come to understand that total comprehension of a text is not the goal and that translation from the target language of the text into one's first/strongest language does not constitute comprehension or interpretation. In fact, translation is a strategy that should be discouraged in the interpretation process. (See Chapter 2 for a full discussion about the rationale for using English in some of the interpretive tasks and an explanation of how this use of English for assessment of comprehension does *not* equate to engaging learners in rote translation.)

Strategies such as skimming for the main idea and scanning for details will help learners understand the literal meaning of texts. Additionally, learners should gain experience in engaging in interpretive comprehension by learning to use the context and organizational features of the text as clues to meaning as well as exploring inferences, author perspectives, and cultural insights with their classmates. Learners often gain new insights about a text as a result of text-based discussions that they have with their peers. This social view of the interpretive process reflects the sociocultural view of language learning, in which learners and instructor co-construct meaning, and it "mirrors the way in which comprehension is constructed socioculturally in the world outside the classroom" (Shrum & Glisan, 2016, p. 178).

In sum, preparing learners to comprehend and interpret an authentic text in the IPA requires using a number of instructional strategies that will give them confidence in dealing with the target language in its authentic form. Some specific strategies that the instructor might use include:

- Integrating authentic texts into instruction on a regular basis
- Providing opportunities for learners to explore an authentic text to glean either the main idea or specific details (skimming or scanning), but without having to demonstrate an understanding of the entire text
- Preparing learners for the task by activating their background knowledge and engaging them in anticipating the main idea of what they will listen to/read/view
- Encouraging learners to develop their own purposes for listening to/reading/viewing an authentic text
- Providing learners with strategies for comprehending authentic printed texts such as using contextual clues, using word families as clues to figuring out the meaning of new words, identifying key words that provide meaning clues, and using titles and visuals that appear with the text as clues to meaning
- Providing opportunities for learners to check their initial guesses about meaning against the context and revise them as necessary
- Engaging learners in gleaning meaning from visuals that are included to support the meaning of the text
- Providing learners with strategies for comprehending authentic oral texts such as listening to the segment multiple times (each time for additional information), pausing the recorded segment to give time for recalling what was heard, and listening for key words only
- Designing interpretive activities that include pair and group collaboration
- Using interpretive tasks as the basis for interpersonal and presentational communication
- Assisting learners in moving from literal comprehension (key word, main idea and supporting detail detection) to interpretive comprehension (word and concept inferences, organizing principles, author perspective, and cultural perspectives of the text)
- Facilitating the interpretive task by enabling learners to collaborate with one another, construct meaning together, use teacher and peer feedback in refining hypotheses, and accept an active role in developing their interpretive abilities
- Providing opportunities for learners to select their own authentic texts of interest and demonstrate their comprehension and interpretation of them (Shrum & Glisan, 2016).

Factors To Consider When Selecting Authentic Texts for the Interpretive Tasks

Another important aspect of preparing learners for interpretive tasks is the selection of the appropriate text for both classroom learning activities and use in the IPA (Glisan et al., 2003). Instructors can use various sources from the target language culture to find the oral, printed, and video texts required for the interpretive tasks, both for the classroom practice that prepares learners for the IPA and for the IPA itself. The texts selected should be *authentic*; that is, texts that are "produced *by* members of a language and culture group *for* members of the same language and culture group" (Galloway, 1998, p. 133). Authentic texts such as announcements and invitations distributed by churches to those in the community or public service announcements issued by health agencies can also be found in local communities in which the target language is spoken. The selection of these types of resources enables learners to connect to socially varied forms of the target language spoken by immigrant/heritage communities while motivating them to engage in communication within their own local areas (Zapata & Ribota, 2021).

While instructors may find it intuitively appropriate to simplify or edit authentic texts to make them easier for learners to interpret, particularly for those in beginning language classes, research indicates that learners demonstrate a higher level of comprehension on texts that are read in their authentic, unedited versions in contrast to versions that are simplified through lexical changes such as substituting known vocabulary for original vocabulary contained in the text; see for example Allen et al., 1988; Oguro, 2008; Young, 1999. Simplifying a text for learners may in reality be counterproductive, given that the natural redundancy of the authentic context facilitates comprehension (Shrum & Glisan, 2016). An alternative to changing the text and sacrificing its authenticity is to teach learners strategies for interpreting authentic texts such as using their background knowledge, the context of the text, and word families to hypothesize meaning. Note that the oral and printed texts included as part of a textbook program are often not authentic; that is, they are prepared by textbook authors for instructional purposes.

According to Shrum & Glisan (2016), two types of factors should be considered when selecting an authentic text: reader- and listener-based factors and text-based factors. For reader-based factors, several important research-based findings deal with what the reader/listener/viewer brings to the interpretive task:

1. Topic familiarity and purpose for listening/viewing/reading: Learners will have greater success if the selected texts deal with familiar topics and if learners themselves establish a purpose for exploring these texts.

2. Short-term or working memory: Learners may experience a cognitively challenging load on memory during a comprehension task, and instructors should plan to control for this by allowing learners to have the printed text available while completing a reading comprehension task and allowing them to listen to an oral text or view a video text multiple times.

3. Strategies for increasing comprehension/interpretation and reducing anxiety: Learners have more success in interpreting texts if they are taught to interact with the text through the use of both bottom-up processes (comprehending pieces of the text in a linear fashion) and top-down processes (interpreting the whole, the big ideas of the text). Learners' comprehension will increase if they are trained to use strategies such as activation of background knowledge, contextual guessing, and use of nonverbal cues, which will also serve to lessen their anxiety. Instructors should encourage learners to self-report periodically while listening, reading, and viewing so that instructors will be informed about the comprehension strategies their learners are using (Shrum & Glisan, 2016, pp. 181-184).

Selecting an appropriate text is no simple task, as the instructor must also keep in mind several important considerations regarding text-based factors:

1. The text should be context-appropriate: Texts should reflect contexts and content areas that learners are exploring in the language class or program so that background knowledge can be activated. For example, a text on good nutrition habits would be context-appropriate within a unit on maintaining a healthy lifestyle, while learners are acquiring vocabulary on food, learning about food preparation and exercise, and exploring the perspectives of the target culture relative to staying healthy. Presentation of such a text in the absence of this contextual foundation would likely result in frustration and lack of interest for learners. In this vein, learners' interest level has been

found to be a key factor in text selection to the extent that they may be able to interpret at a higher level when the text is more interesting to them (Dristas & Grisenti, 1995).

2. The text should be age-appropriate: Learners in elementary school, for example, might not be able to relate to authentic soap operas, talk shows, or newspaper editorials, because cognitively these texts would be too complex and would not capture the interest of a typical younger learner. At this age, learners might respond more effectively to stories, fairy tales, folktales, and legends; concrete descriptions of people and places; personal letters; conversations between young people or interviews.

3. The text should be appropriate for the linguistic level of the learners: This does not mean that instructors should select only texts that have the exact grammar and vocabulary that learners have acquired (this would be impossible anyway). It means that the text should have enough language that learners can recognize so that they can use these recognizable portions as scaffolds to meaning. Readers, listeners, and viewers may pay more attention to words that carry content than they do to grammatical markers such as verb endings. An important factor to consider when selecting texts is the degree of contextual support. For example, some longer texts may be easier for learners to comprehend than shorter ones because they provide more of a context from which meaning may be inferred. Additionally, the organization of the text may affect ease of interpretation; texts with story-like features (those that have a beginning, middle, and end) and signaling cues may facilitate comprehension. Linguistic signaling cues such as connectors and transition words such as *in addition to, on the other hand,* and non-linguistic signaling cues such as charts, graphs, pictures, and subtitles, provide additional support to assist learners in drawing meaning from the text.

4. Learners should be able to have success in interpreting the text if the instructor edits the task and not the text. That is, instructors should take great care to design interpretive tasks that are appropriate to the linguistic level of learners, while challenging them to stretch and develop their interpretive abilities further.

In sum, instructors may find it helpful to remember the acronym CALL-IT to recall these text-based factors:

C	=	Context
A	=	Age
LL	=	Linguistic Level
IT	=	Importance of Task

Instructors are encouraged to consider the CALL-IT factors very closely as they select authentic texts, and to edit the task, not the text.

This third edition of the IPA manual reiterates that any text can be interpreted at a variety of linguistic levels. There is nothing inherent in the text itself to make it Novice, Intermediate, Intermediate-High, or Advanced. Consequently, a given text is not static in terms of how it might be interpreted. What enables a text to be interpreted is what the listener/reader/viewer brings to the interpretive task— that is, how the learner interacts with the text. For instance, some authentic travel brochures may be more accessible to some readers than to others based on age of the learner and linguistic level, the familiarity of the learner with the destination described, background experiences in traveling, and learner interest in the interpretive task.

Figure 4.3 depicts an authentic text that deals with the topic of "nomofobia" and its consequences, found on the Conversation website (https://theconversation.com/como-se-si-padezco-nomofobia-miedo-irracional-a-no-tener-el-movil-ni-whatsapp-168028#:~:text=Hay%20varias%20variables%20que%20pueden,a%20usar%20el%20tel%C3%A9fono%20m%C3%B3vil). Mr. Carnevali used this text in his unit Social Media and Bullying, where it was context-appropriate and built upon what students were learning in terms of content and culture throughout the unit. Although the text could be used with learners at any level, it fits well within an Intermediate-level IPA, given the types of tasks that these learners should be able to do in the interpersonal and presentational modes. The text and topic are ideal for middle-school or high-school learners, since they often grapple with issues related to technology in their lives and it could well be of personal interest to them. Having some language beyond the Novice level would be helpful in interpreting this particular text, which includes language

Figure 4.3 Authentic Text in Spanish: "Cómo sé si padezco 'nomofobia', miedo irracional a no tener el móvil (ni WhatsApp)?"

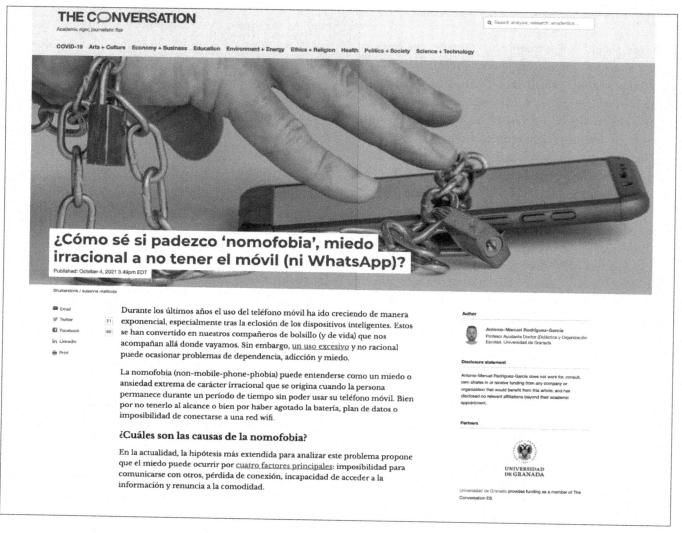

beyond simple vocabulary and cognates. Nevertheless, the text could also be used with Novice-level learners, provided that the tasks were designed to focus on identifying the main ideas and using familiar vocabulary to glean meaning. Additionally, the text is attractively organized, with visuals and subtitles in the form of questions—all of which entice the reader and facilitate the comprehension and interpretation processes.

The following is a list of some types of authentic texts that instructors might consider incorporating into work on the interpretive mode and into IPAs.

Interpretive listening/viewing task examples:

- Interviews or surveys from youth-oriented TV programming
- Straightforward conversations taped from a youth-oriented music program on TV or radio
- Segments from social media platforms
- Youth-oriented podcasts
- Product commercials from TV or radio
- Public service announcements on radio or TV, such as anti-smoking or anti-drug campaigns
- Authentic resources available in repositories such as the Center for Open Educational Resources and Language Learning (COERLL, https://www.coerll.utexas.edu/coerll/)

- Songs by artists from the target culture based on familiar contexts or themes
- Animated cartoons
- Segments from soap operas or other television programming
- Interviews from talk shows from the target cultures

Interpretive reading task examples:
- Social media posts
- Youth-oriented blogs
- Simple biographies or descriptions of people from a popular culture magazine or newspaper
- Product ads in target language publications and websites
- Public service announcements in magazines and newspapers such as anti-smoking or anti-drug campaigns
- Product advertisements or sales advertisements from a supermarket
- Interviews or surveys from youth-oriented magazines
- Short stories
- Photo stories with captions, such as "fotonovelas"
- Essays or editorials in authentic target culture newspapers
- Authentic songs or poetry by artists of the target culture
- Comic strips

Learning Activities to Prepare Students for the Interpersonal Task

During an interpersonal task, two learners exchange information with each other, expressing feelings, emotions, and opinions about the theme or task. Each of the two speakers comes to the task with information that the other person may not have, thereby creating an information gap, or a real need to provide and obtain information through the active negotiation of meaning (Henshaw & Hawkins, 2022; Lee & VanPatten, 1995; Shrum and Glisan, 2016; Waltz, 1996). Spontaneous conversation in the IPA requires a number of instructional strategies to help learners develop communication tactics. Some specific strategies that an instructor might use include the following:
- Beginning with warm-up activities that lower the affective filter and provide learners with planning time
- Providing learners with pre-thinking exercises or graphic organizer to activate the thought process
- Providing learners with videotaped models of interpersonal communication and engaging them in analysis of the models

- Weaning learners gradually from using a written script or notes in their oral communication and moving to more spontaneous interactions
- Providing multiple opportunities for learners to practice "thinking on their feet" without the pressure of being evaluated constantly
- Providing learners early on with conversational gambits in the target language as a means of negotiating meaning (for example, *Could you repeat that please? Do you mean to say that…?*); a list of these expressions could be displayed in the classroom for part of the year until learners are able to use them without reference to the list
- Including as a regular classroom feature opportunities for the instructor to engage learners in interpersonal communication on topics of school and individual interest, both with the instructor and with fellow classmates (for example, opening class by sharing opinions about the upcoming basketball championship game)
- Integrating ongoing opportunities for learners to ask questions in the target language within tasks where there is an information gap, thus motivating learners to make inquiries for real-world purposes
- Including activities in which learners communicate with one another on some aspects of an interpretive task such as an authentic reading or tape-recorded segment
- Providing opportunities for each learner to interact with a variety of peers who may have the same, lower, or higher language proficiency; this ensures learners will at times assist lower-level classmates while at other times they are challenged by classmates at their own or higher levels (Glisan et al., 2003, pp. 31-32)

Learning Activities to Prepare Students for the Presentational Task

In the presentational task learners communicate a message to an audience of listeners or readers. Since the audience is not usually able to negotiate meaning with the creator of the message, presentational communication is referred to as one-way communication. In the IPA, learners communicate messages by means of products that include oral public service announcements, short speeches, written essays or letters, and written magazine articles. These products are often the culminating phase of the IPA and build upon the interpretive and interpersonal tasks.

The rubrics used to evaluate presentational communication include the criterion of impact, which refers to the degree to which the message maintains the attention of the reader or listener. The instructor should explore with learners strategies for creating presentational products that have impact, such as selection of topic, use of visuals, choice of words, and visual layout.

Preparing learners to perform presentational tasks in the IPA requires a number of instructional strategies to help them produce messages that are clear and address the targeted audience. Some of those strategies include:

- Beginning with warm-up activities that lower the affective filter and provide learners with planning time
- Incorporating a process-oriented approach to presentational tasks with phases for drafting, peer editing, revising, and re-writing
- Offering feedback to learners that includes attention to the message itself in addition to linguistic accuracy
- Providing periodic opportunities for learners to judge the impact of the presentational messages of others so that they become more familiar with this aspect of their work
- Providing periodic opportunities for learners to share their work with audiences other than the instructor and receive feedback from them
- Periodically videotaping learners' presentations and having them analyze their own work.

Conclusion: Realizing the Potential of the IPA and UbD

This chapter has outlined the use of the IPA within the UbD approach to unit planning. The examples, tools, and guidelines provided here are intended to provide instructors at any stage of IPA use with new insights on design and implementation. In addition, the chapter has explored the integration of FIP at various aspects of planning and instruction, in the hope that linking to this important Special Education framework will allow the IPA and its related instructional practices to increase the inclusion of learners with disabilities in world language classrooms. Finally, as Chapter 6 will further outline through various exemplars, the IPA can also be a vehicle for realizing assessment, instruction, and learning that center diversity, equity, and inclusion as well as social justice through the choices of texts, content, and tasks that instructors make in the design of IPAs for their learners.

Chapter 5

Modeling and Feedback in the IPA

From the beginning, the IPA was designed and implemented as part of a new paradigm in teaching and learning in which assessment and instruction are integrated to enhance learning (Glisan et al., 2003; Shepard, 2000; Shrum & Glisan, 2016). In this view, learning is ultimately connected to rigorous standards (Hamilton, 2003; National Council on Education Standards and Testing, 1992) and the tests that assess them. In their description of assessment and learning in the paradigm called "the thinking curriculum," Resnick and Resnick (1992) remind us that we get what we assess, we don't get what we don't assess, and we must design tests worth teaching to (p. 59). Wiggins (1998) echoes this tenet when he states, "Tests in their form and content teach students what kinds of adult challenges we value" (p. 21). The current paradigm as outlined in the research on educational testing and accountability (Black & Wiliam, 1998; Hattie, 2008; Hattie & Timperley, 2007; Resnick & Resnick, 1992; Shepard, 2000, 2003; Stiggins et al., 2007; Wiggins, 2012) proposes a role for assessment that is

- Part of a learning culture
- Dynamic and ongoing
- A tool for evaluating prior knowledge
- An ongoing feedback cycle between learners and instructors
- Feedback considered as teaching/learning
- A vehicle for transfer of knowledge and skills
- A communicator of explicit criteria
- A means for student self-assessment
- An evaluative and self-reflective tool for instructors
- The locus of research.

The IPA is well situated within this paradigm on teaching and learning. Given the historical context and the role of feedback in a learning culture as described by Shepard (2000), this chapter considers the critical role of modeling and feedback in the IPA. In the first edition of this manual, the IPA was presented as a cyclical approach of modeling,

practicing, performance, and feedback phases (Glisan et al., 2003; Wiggins, 1998) as depicted in Figure 5.1.

Figure 5.1. A Cyclical Approach to Second Language Learning and Development

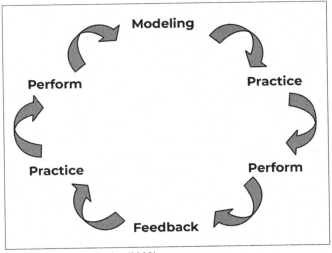

Source: Based on Wiggins (1998).

Addressing the Needs of All Learners: The IPA as a Means for Enacting Formative Instructional Practices

For decades, learners with learning disabilities have been excluded from world language classrooms in favor of focusing on core content areas such as reading and mathematics (Kleinert et al., 2007). Numerous researchers and world language instructors view exclusion of learners with disabilities from world language education as a social justice issue (Graham-Day et al., 2020). These researchers are calling for best practices in world language assessment that would facilitate the inclusion of more learners with disabilities into the world language classroom. This section briefly describes the special education paradigm of formative instructional practices (FIP) and how it interfaces with IPA to promote inclusivity in the world language classroom.

Special education has a rich history of data collection, such as the Individualized Education Program (IEP) process, to provide ongoing evidence of learning and progress. To this end, the field has stressed the importance of FIP (Fuchs & Fuchs, 2006; McLeskey & Brownell, 2015). As introduced in Chapter 1, FIP refers to the formal and informal practices that instructors enact to gather information about learning and engage with learners about it. More than formative and summative assessment, FIP involves the design of an ongoing dialogue between instructors and learners that identifies and responds to gaps in learning (Graham-Day et al., 2014; Graham-Day et al., 2020). Graham-Day et al. (2020) outline the features of FIP and link them to the work of world language education and the IPA. First, instructors create and communicate to the learners *clear learning targets* based on content standards. In world language education, the NCSSFL-ACTFL Can-Do Statements (ACTFL, 2017) and other targets linked to the World-Readiness Standards (National Standards Collaborative Board, 2015) delineate what learners need to know and be able to do by the end of a lesson or a unit of instruction. Next, instructors make a plan for to how to *collect and document evidence of learning*. In designing this plan, which references the learning targets, instructors typically create a variety of informal and formal instructional activities and use learner responses and performances in these activities to plan future instruction. Third, providing *effective feedback* is central to FIP. Effective feedback is specific, connected to the focal learning target(s), focused on success, provided to learners as quickly as possible, and related to new learning or previous performance on the target. Finally, successful implementation of FIP requires *a plan for learner involvement in monitoring progress* in realizing the learning targets. Chan et al. (2014) maintained that learner involvement in FIP can be accomplished in a variety of ways, such as through self-monitoring, self-evaluation, or the implementation of peer tutoring models. These major tenets of FIP (learning targets, collection and evidence of learning, effective feedback, and a plan for learner involvement in monitoring progress) have been central to the principles of IPA design (Adair-Hauck et al., 2006; Glisan et al., 2003).

The following section addresses best practices in providing effective feedback for all learners within the context of the research and practice related to FIP. First, modeling in the IPA is presented and discussed from a social construc-tivist approach. Second, the same theoretical approach is applied in an expanded description of the Co-Constructive Approach to Feedback, and research describing the features of the discourse between instructor and learners in this approach is summarized. Third, based on those discursive features, characteristics of the Co-Constructive Approach to IPA feedback are outlined to assist instructors in providing quality descriptive feedback on learner performance. Finally, those characteristics are applied to an example of Co-Constructive IPA Feedback sessions to actualize the characteristics of the approach. As Graham-Day et al. (2020) have highlighted, the IPA and the integral role of feedback within it embody the essence of FIP.

Modeling: Establishing Clear Learning Goals

The IPA framework of instruction and assessment assumes that learner performance is anchored to performance models. Before learners begin a unit of study, they view examples of the type of performance that is the goal of the instructional process (Adair-Hauck et al., 2006; Glisan et al., 2003; Hattie & Timperley, 2007; Shrum & Glisan, 2016; Wiggins, 1998; Wiggins & McTighe, 2005). Tharp and Gallimore (1988) described the importance of this component:

> Modeling is a powerful means of assisting performance, one that continues its effectiveness into adult years and into the highest reaches of behavioral complexity… Often teachers demand that students perform skills without having observed an expert performance of those skills within a relevant task context. (p. 49)

When an IPA and associated instructional activities are planned according to the Understanding by Design template described in Chapter 4, instruction can be linked to clear exemplars of performance that meet, exceed, or do not meet the standards.

In addition to articulating the desired performance, models serve a purpose in the feedback loop by anchoring the feedback in the domains, criteria, and descriptors articulated in the relevant rubric (Glisan et al., 2003; Shrum & Glisan, 2016; Wiggins, 1998). Adair-Hauck and Troyan (2013) described two types of modeling that occurred during a unit of instruction linked to the IPA. The first type was at the beginning of the unit when learners assessed interpersonal IPA tasks from the previous year. Using the Intermediate Interpersonal Rubric (see Appendix F-2), learners rated videotaped performances and subsequently discussed the rating with the teacher. In their discussions, they referenced the specific domains or criteria (such as language function and text type) on the rubric. This group rating process allowed the teacher and learners to collectively identify the targeted performance before instruction began (Shrum & Glisan, 2016; Wiggins & McTighe, 2005).

The second type of modeling often occurred at the beginning of class when the teacher and a learner modeled a speaking activity related to the theme. Once the modeling was completed, teacher and learners group-rated the performance using the interpersonal rubric. Similarly, sometimes two learners performed or modeled an interpersonal speaking activity for the class; the performance was videotaped by the teacher and followed up with group-rated feedback. The teacher asked questions to guide the group-rated feedback: "Did they complete the task?" "Was their speech at word, sentence, or paragraph level?" "Did you see any negotiation of meaning?" and so on. Through modeling, the learners were able to "see" and better comprehend the criteria of the interpersonal speaking rubric. After the modeling phase, the learners had time to practice through meaningful, interpersonal theme-based speaking activities. These interpersonal tasks involved teacher-to-learner and learner-to-learner interaction in tasks that were similar or parallel to the summative speaking task in the IPA. During the practice speaking activities, learners were able to make adjustments to try to improve their performance. Throughout the modeling and practicing phases, learners were engaged in self-assessment, peer assessment, and co-constructive feedback discussions with the teacher using the IPA rubrics. This use of the IPA rubrics familiarized learners with the rubric language, the types of performance associated with that language, and the procedures for the feedback that occurred during the IPA (Adair-Hauck & Troyan, 2013).

The Feedback Loop: Co-Constructing Performance Assessment Descriptions

In the first edition of this manual (Glisan et al., 2003), the feedback loop was presented as "responsive assistance" as the teacher guides a classroom of learners through a feedback session related to their interpretive mode performance on the IPA. See Appendix H for a discussion of the differences between explicit and co-constructive (responsive) feedback for the interpretive mode.

In the second edition, the discussion of the feedback loop was expanded to account for feedback on interpersonal tasks (Adair-Hauck & Troyan, 2013). From a social constructivist perspective, the "feeding-back" (Tharp & Gallimore, 1988) of information related to performance is a process that occurs between the individual expert (the teacher, a parent, some other mentor) and the learner through guided participation in communities of practice (Duff, 2003; Gutiérrez et al., 1999; Hattie & Timperley, 2007; Lave & Wenger, 1991; Rogoff, 1990, 1994, 2003). Contrary to traditional forms of teacher-learner feedback—which have traditionally been tests, scores, and other marked papers—a social constructivist perspective views feedback as dialogic interaction in which the expert (the teacher) and the apprentice (the learner) co-construct a performance assessment (Adair-Hauck & Troyan, 2013). Many scholars have advocated such a constructivist approach to feedback in assessment because it involves the learner more closely in the assessment process (Muñoz & Alvarez, 2010; Shepard, 2000, 2003; Tunstall & Gipps, 1996). Pryor and Torrance (2000) point out that assessment is not something that teachers do *to* learners; rather, they propose that it is

> accomplished by means of social interaction in which the practices of the participants have a critical effect on the outcome. The outcomes of assessment are actively produced rather than revealed and displayed by the assessment process. Moreover, each participant brings to the event understandings not only of the cognitive agenda, but also of the kind of social relations and practices that are legitimate in the circumstances. (p. 126)

The co-construction of a performance assessment description between the instructor and a learner is the essence of the feedback loop of the IPA. This section presents the Co-Constructive Approach to the IPA Feedback Loop (Adair-Hauck, 2003; Adair-Hauck & Troyan, 2013) as a way of enacting co-constructed performance assessment descriptions in world language teaching. To support instructors in using this approach, a community of practice for providing feedback can be developed over time through mentoring in questioning techniques and other discourse strategies.

The Power of Feedback
Research has provided insight into the types of feedback that may be the most effective for improving learner perfor-

mance. Hattie and Timperley (2007) found feedback to be in the top five of the ten factors affecting achievement that they analyzed. Beyond identifying the power of feedback, they maintained that the effect of feedback on performance varied by type: task feedback showed the highest effect sizes, whereas praise, rewards, and punishment had lower associated effect sizes. The most effective types of feedback offered assistance such as cues and reinforcement, utilized technology in feedback delivery, and connected to goals.

Kluger and DeNisi (1996) went well beyond the realm of feedback in the classroom in their synthesis of feedback studies in work, school, and other performance situations. They concluded that feedback is a highly complex process that is context dependent, and they derived several practical suggestions from their analysis. Feedback is most effective when it features

- Tasks that are familiar to learners and connect to standards and analogous tasks
- Cues that support future learning
- A focus on the task and not the learner
- Consistency in feedback practices (Kluger & DeNisi, 1996).

These studies provide an overall picture of the impact of feedback on learning using statistical analyses. Furthermore, they reinforce the critical role of modeling and feedback in the IPA. However, a full understanding of the complexity of feedback as a social practice also requires the use of qualitative research approaches.

The Discourse of Feedback

To unpack the discursive nature of co-constructive feedback, it is important to describe the interaction between teacher and learner qualitatively. Building on Sadler's (1989) research, which outlined the ways in which instructors might use feedback to articulate the standards to be achieved and move learners toward "evaluative expertise" (p. 143), Tunstall and Gipps (1996) described a typology of feedback based on their qualitative study of 49 Year 1 and Year 2 children and eight teachers across six London schools. Their analysis identified four types of feedback (A, B, C, and D) that were identified along a continuum from evaluative to descriptive. The evaluative types were A1–Rewarding; A2–Punishing; B1–Approving; and B2–Disapproving. The descriptive types were C1–Specifying attainment; C2–Specifying improvement; D1–Constructing achievement; and D2–Constructing the way forward.

Types C and D are the most salient for the current discussion, as they correspond to the standards-based, social constructivist model of feedback advocated for IPA feedback (Adair-Hauck & Troyan, 2013). To simplify this typology for the IPA Feedback Loop, Types C and D have been renamed Type 1 and Type 2, respectively, and are depicted in the continuum in Figure 5.2 below.

Figure 5.2 Continuum of Feedback Types in the IPA Feedback Loop

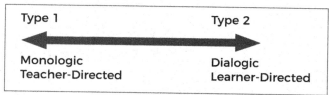

In Type 1, the learner is provided with models for desired performance, and improvements are suggested based on those models. This is the moment when the instructor can articulate a clear performance goal and secure the learner's commitment to achievement (Kluger & DeNisi, 1996, p. 260) by communicating the standards during modeling activities (Sadler, 1989; Wiggins, 1998). Type 1 is monologic, however, and does not allow for learner participation, whereas Type 2 engages learners and empowers them in the process of identifying "aspects of competence" that emerge in their work (Tunstall & Gipps, 1996, p. 399) through a co-constructed description of performance (Adair-Hauck & Troyan, 2013). Type 1 exchanges may be more characteristic of early conversations when performance standards and/or the feedback process are new to the learner. As learners complete tasks and become more familiar with the descriptors associated with the standards, they gain more competence in identifying their own gaps in performance, moving gradually toward the Type 2 exchanges that are the goal in the Co-Constructive Approach to IPA Feedback.

The Role of Questions in the Co-Constructive Approach

Questioning is at the core of the Co-Constructive Approach. Tharp and Gallimore (1988) identified two types of questions: assessing and assisting. Assessing questions determine the level at which the learner can perform without assistance, whereas assisting questions support the learner in reaching a level of performance that they could not reach unassisted. Instructors can use assessing questions to determine the appropriate level of instruction, or to move into the learner's zone of proximal development (ZPD), "the distance between the learner's actual developmental level as determined by independent problem-solving (unassisted performance) and the level of potential development as determined through problem-solving under adult guidance (assisted performance)" (Vygotsky, 1978, p. 86). Assessing questions, although they provide the instructor with vital information for instruction, serve a limited role because they do not assist learning. Assisting questions, on the other hand, function within the learner's ZPD, allowing production of language that the learner is unwilling or unable to construct alone (Tharp & Gallimore, 1988). Although both types of questions serve essential roles, assisting questions are the predominant type in the IPA feedback model articulated here.

Adair-Hauck and Troyan (2013) described the features of the Co-Constructive Approach to IPA Feedback related to learner's interpersonal mode performance. The three tasks of the intermediate-level IPA completed by the learners are summarized in Box 5.1. The IPA was administered at the end of a high school French unit exploring famous persons of the Francophone World. The study presented discourse analysis of an IPA interpersonal task feedback session between the teacher and a learner who met expectations on the Intermediate Interpersonal Rubric. The exchange between the learner and the teacher featured the following:

- Dialogic and bi-directional feedback mediated and negotiated by the teacher and the learner through language
- Ample assisting questions and cognitive probes to help the learner self-assess, self-reflect, and self-regulate
- Discourse mirroring everyday language used outside of instructional settings

Box 5.1

Famous Persons of the Francophone World Intermediate Level

IPA Task Overview

You are conducting research to learn about people from across the Francophone world. After reading about a famous Francophone from a magazine article, you will discuss with your partner the characteristics and personality traits of your famous person. Together, you and your partner will decide which of the two should be honored by naming the French club after them. Finally, you will write a letter of nomination of approximately 200 words (three paragraphs) for naming your school's language club chapter after a famous person from the Francophone cultures.

Interpretive

Your teacher will give you a reading dealing with the life of a famous person from the Francophone world. Your job is to understand as much of it as possible so you can use the information in a letter. Take up to 20 minutes to read and show your understanding of the article.

Interpersonal

You and your partner have to decide the name of the French Club. Based on the research that you have conducted on a famous person over the past weeks, you will now talk to your partner and decide which of your two people the club will be named after. Decide on one of the two and give good reasons for the choice that you make.

Presentational

Based on information you have read as well as your discussion with your classmate, write a letter of nomination of approximately 200 words (three paragraphs) for naming your school's language club chapter after a famous person from the Francophone cultures. Briefly describe their personal life and professional accomplishments. Write about why the person is popular in their own country and also in the U.S. Be sure to make the case why you want to name your club after this person. Remember that you are writing to members of your language club. Take up to 40 minutes to prepare your letter of nomination.

Based on their analysis of the interaction, Adair-Hauck and Troyan summarized the discourse features and characteristics of the Co-Constructive Approach to IPA Feedback. Box 5.2 outlines the major discourse patterns observed in the interaction. Box 5.3 provides a summary of the characteristics of co-constructive feedback to guide instructors in implementing this type of feedback in their classrooms.

Box 5.2

Discourse Features used to Facilitate a Co-Constructive Approach to IPA Feedback

1. Dialogic or symmetrical combination of instructor and learner talk

2. Judicious use of explicit directives and metastatements; mainly used initially to define task and establish a context

3. Use of first person collective pronouns ("we") for joint-problem solving

4. Sparse use of assessment questions

5. Abundance of assisting questions and cognitive probes

6. Use of presuppositions, ellipses, and abbreviated speech (mirroring everyday language)

7. Language, especially questions, that are attuned to the level where performance requires assistance

Source: Adair-Hauck & Troyan (2013)

Box 5.3

Characteristics of a Descriptive and Co-Constructive Approach to IPA Feedback

1. Focus on learner performance compared to model performance

2. Language development as a work in progress

3. Questioning as part of the discussion

4. Mutual appraisal of performance is integral to descriptors

5. Shifting responsibility of learner's own role in learning/assessing

6. Brainstorming of strategies to improve performance

7. Active participation of learner to self-assess and self-regulate

8. Reflective process for both instructor and learner

9. Lack of evaluative or judgmental statements

Source: Adair-Hauck & Troyan (2013)

Exploring the Discourse Features of Co-Constructive IPA Feedback

This section presents the discourse between an instructor, Francis, and a learner, Lindsay, who engaged in co-constructive IPA feedback. The data are from Francis's high school French classroom, also described in Adair-Hauck and Troyan (2013), a study which depicted and analyzed the feedback discourse between Francis and a learner named Ashlie. This section has two goals. First, the feedback discourse presented here features Lindsay, who was Ashlie's partner for the interpersonal task. It thus provides an additional example of the use of the Co-Constructive Approach to IPA Feedback for the interpersonal mode. Second, the examples feature the assessment of two learners at different performance levels: Ashlie rated as meeting expectations, while Lindsay rated as

exceeding expectations on the Intermediate Interpersonal Rubric. Collectively, these exemplars serve as models for instructors implementing this approach to feedback.

Francis facilitated this co-constructive IPA feedback after the learners had performed the interpersonal Famous Person task with a partner. First, each learner viewed her performance from the videotape of the interpersonal task. Then the learner and Francis assessed the performance separately. Finally Francis and the learner co-constructed IPA feedback.

This process for interpersonal assessment aligns with Kluger and DeNisi's (1996) research on feedback, which underscores that the most effective types of feedback offer assistance such as cues and reinforcement, use technology in feedback delivery, and connect to goals.

The discourse examined in Figure 5.3 came from a co-constructive IPA feedback session for the Famous Person IPA depicted in Box 5.1 above. At the time of the study, this learner was in 10th Grade and had been studying French for 4 years. The Famous Person IPA was her third IPA. In the IPA feedback protocol below, the key discursive features outlined in Tables 5.2 and 5.3 are highlighted to illuminate the nature of co-constructive feedback.

The co-constructive IPA feedback session depicted in Figure 5.3 above has many of the characteristics underscored by Adair-Hauck and Troyan (2013). First, the focus of the IPA feedback session was on comparing the learner's performance with model performance, not with some other learner's performance or to a set of statistical norms. The rubric outlined for both Francis and the learner the criteria to judge the performance as well as the range in quality of the performance. Second, a lack of judgmental statements such as "good," "great," or "well done" was evident in the feedback session. Francis, using the rubric as a language learning tool, provided rich and descriptive feedback that highlighted what the learner can do with the language in spontaneous, unscripted discourse. Third, since a major goal of Francis was to encourage the learner to self-assess, he used assisting questions to encourage the learner to self-reflect, self-assess, and reflect on her language performance. Through language and co-constructive feedback, Francis empowered the learner by shifting the responsibility for the IPA assessment from him alone to both of them.

The protocol exemplifies learners as "apprentices in thinking" (Rogoff, 1990). At first, the learner underrated her interpersonal language performance; she rated herself as *weak meets* for both Language Function and Text Type. Francis gave the learner the latitude to rate herself first. In this way, she was able to share her thoughts without any predispositions. After the learner shared her self-assessment, Francis explained why she had underrated herself in two critical domains for Intermediate Interpersonal Speaking (Language Function and Text Type). However, the learner was not that far off in her self-assessment because she rated herself at the Meets level for Intermediate Interpersonal Speaking. In a sense, she was just a sub-level off for each of these two domains. In many ways, the discourse highlights that this learner was moving toward evaluative expertise. That is, she was assuming more control over her own

performance and the assessment of that performance. In the process, she gained a clearer sense of exactly where she was in the continuum of performance toward proficiency. Her ability to summarize this awareness was facilitated by the Co-Constructive Approach. The discourse in Figure 5.3 highlights how co-constructive IPA feedback encourages mutual appraisal of performance and, therefore, how it can be a reflective process for both instructors and learners. (Appendix I provides an additional sample of IPA feedback discourse for a learner who did not meet expectations.)

After this feedback session, Francis viewed the videotape again and noticed that he had forgotten to encourage the learner to think about how she was going to improve her language performance, that is, to provide feedback for constructing the way forward ("where to next?" feedback) (Hattie & Clark, 2019; Hattie & Timperley, 2007). Being able to view his co-constructive feedback performance using the videotaped feedback session made him more cognizant of the need to include this important feature of feedback in subsequent IPA feedback sessions.

Improving Learner Performance through IPA Assessment and Feedback

As more instructors explore the use of IPA assessment and co-constructive feedback, various approaches are being applied in different instructional contexts. For example, some instructors prefer to co-construct IPA feedback with pairs of learners. Others have reported that once learners are familiar with the rubric descriptors, co-constructive IPA peer assessment can be an effective means to assist learners in thinking about their language performance. In other words, through modeling and frequent dialogic instructor-to-learner or learner-to-learner IPA feedback, learners become effective self- and peer assessors.

To this end, Hattie and Timperley (2007) offer three questions that instructors can use to guide learners in using the IPA process and co-constructed feedback as they work to meet the goals of the standards:

- Where am I going?
- How am I going?
- Where to next?

Using these three guiding questions, Adair-Hauck and Troyan (2013) suggest the guidelines presented in Box 5.4 for co-constructive IPA feedback.

Figure 5.3 Co-Constructive IPA Feedback Session: Meets Expectations Feedback Loop Example 1 – Lindsay

Lindsay completed the interpersonal task with Ashlie, the student featured in the Adair-Hauck and Troyan (2013) study.

Part 1: Lindsay assesses her overall *task completion*

T: So in the end, you decided on your person. So that gets to my question: *Did you complete the task that was asked of you?* — Assessment question to define the task.

S: I think so.

T: Okay. And how so? — Assisting question probing student to explain "why".

S: Because we picked a person…and there was a reason why.

T: How do you in English just recap what that reason was?

S: It was because um we thought that my person was like a better role model for um people, especially like young girls because she is like a real person, like relatable whereas like she wasn't you know, crazy with being a celebrity or anything, whereas Ashlie's person was kind of, you know, very, kind of fake and not a very good person, so… — Student defends why she thinks she completed task.

T: Let's start with the top part, *Language Function.* — "Let's" denotes joint problem solving.

S: Um… I said that I created in a basic way or created language in a basic way because I felt like I didn't I wasn't necessarily expressing all that I could expressing all that I could express or what I wanted to so I thought it was just kind of basic. It wasn't extraordinary or whatever. Um… for *Text Type, I said simple sentences and some strings of sentences.* A lot of times, I was just kind of explaining little bits and pieces. I wasn't necessarily explaining the whole picture all at once. So yeah… that's why I picked that. Umm…the next one [*Communication Strategies*] is kind of the same thing, I guess. — Learner self-reflecting & self-assessing

T: yeah? — Teacher's rising intonation asking for more information.

S: By asking and answering questions, both Ashlie and I like would ask clarifying questions if we needed to or so it was the same.

T: What kind of clarifying questions did you ask?

S: Well, there was a verb that she used that was like "to act" like the actual verb "acting". And I didn't know what that meant and I had to clarify what that was and she had to negotiate the meaning of that. And she also had to ask me a couple of questions about what I was talking about just like the movie or whatever she was saying. — Learner reflects on how she negotiated meaning by questioning.

T: When you had to, you were able to clarify for meaning, right? — Assisting question to encourage learner to reflect on her ability to ask questions.

S: yeah…so that was good. And then… — Learner responds and evaluates her performance.

Figure 5.3 (cont.) Co-Constructive IPA Feedback Session: Meets Expectations
Feedback Loop Example 1 — Lindsay

T: Did you ever clarify by paraphrasing, using different words?

> Assisting question regarding use of paraphrases as a communication strategy.

S: Ahhh…no. I don't think so. I don't really know. There wasn't a bit time where I had to do that. I was more like just answering questions she had…so…

> Learner explains she didn't need to paraphrase.

T: Okay. Okay.

S: Um…and I thought I was generally understood by those *accustomed with the interaction with language learners because I mean Ashlie is also a language learner and*… she understood me or whatever, so….That was that. Um….I thought I was on the weaker side of the meets section for language control because I was able to like, do little…make little sentences…but it wasn't necessarily like a full thing. So, it was mostly just kind of like simple sentences….nothing big.

> Learner reflects on her comprehensibility.

T: And…What did we miss here?

S: Nothing.

T: How was your…were you mainly working in the present tense? Past tense?

> Assisting question asking learner to reflect on her use of present/past tense.

S: Uh…I did both. Because I talked about how when she was younger, like how she *became* an actress and how she wanted to sing but um she got into acting because of her parents. And then I talked about presently, she's in the movie *La Vie en Rose* and kind of that presently, she's a good role model.

> Learner's reflection on tense use.

T: So, just to come back up here [**points to the top of the Rubric:** *Language Function and Text Type* **where the student had rated herself as** *weak meets*.], I think you're a little hard on yourself here. And it is true that you are working with someone who is [makes a gesture indicating that her speaking partner was a higher level than her]…so working with Holly [Lindsay's partner in the mid-year IPA] at one end and working with Ashlie at the other end…um… you handled yourself well. You could tell you were nervous working with her, just because of your body language, but you still, you're still working in the *strong meets* um…things where maybe that there just weren't opportunities to clarify by paraphrasing…but you definitely clarified by asking questions …and uh…that's clear. Umm…and I mean… definitely understood by someone *accustomed to working with language learners,* if not beyond that. So, I think you… you're selling yourself a little short there. Um…but um…it's just important for you to know that you can survive in those newer situations where you're speaking with someone who is more advanced. You're going to encounter that in France when you go there soon. So…okay?

> Teacher offers his assessment compared to learner's self-assessment and explains *why* the learner needs to adjust her rating.

> Teacher compares learner's performance to past performance.

> Authentic use of language in IPA related to real-world use of language.

S: Mmm Hmm.

T: Anything else that you wanted to mention?

S: No

T: Thank you.

Box 5.4

Instructors and Learners as Co-Constructors of IPA Feedback

1. To set the learners up for success, ensure that they are familiar with the IPA rubrics. Providing models of learner performance across the modes will enable them to better understand the questions, "Where am I going?" and "What are the goals?"

2. During the feedback loop, both the instructor and the learner should review interpersonal language performance using audio or video and then assess the performance individually using the IPA rubric. Allowing the learner the opportunity to self-assess first will shift more of the responsibility for determining appropriate ratings onto the learner. When a learner is not sure how to assess their performance or is otherwise confused, the instructor's assisting questions may help the learner to better understand and assess performance. After the learner provides their appraisal, the instructor provides an assessment and notes how it aligns with the learner's. Most importantly, instructor and learner should assess and acknowledge *why* the performance is at a particular level, that is, answer the "How am I going?" question.

3. Through the use of the instructor's critical assisting questions or cognitive probes, co-constructive IPA feedback shifts or places the responsibility on the learner to appraise and assess their performance.

4. Cognitive probes will also prompt and support learners in perceiving, observing, and examining their work, that is, in thinking about their progress in language learning.

5. Instructor and learners together discuss strategies that will help to improve performance and plan for future achievement/performance, or "Where to Next?"

6. Co-constructive IPA feedback facilitates learning for both the instructor and the learners..

Source: Adair-Hauck & Troyan. 2013

Conclusions: The Potential of the Feedback Loop

In its role as a key component in an innovative support system for learning in the 21st century, the IPA and the Co-Constructive Approach to Feedback hold the potential to shift the learning mindset of world language learners (see for example Lou & Noels, 2019). The psychological research on mindset by Dweck and her colleagues (Blackwell, Trzesniewski, & Dweck, 2007; Dweck, 2006, 2007) identified two mindsets: The fixed mindset and the growth mindset. In the fixed mindset, the learner views intelligence as unchangeable. By contrast, learners with a growth mindset perceive challenges as opportunities to learn by working hard to develop new areas of language use. The feedback loop of the IPA—and its focus on building learners' ability to self-assess their level of performance in the world language—is one important aspect of a classroom assessment culture that can foster a growth mindset in world language learners. Finally, in terms of FIP, the Co-Constructive Approach to Feedback is a key aspect of enacting more inclusive assessment and instruction for learners with disabilities, who have had fewer opportunities to participate in world language learning (Wight, 2015). Following the principles and practices for feedback described in this chapter, instructors can assist world language learners by designing an ongoing dialogue with them that identifies and responds to gaps in learning (Graham-Day et al., 2014; Graham-Day et al., 2020). In this way, the Co-Constructive Approach to Feedback is another example of the how the IPA can serve as a vehicle for instruction and assessment for equity, diversity, and inclusion in the world language classroom.

Chapter 6

Examples of IPAs from the Field

This chapter presents a collection of IPAs from instructors in K–12 and university classrooms. Representing a range of languages, these IPAs are meant to serve as exemplars for the field. While these IPAs are presented here as models, they were originally created for specific instructional contexts. Therefore, the exact texts, tasks, and content may not be applicable in all classrooms. The intention is that these IPAs will serve as inspiration for other teachers in the design and implementation of their own IPAs.

For research-based reasons discussed in Chapters 2 and 4, several interpretive tasks suggest or provide the option of using English as a means to assess comprehension. However, the decision of whether to use learners' strongest language or the target language is always up to individual instructors based on the levels of their learners and their specific instructional contexts.

The IPAs shared in this chapter target a range of performance levels including the Novice-High, Intermediate, Intermediate-High, and Advanced. ***Please note that for Spanish, IPAs are included across the levels.*** The language educators who designed the IPAs have used them in their classes and provide the overview and details on all three tasks. For each IPA, the authentic text is shared or, in the case of a video or audio resource, a link is provided to access it. In the event that print texts become unavailable online, pdf files can be accessed at the following link: go.osu.edu/ipatexts

Sample Integrated Performance Assessments

Novice High
- Holidays (Mandarin), Na Lu-Hogan
- Taking a Gap Year (German), Daniel S. Ferguson
- Let's Protect our World (Spanish), José Pan

Intermediate
- Social Justice in Japan (Japanese), Iya Nemastil
- Technology (French), Margaret Newcomb
- Social Media and Bullying (Spanish), Jesse Carnevali (see description in Chapter 4)

Intermediate High
- Providing Emergency Room Care (Spanish), Sarah Peceny and Dr. Eva Rodrigues-Gonzalez
- Introduction to Hispanic Heritage Month and History of Latin America (Spanish), Tammy Lyons
- Human Rights (Spanish), Naysa Altmeyer

Advanced
- Social Issues in Arabic Speaking Countries (Arabic), Dr. Myriam Abdel-Malek
- Language and Racial Ideologies (Spanish), Lauren Miranda

**Sample Integrated Performance Assessments:
Novice-High**

Holidays (MANDARIN)

Instructor: Na Lu-Hogan
Ottoson Middle School, Arlington, MA
Languages and Levels Taught:
Mandarin Chinese 1, 2, 3, Exploratory

IPA Theme: Holidays
Language: Mandarin
IPA Level: Novice High
Class Level/Size: Mandarin Chinese 1 / 20 Students

Standards Addressed:
Communication (Interpersonal, Interpretive, Presentational)
Cultures (Relating Cultural Practices to Perspectives; Relating Cultural Products to Perspectives)
Connections (Making Connections; Acquiring Information and Diverse Perspectives)
Comparisons (Cultural Comparisons)
Communities (School and Global Communities)

Task Overview
What are some similarities and differences between the Chinese Mid-Autumn Day holiday and Thanksgiving Day as celebrated in the US?

Holidays play an important role in learning any language and culture. In this unit, you will be learning about a particular Chinese holiday, known as Mid-Autumn Festival, also known as Mid-Autumn Day and Moon Festival.

Interpretive Task
In the first part of the unit, before the assessment, you will be learning about which countries celebrate Mid-Autumn Day, why, and how people celebrate the holiday: with lantern lighting, making pomelo hats, enjoying mooncakes while appreciating the full moon with family, etc. For the interpretive task, you will watch a Chinese TV news broadcast regarding Mid-Autumn Day celebrations which includes interviews of young learners of Chinese who are celebrating Mid-Autumn Day in their class. After watching the news broadcast several times, you will answer questions to check for your comprehension.

Interpersonal Task
Next, you will have a conversation in Mandarin Chinese with a partner to compare and contrast Mid-Autumn Day with Thanksgiving in the United States.

Presentational Task
For your presentational task, you will write to your pen pal in Wenzhou, China. In your letter, you want to let your pen pal know some of the similarities and differences between Mid-Autumn Day and Thanksgiving Day.

Instructions and Materials for the IPA

中秋节 Interpretive Assessment
Theme: Holiday
Link to the authentic video: <u>go.osu.edu/ipatexts</u>

I. Key Word Detection

As you watch the video segment, jot down a list of 8 content words/phrases that you hear that convey meaning related to the theme of the video, such as key nouns and verbs. Avoid listing words/phrases such as prepositions (*of, from, in, out, etc.*) and conjunctions (*and, but, or, etc.*), which do not carry much meaning. Then provide an English equivalent to the right of each word you listed.

_____   _____
_____   _____
_____   _____
_____   _____

II. Main Idea

Using information from the video clip, describe in English the main purpose of this video clip.

_____
_____
_____
_____

III. Supporting Details

Circle the letter of each detail that is mentioned in the video clip (not all are included!)
Write the information that is given in the video clip in the space provided next to the detail below.

A. The holiday kids in the video are celebrating: _____
B. The fruit that is often consumed on this holiday: _____
C. An accessory kids make out of a type of fruit: _____
D. An animal that has significance to the holiday they are celebrating: _____
E. The date of this holiday: _____
F. People with whom the kids celebrate this holiday: _____
G. At least two activities kids do to celebrate this holiday: _____
H. Types of flavors of moon cakes kids have: _____

IV. Organizational Features

How is the text organized? Choose all that apply and explain briefly why you selected each feature.
A. Chronological _____
B. Pros and cons _____
C. Cause and effect _____
D. Compare and contrast _____
E. Informational _____
Justification from video clip:

_____
_____
_____
_____

V.   Guessing Meaning from Context
Based on this video clip, what do the following three words/phrases probably mean in English? Please match.

jué d e 觉得	game
yóu x ì 游戏	the first time
d ì y ī c ì 第一次	to think; to consider

VI. Inference
"Read between the lines" to answer the following question, using information from the video clip. Your answer should be in English.

Why do you think Chinese people find this holiday interesting and important? (Please provide a few reasons)

_____
_____
_____

VII. Producer's Perspective
Select the perspective or point of view you think the producer of this video clip adopted as they created this video and justify your answer with information from the clip.

    A.   Comic
    B.   Moral
    C.   Informative

Justification _____
_____
_____
_____

VIII. Compare Cultural Perspectives
Answer the following question in English:
How does this Chinese holiday compare to a holiday you know of?

_____
_____
_____

IX. Personal Reaction to the Video Clip
Using specific information from the video, describe your personal reaction to the video clip *in Mandarin*. Be sure to provide reasons/details that support your reaction.

_____
_____
_____
_____

Taking a Gap Year (GERMAN)

Instructor: Daniel S. Ferguson
Dublin City Schools, Dublin OH
Languages and Levels Taught:
German 1, 3, 5/AP at Olentangy
Liberty High School, Delaware OH

IPA Theme: Taking a Gap Year
Language: German
IPA Level: Novice High
Class Level/Size: German 1/15 Students

Standards Addressed:
Communication (Interpersonal, Interpretive, Presentational)
Cultures (Relating Cultural Practices to Perspectives, Relating Cultural Products to Perspectives)
Connections (Acquiring Information and Diverse Perspectives)
Comparisons (Cultural Comparisons)

Task Overview
In your German class, you have been studying the benefits of taking a gap year. As a reminder, a gap year is typically defined as a year taken between high school and college that might include travel, work, study, volunteering, or research. This break has the potential to help fight against academic burn-out, while allowing you to explore the world and gain valuable experience during your transition into independence. Taking a gap year is indeed quite the undertaking. Although challenging oneself and getting outside of one's comfort zone is not an easy task, an essential benefit of a gap year is the one-in-a-lifetime opportunity to experience another culture first-hand, build confidence, and grow before you venture into life after high school.

In this unit, we will explore and discover answers to the following questions:
1. How does the amount of space available in a country or city determine the housing options?
2. How does lifestyle play a role in searching for housing?
3. What do you need to know in order to begin searching for housing in a different country?
4. What amenities are considered important to members of the German-speaking world?
5. What kinds of life skills can you gain from living abroad?

We will watch several short videos in which youth discuss the pros and cons of taking a gap year and read about a European government program called Erasmus. We will discuss the motives and various activities you can do during a gap year. We will also examine differences in living spaces (measuring systems and blueprints), living arrangements (shared housing such as a "Wohngemeinschaft"), and common housing amenities. Before the interpretive assessment, you will learn the vocabulary necessary to navigate housing websites and advertisements in the German-speaking world. Next, we will learn forms of language that will allow you to compare and contrast facts and opinions. Accordingly, the interpersonal speaking assessment will require you to discuss with a partner the advantages and disadvantages of two apartments before deciding on a place to live. Lastly, we will deconstruct the genre of an online review and co-construct a housing review similar to what you might have seen on websites such as Hostel World, Airbnb, etc. Your presentational task will require you to use your imagination (and details from the advertisement) to write a review of your chosen apartment, taking into consideration how this living space suited your needs and activities for your gap year.

Interpretive Task
You and your best friend have made the decision to take a gap year between high school and college. You have decided to live in Germany for a year. In preparation for your departure, you get on the internet and start researching places to live. One of your web searches takes you to a shared apartment advertisement shown below.

Interpersonal Task
Both you and your best friend are having trouble deciding on an apartment in Germany for the upcoming year. Neither of you can find an accommodation you like; so, you expand your search to Austria. After weeks of searching on the internet, you both meet up at Staufs coffee shop to continue your

search for apartments together. Sitting across from one another and situated behind your laptops, you both find an apartment you like in the city of Graz. Describe the features of the apartment you found to your friend. Then listen to the description of their apartment. Finally, compare and contrast the differences and decide which apartment will be best for the two of you.

Presentational Task

You've arrived to Austria safe and sound! You've just got off the plane in Graz and take a taxi to your new place. You look around and the apartment is NOT what you expected. Write a review on the website describing differences in the layout, amenities, and location. Don't forget to attach pictures of the apartment to really show them how terrible your apartment is.

Instructions and Materials for the IPA

German: Interpretive Task for WG-Gesucht Advertisement

Task: Read and interpret the advertisement, and then answer the following questions in English as best you can.

I. Key Word Recognition

Find in the advertisement the German word/phrase that best expresses the meaning of each of the following English words/phrases:

1. Cellphone Number: _____
2. Room: _____
3. Available: _____
4. Starting from: _____
5. Luxury Shared Apartment: _____
6. Home Phone Number: _____
7. Street: _____
8. Square meters: _____

II. Main Idea(s)

Using information from the advertisement, provide the main idea(s) of the ad in English.

_____

_____

_____

_____

III. Supporting Details

1. Circle the letter of each detail that is mentioned in the ad (not all are included!).
2. Write the letter of the detail next to where it appears in the text.
3. Write the information that is given in the advertisement in the space provided next to the detail below.
    A. The price of a room: _____
    B. The size of the shower: _____
    C. The number of roommates: _____
    D. The move-in date: _____
    E. The phone number of a roommate: _____
    F. The address / location of the shared apartment: _____
    G. The amenities of the shared apartment: _____
    H. Due date for monthly rent: _____

IV. Organizational Features

How is this text organized? Choose all that apply and explain briefly why you selected each organizational feature—what were the clues in the text?
    A. Chronological
    B. Cause/Effect
    C. Compare/Contrast
    D. Biography/Autobiography
    E. Storytelling
    F. Description
    G. Problem and Solution
Justification from text:

_____

_____

_____

_____

_____

V. Guessing Meaning from Context

Based on the advertisement, indicate the meaning of the following from the context in the advertisement in English.
06844 Dessau Nord, Friedrich-Schneider Str. 8a

_____

_____

_____

VI. Inferences

Answer the following question by providing as many reasons as you can. Your responses may be in English or in German. *Use details from the advertisement to support your answers*.

If you were moving to Germany, why would you choose to move into this shared apartment? Or why wouldn't you want to move into this apartment?

_____

_____

VII. Author's Perspective

Select the perspective or point of view you think the author adopted as they created this advertisement and justify your answer with information from the ad.

A. Comic

B. Factual

C. Moral/Religious

Justification from text:

_____

_____

_____

_____

VIII. Comparing Cultural Perspectives

Answer the following question:

What did you learn about the target culture from this advertisement?

_____

_____

_____

_____

_____

IX. Personal Reaction to the Text

Using specific information from the advertisement, describe your personal reaction to the advertisement **in German**. Be sure to provide reasons that support your reaction.

_____

_____

_____

_____

_____

_____

_____

German: Interpersonal Task for WG-Gesucht Advertisement

German I: STUDENT A

Kosten

Miete:	**395€**
Nebenkosten:	**n.a.**
Sonstige Kosten:	**20€**
SCHUFA-Auskunft:	**Online anfordern**[1]

Adresse

Merangasse 53
8010 Graz Graz
Umzugsfirma beauftragen[1]

Verfügbarkeit

frei ab: **01.02.2017**

frei bis: **30.06.2017**

Online: 11 Minuten

WG-Details

DIE WG

22m² Zimmer in 3er WG
Wohnungsgröße: 97m²
3er WG (0 Frauen und 2 Männer)
Bewohneralter: 20 bis 21 Jahre
Rauchen nicht erwünscht
Studenten-WG, gemischte WG
Sprache/n:

GESUCHT WIRD

Frau oder Mann zwischen 19 und 24 Jahren

Angaben zum Objekt

Badewanne, Dusche

WLAN

Kabel

Parkett, Fliesen

gute Parkmöglichkeiten

1 Minute zu Fuß entfernt

Waschmaschine, Spülmaschine

German I: STUDENT B

Kosten

Miete:	**300€**
Nebenkosten:	**40€**
Sonstige Kosten:	**0€**
Kaution:	**400€**
SCHUFA-Auskunft:	**Online anfordern**[1]

Adresse

Sandgasse
8010 Graz Jakomini
Umzugsfirma beauftragen[1]

Verfügbarkeit

frei ab: **06.02.2016**

frei bis: **31.07.2017**

Online: 3 Stunden

WG-Details

DIE WG

13m² Zimmer in 3er WG
Wohnungsgröße: 96m²
3er WG (0 Frauen und 1 Mann)
Bewohneralter: 20 bis 35 Jahre
Rauchen auf dem Balkon erlaubt
Studenten-WG, Berufstätigen-WG, gemischte WG
Sprache/n:

GESUCHT WIRD

Frau oder Mann zwischen 20 und 35 Jahren

Angaben zum Objekt

Badewanne, Dusche

DSL, Flatrate, WLAN

Parkett

Fernwärme

schlechte Parkmöglichkeiten

1 Minute zu Fuß entfernt

Waschmaschine, Spülmaschine,
Terrasse, Keller, Fahrradkeller

Let's Protect Our World (SPANISH)

Instructor: *José Pan*
Edison High School, Edison Twp., NJ
Languages and Levels Taught:
Spanish 1, 2, 2H, 3, 4, 5, 5H, & AP

IPA Theme: *Let's Protect our World*
Language: *Spanish*
IPA Level: *Novice High*
Class Level/Size: *Spanish 2 / 25 students*

Standards Addressed:
Communication (Interpersonal, Interpretive, Presentational)
Cultures (Relating Cultural Practices to Perspectives)
Connections (Making Connections; Acquiring Information and Diverse Perspectives)
Comparisons (Cultural Comparisons)
Communities (School and Global Communities)

Task Overview
What can we do as students and members of the community to help better our environment?

In Spanish class, we have been studying the environment in our community. We have seen the type of ecosystems that exist, the problems threatening them, and solutions we can implement as students and as well as community members to help better the situation. To encourage others to participate in your cause to help save the environment, you will be writing a postcard to your overseas pen pals explaining problems that are threatening our environment. Your postcard should also try to encourage your pen pal to follow your advice on what they can do to help better the planet. First you will watch a short YouTube video titled "Cuidado del agua" by UNESCO and answer questions to show your comprehension. Then you will hold a conversation with a partner in class to discuss who has the better suggestions on how to motivate students to change their ways to help the environment. Finally, you will write a postcard to your friends describing what to do to help the environment in their community.

Interpretive Task
You will watch the video "Cuidado del agua" by UNESCO several times. As you listen and watch, you will answer several types of questions about what you are hearing and seeing.

Interpersonal Task
After watching the video "Cuidado del agua" and continuing to learn about what can be done to help combat environmental issues in the community, you will hold a discussion with a partner to debate who has the better message to help motivate students in your school to become involved in taking care of the environment. Remember that the posters can only be hung in a specific area of the school, and there is limited space. Therefore, the most impactful posters will be hung in the school hallways, and the others will be displayed in the classroom.

Presentational Task
After seeing the video and debating over the poster with a partner in class, you decide to send your pen pal in Colombia a postcard describing some environmental issues you are concerned about and what they can do to help the situation in their community. The purpose of your postcard is to give them information on environmental issues and to provide them with suggestions on what they can do to help make a positive change.

Instructions and Materials for the IPA
Spanish: Interpretive Task for YouTube video "Cuidado del Agua"
Youtube link: go.osu.edu/ipatexts
(assessment is based on the first two story sections up until 3:19)

I. Key Word Recognition

As you watch the video segment, jot down a list of 8 content words/phrases that you hear that convey meaning related to the text, such as key nouns and verbs. Avoid listing words/phrases such as prepositions (*of, from, in, out, etc.*) and conjunctions (*and, but, or, etc.*), which do not carry much meaning. Then provide an English equivalent to the right of each word you listed.

_____   _____

_____   _____

_____   _____

_____   _____

II. Main Idea(s)

Using the information from the video, provide the main idea(s) of the video selection in English.

_____

_____

_____

_____

III. Supporting Information

For each of the following statements

1. Circle the letter of each detail that is mentioned in the video (not all are included!).

2. Write the information that is given in the video in the space provided next to the detail below.

    A. At the beginning of the story what the character needs to do to the carrots _____

    B. The type of animal who says water is not a valuable resource _____

    C. Water on the ground when it evaporates gets converted to _____

    D. The water drops state he is mean and aggressive _____

    E. He states water is a valuable resource _____

    F. They decide to go on an outing along the river current _____

    G. At the end of the river they find a family of fish named _____

    H. What the family in the lake asks the water drops to do _____

    I. What the water drops see as they go down the river _____

    J. The drops realize that water is very useful to only these animals _____

IV. Organizational Features

How is this video organized? Choose all that apply, explain briefly why you selected each organizational feature, and identify the clues in the text.

    A. Chronological order

    B. Pros and cons

    C. Compare/contrast

    D. Biography/Autobiography

    E. Problem and solution

    F. Storytelling

Justification from selection:

_____

_____

_____

V. Guessing Meaning from Context

Based on this clip, write what the following four words or phrases mean in English.

1. Regar _____

2. Desperdiciado todo el agua _____

3. Escasea_____

4. Sequía _____

VI. Inferences

"Read between the lines" to answer the following questions, using information from the article. Your responses may be in English or in Spanish.

1. What could happen if people do not take care of water on the planet?

_____

_____

_____

2. How could this affect the planet?

_____

_____

_____

VII. Author's Perspective

Select the perspective or point of view you think the author adopted as he wrote this article and justify your answer with information from the text.

    A. Comic

    B. Factual/Historical

    C. Moral

    D. Story

Justification from text:

_____

_____

_____

VIII. Comparing Cultural Perspectives

Answer the following question in Spanish or English.

Would this video have been different if it were produced for a US audience? Explain.

_____

_____

_____

IX. Personal Reaction to the Text

Using specific information from the video, describe your personal reaction to its content **in Spanish**. Be sure to provide reasons that support your reaction.

_____

_____

_____

Interpersonal speaking assessment: Pre-speaking co-constructed content scaffolding for Novice level learners

Note to teachers: *Only for Novice level learners*, the teacher builds in this content scaffolding activity to help the learners organize their thinking before speaking. The pre-speaking chart is completed by the students individually. Then as a class, have students think out loud about general ideas/content that they would include in their interpersonal conversation. For example, a general idea they could write down in the content box would be "solutions for environmental problems". Help them come up with several ideas they could incorporate in their conversation for the content column.

Once they fill out the content column, instruct the students that they now have exactly one minute to fill out individually the vocabulary column in silence. In this column, the students should write any vocabulary or structures they will use in the conversation. For example, in the vocabulary column next to "solutions to environmental problems" they could write, "conserve water" or "plant more trees." They basically will write out anything they wish to use in their conversation. Once the minute is up, they are to put their pencils/pens down. Have them focus on the conversation and their partners to start the recording. **Note: Students are not allowed to look at their pre-speaking charts during the conversation.**

PRE-SPEAKING

CONTENT	VOCABULARY

Interpersonal Task
TÍTULO: Mi mensaje para la escuela
Hold a conversation with your partner regarding who has the better ideas to take care of the environment as well as whose poster should be displayed in school. Discuss each other's posters and ideas by asking questions about what you see on their posters and answer any questions you might be asked about yours. Remember that our class needs to pick the most impactful posters for the school hallway and the rest will be hung in our class. Therefore, make sure to decide who has the better poster to display in school so you could recommend it to the teacher

Presentational Task
NUESTRO MUNDO
Título: ¡¡¡AYUDA AL MEDIO AMBIENTE!!!!
The environment in our community is constantly being threatened by the actions of human beings all over the world. Seeing that today is Earth Day, you decide to write a postcard to your pen pal in Colombia to explain what we can do to help make the world a better place.

On one side of the postcard paper, draw an image of what you think is the most important problem facing the environment today. Also address the postcard to your friend.

On the other side of the postcard, you are going to write a message to your friend. Make sure to include the following information (use the following as a checklist):

1. _____Greet your friend.

2. _____Tell them today is Earth Day and we should all do something good for the planet.

3. _____Tell them what you think is the most serious problem in the environment and why

4. _____Explain how it affects people

5. _____Describe 2 things that can be done to help the situation.

6. _____Ask them what problems their community is facing.

7. _____Include a farewell.

¡¡¡¡¡EL PLANETA TE NECESITA!!!!

Sample Integrated Performance Assessments: Intermediate

Social Justice in Japan (JAPANESE)

Instructor: Iya Nemastil
Dublin Jerome High School,
Dublin, OH
Languages and Levels Taught:
Japanese 1, 2, 3, 4/AP

Standards Addressed:
Communication (Interpersonal, Interpretive, Presentational)
Cultures ((Relating Cultural Practices to Perspectives, Relating Cultural Products to Perspectives)
Connections (Acquiring Information and Diverse Perspectives)
Comparisons (Cultural Comparisons)

Task Overview
In your Japanese class you have been studying some of the problems that exist in Japan, as well as in the United States, such as poverty, racism and discrimination, childhood hunger, access, cost of living and income, and ideal living conditions. To help raise awareness of the low-income families and food access in your hometown, you will first research these issues, and then you are going to make a slide-show presentation for the students at your sister city school in Japan, in which you describe steps that Dublin, Ohio can take that Japan already has in place in order to benefit its citizens. You will also come up with new suggestions and solutions. You will then also read a short article from a Japanese website describing a Japanese children's kitchen and its amenities to give you some ideas.

In this unit, you will watch several short videos where Japanese people talk about why they love where they live. You will also go on various Japanese city websites as well as apartment and housing information to learn about their specific positives and negatives, ease of living, food, and amenities. Before the IPA interpretive task, you will learn about childhood poverty and hunger and how Japan utilizes children's kitchens to feed underprivileged families. You will also learn information about common living conditions and housing statistics such as crime rate, safety, homelessness, etc., before the interpretive assessment. The interpersonal assessment involves speaking with your classmates about what you find important in your ideal city, such as safety, schools, access to things, and giving reasons for your thoughts. The final part of the unit focuses on visiting several websites to see what is considered ideal ease of living for Japanese people. For the presentational task, you will create an ideal city encompassing all things you find important and present it to the class.

Interpretive Task
After learning about the different children's kitchens/cafeterias that Japan has popped up all over the country, you will read a short article website description of a children's cooking kitchen and answer the interpretive questions that go along with it.

Interpersonal Task
Now that you have some more ideas for what types of things Japan utilizes to keep its country safe, and how childhood hunger affects both Japan and the U.S., discuss with your partner what you find to be necessary in order to live easily and comfortably in a city.

Presentational Task
Based on the information that you spoke about with your partner, where you discussed your reasoning for why you chose to incorporate certain aspects in your ideal city, you will make a slide-show presentation for your class describing your ideal city and living situation and how specific amenities and equitable access can help the citizens living in that city.

Instructions and Materials for the IPA

Japanese: Interpretive Task for
あきしま　こどもクッキング
Link to text: go.osu.edu/ipatexts

あきしま こどもクッキング

パパたちによる「こどもクッキング」でみんなでごはんを食べよう。

あきしまこどもクッキングとは？

ご協力のお願い

活動報告

お問い合わせ

あきしまこどもクッキング
about 2 years ago

6月開催中止のお知らせ

開催を予定しておりました、あきしまこどもクッキングですが、新型コロナウイルス感染防止により会場の臨時休館が続いております。先日6/14(日)まで再延長が決定いたしました。つきましては6/10(水)の開催を、中止させていただくこととなりました。
ご参加をご検討いただいた皆様にご迷惑をおかけする事となり、大変申し訳ございません。
なお、7月以降の開催につきましては未定です。 ... See more

👍 2   💬 Comment   ➦ Share

あきしまこどもクッキング

あきしまこどもクッキングってなあに？

- みんなで一緒に料理を作って、食べるサークルです
- こどもが1人でも参加できます。（高校生まで）
- 大人300円　こども無料　栄養バランスのとれた夕食を食べられます
- 学習支援もはじめました。宿題したり本を読んだり、食後を自由に過ごしてください。

スケジュール

5月開催中止のお知らせ

開催を予定しておりました、あきしまこどもクッキングですが、新型コロナウイルス感染防止により会場の臨時休館が続いております。先日5/31(日)まで再延長が決定いたしました。
つきましては5/13(水)の開催を、中止させていただくこととなりました。
ご参加をご検討いただいた皆様にご迷惑をおかけする事となり、大変申し訳ございません。
なお、6月以降の開催につきましては未定です。

何卒ご理解のほどよろしくお願いいたします。

あきしまこどもクッキングの開催場所はこちら

昭島市公民館　3階　実習室
〒196-0012 東京都昭島市つつじが丘3丁目7-7

KOTORIホール(昭島市民会館)
〒196-0012 Tokyo, Akishima, Tsutsujigaoka, 3 Chome-7-7 昭島市民会館
3.6 ★★★★☆　289 reviews
View larger map

City Kaikan Park

SHOWACHO Google
Keyboard shortcuts　Map data ©2022　Terms of Use　Report a map error

I. Key Word Recognition

Find in the article the Japanese word/phrase that best expresses the meaning of each of the following English words/phrases:

1. make cuisine: _____
2. club: _____
3. participate: _____
4. free of cost: _____
5. dinner: _____
6. freely: _____
7. spend time: _____
8. every month: _____
9. single parent: _____
10. goal/purpose: _____
11. to raise (a child): _____
12. children's kitchen: _____
13. enough: _____
14. to watch over: _____
15. place: _____
16. home: _____

II. Main Idea

Using information from the article, provide the main idea of the article in English.

_____

_____

_____

III. Supporting Details

Circle the letter of each detail that is mentioned in the article (not all are included!).

Write the letter of the detail next to where it appears in the text.

Write the information that is given in the article in the space provided next to the detail below.

   A. The address and city that the Akishima Children's Kitchen is located in: _____

   _____

   B. The goal/purpose of the Akishima Children's Kitchen: _____

   _____

   C. Akishima Children's Kitchen open weekday schedule for the month of May: _____

   _____

   D. The price for attendance for high school children: _____

   _____

   E. The types of foods that can be cooked at this kitchen: _____

   _____

   F. The two ACTION reasons for why the author wanted to make the children's kitchen: _____

   _____

   G. The dates that the kitchen will be closed and events canceled: _____

   _____

IV. Organizational Features

How is this text organized? Choose all that apply and explain briefly why you selected each organizational feature—what were the clues in the text?

    A. Alphabetical order

    B. Letter/message

    C. Informational

    D. Description

    E. Chronological

Justification from text: _____

_____

_____

V. Guessing Meaning From Context

Based on this passage, write what the following three words/phrases probably mean in English:

1. 『場』があり、絆が出来れば、いくらでもおせっかいが焼けます

_____

2. 子供らに無料や低価格で食事を提供する場所です。

_____

3. 宿題したり本を読んだり、食後を自由に過ごしてください。

_____

VI. Inferences

"Read between the lines" to answer the following questions, using information from the article. You may respond in Japanese or English.

1. True or False: Circle one and provide evidence from the text.

    Children can come here and cook and eat without a parent. _____

_____

_____

2. True or False: Circle one and provide evidence from the text.

    Raising children in the community is important. _____

_____

_____

VII. Author's Perspective

Select the perspective or point of view you think the author adopted as they wrote this article and justify your answer with information from the text. You may respond in Japanese or English.

    A. Clinical/scientific

    B. Moral/Religious

    C. Factual

Justification from text: _____

_____

VIII. Comparing Cultural Perspectives

Answer the following questions in Japanese or English:

1. What are the cultural similarities and differences between this Children's Kitchen and the soup kitchens we have for low-income families in the United States?

_____

_____

_____

_____

2. How would this website article have been different if it were written for a U.S. audience?

_____

_____

_____

IX. Personal Reaction to the Text

1. Using specific information from the text, describe your personal reaction to the article **in Japanese**. Be sure to provide reasons that support your reaction.

_____

_____

_____

2. In your opinion, do you think that having places such as this readily available for the community is sustainable and possible in Dublin, Ohio?

_____

_____

_____

Technology (FRENCH)

Instructor: Margaret Newcomb (retired)
Bishop Blanchet High School, Seattle, WA
Languages and Levels Taught:
French 1, 2, 3, & 4/AP

IPA Theme: *Technology*
Language: *French*
IPA Level: *Intermediate*
Class Level/Size: *French 3/15 Students*

Standards Addressed:
Communication (Interpersonal, Interpretive, Presentational)
Cultures (Relating Cultural Practices to Perspectives; Relating Cultural Products to Perspectives)
Connections (Making Connections; Acquiring Information and Diverse Perspectives)
Comparisons (Cultural Comparisons)
Communities (School and Global Communities)

Task Overview
How can we positively manage technology in our day-to-day lives?
In your French class, you have been using online interactive resources for your French language acquisition and have been studying various forms and uses of technology in the classroom and throughout the world. To help put in perspective the pros and cons of living in a wired world, you will write a digital story incorporating video and sound in collaboration with the students at the *lycée of Sainte Marie du Port*, your partner school in France. One aspect of the conflict in the story you create will involve positive and negative consequences of technological dependence. First, you will listen to an audio clip concerning descriptive and proscriptive usage of a technological device. To make the experience come alive and to give you more ideas for your final digital stories, you will participate in a role-play situation (one partner is a parent, the other is a middle schooler) to discuss the advantages and disadvantages of technology. Lastly, you will collaborate with two classmates and one French correspondent to put together a story board, in French, for your digital story, developing a conflict that

centers on technology. You will publish your digital stories on the classroom blog and share them with the French III students at your high school and the selected class of French students. All student and faculty readers will share their reflections through blog comments.

Interpretive Task
To help you evaluate some of the conflicts associated with the integration of technology into daily life, you will listen to an audio clip from *France Bienvenue*. Listen carefully to the clip two times before completing the accompanying comprehension activity. You may listen again to the clip as needed to help you make your choices.

Interpersonal Task
Partner A: Play the role of a parent who wants their middle schooler to spend less time connected to technology via cell phone (texts, social media, video games, blogs, etc.). Lately, the middle schooler seems anti-social, unhappy and doesn't want to participate in past time activities with the family. Furthermore, your child's grades are slipping and final exams are in a few weeks. Come to a consensus with your child about how much time per day they should be allowed on the cell phone.

Partner B: Play the role of a middle school student who enjoys technology, especially cell phones, texts, video games, social media, blogs, etc. Explain why your cell phone is an advantage and can actually help you with your grades. Address your parent's concerns that lately you seem unhappy, anti-social and do not want to spend past time activities with the family. Come to a consensus with your parent on how much time a day you should be allowed on your cell phone.

Presentational Task
With two partners, identify the technology presently in use by you and your community. Get input from your French correspondent. Brainstorm past uses of technology, now out of use, as well as future possible uses not yet available. Draw from vocabulary lists studied in class, but augment freely with new French vocabulary, including verbs related employing the technology. Using the terms as a starting point, collaborate with your partners to create a story board whose conflict will originate from a technological issue or issues.

Then you will work in groups of three to create the digital story.

Publish the story on the class Google Document page to share with your classmates and invited students from *St. Marie du Port*.

Instructions and Materials for the IPA

Audio Clip: "Jamais sans mon portable" go.osu.edu/ipatexts

French Intermediate Level Interpretive Task Comprehension: Technology

I.   Key Word Recognition

Listen carefully to the audio clip and write eight words that are related to the theme, such as key nouns and verbs. Avoid listing word/phrases, such as prepositions (of, from, in, out, etc.) and conjunctions (and, but, or, etc.), which do not carry much meaning. Then provide the English equivalent to the right of each word.

_____   _____

_____   _____

_____   _____

_____   _____

II.   Main Idea

Using information gleaned from the recording, provide the main idea of the audio clip in English.

_____

_____

_____

III. Supporting Details

Circle the letter of those details, and ONLY those details, that are mentioned in the clip (not all are included!).

In English, write the information that is given in the recording in the space provided next to each circled detail.

A.   What happens to draw attention to the object belonging to the male speaker:

_____

B.   What the object is:

_____

C.   Where the female speaker is employed:

_____

D.   What reason the young man gives for his action:

_____

E.   The assignment given to the young man to complete:

_____

F.   How the young man's behavior differs from his classmates' behavior:

_____

G.   What permission the young woman gives to the young man:

_____

H.   What the young man's offer is to the suggestion from the young woman:

_____

IV. Organizational Features

How is the content of this audio clip organized? Choose all that apply and explain briefly why you selected each organizational feature—what were the clues in the recording?

    A.   Lecture

    B.   Conversation

    C.   Compare / contrast

    D.   Interview

    E.   Debate

Justification from audio clip: _____

_____

_____

_____

V. Guessing Meaning from Context

Based on this recording, write what the following three words probably mean in English:

1.   …je l'ai laissé allumé et.. (near the beginning)

_____

2.   Ils le confisquent ? (closer to the middle)

_____

3.   La prochaine fois, vous l'éteindrez? (near the end)

_____

VI. Inferences

Using the ideas and explanations that come up in the recording to guide you, answer the following questions. Be sure to use issues raised in the clip to ground your answer. You may respond in French or English.

1.   How can the options for online activities and communication sometimes have negative consequences, especially in a learning context? _____

    _____

2.   Why does the male speaker in the clip emphasize the differences between his use of technology and that of his classmates? What personal value does he want to show the young woman that he holds?_____

    _____

    _____

    _____

VII. Recorder's Perspective

Select the perspective or point of view you think the recorder of the clip adopted when she arranged this encounter, and justify your answer with information from the text. You may respond in French or English.

    A.   Cultural

    B.   Humanistic

    C.   Scientific

Justification from text: _____

_____

_____

_____

VIII. Comparing Cultural Perspectives

Answer the following questions in French or English:

1. What do the observations made in this recording reveal about French cultural perspectives?

_____

_____

_____

2. Based on the audio clip, describe some cultural similarities and /or differences between France and the United States.

_____

_____

_____

IX. Personal Reaction to the Audio Clip

Using specific information from the audio clip, describe your personal reaction to the content of the recording **in French**.

_____

_____

_____

_____

Sample Integrated Performance Assessments: Intermediate-High

Providing Emergency Room Care (SPANISH)

Instructor: Sarah Peceny
University of New Mexico,
Albuquerque, NM
Languages and Levels Taught:
Spanish / Beginner I, Beginner II,
Intermediate I, and Intermediate III

Instructor: Eva Rodríguez-González
University of New Mexico,
Albuquerque, NM
Languages and Levels Taught:
Spanish (Spanish I, II, III, IV,
300, 400, 500 and 600 levels) and
English Currently serving as
Spanish language teaching coordinator

IPA Theme: *Providing Emergency Room Care in a real*
Medical Spanish Program in New Mexico
Language: *Spanish*
IPA Level: Intermediate High
Class Level/Size: Intermediate II: Introduction to Medical
Spanish / 25 students

Standards Addressed:
Communication (Interpersonal, Interpretive, Presentational)
Cultures (Relating Cultural Practices to Perspectives)
Connections (Making Connections; Acquiring Information
and Diverse Perspectives)
Comparisons (Cultural Comparisons)
Communities (School and Global Communities)

Task Overview

In our medical Spanish program, we have been preparing you for the possibility of working in an *Emergency Room* with patients who only speak Spanish. To determine if you're ready for this medical position, first, you will listen to a conversation that takes place between a woman and an emergency operator to report a motorbike accident and respond to questions to check your comprehension. Then, you will read an Emergency

---

Room patient's medical chart with clinical notes and answer questions for comprehension. Next, interview a family member or friend and ask them about a hypothetical or actual emergency care situation they have experienced and how the situation was dealt with in the hospital. Make sure you ask questions that add details to the situation described. Upload the interview once you are done. Next, imagine that you work in a TV station and you have been tasked with the creation of a short 2-minutes video clip regarding the danger of cell phone use while driving by means of sharing a testimonial. Prepare a video clip with at least 3 images/pictures that describe the example of a distracted driving case and the hospitalization of the patient in the Urgent Care unit. Feel free to make up the case and the actors. You might create your own images or find them here: https://www.flickr.com/creativecommons/. And finally, imagine that you are the patient from the article you have read above (clinical note). After being hospitalized, you come back home and decide to email one friend/ family member to describe what happened to you. Write a description of where you were, when you had the accident, who you were with, what happened on the road and then in the emergency room. You may want to provide details regarding your feelings as well and your actual emotional and physical state of being right after the accident, while being in the hospital, and finally now being home.

Instructions and Materials for the IPA

At the Emergency Room

Interpretive Listening
Listen to the following conversation that takes place between a woman and an emergency phone operator to report a motorbike accident.
Link to listening passage (Instructors: See Appendix J for transcription): go.osu.edu/ipatexts

I. Key Word Recognition

As you listen to the recorded segment, jot down a list of 10 content words/phrases in Spanish that you hear that convey meaning related to the content, such as key nouns and verbs. Avoid listing words/phrases such as prepositions (of, from, in, out, etc.) and conjunctions (and, but, or, etc.), which do not carry much meaning. Then provide an English equivalent to the right of each word you listed:

_____	_____
_____	_____
_____	_____
_____	_____
_____	_____

II. Main Idea(s)

Using information from the segment you heard, provide the main idea(s) of it in English.

_____

_____

_____

III. Supporting Details

1. Circle the letter of each detail that is mentioned in the segment (not all are included!).
2. Write the information that is given in the segment in the space provided next to the detail below.

   A. Name two types of vehicles involved in the accident:

   _____

   B. The age of the injured person:

   _____

   C. The relationship of the injured person to the caller reporting the accident:

   _____

   D. The location where the accident occurred:

   _____

   E. Name two symptoms that the caller is complaining about:

   _____

   F. The destination to where the caller and the other person were heading at the time of the accident:

   _____

   G. What caused the accident:

   _____

   H. The types of first aid that the caller is told to administer:

   _____

IV. Organizational Features

How is this segment organized? Based on the purpose of this segment, identify the organizational structure. Choose all that apply and explain briefly why you selected each organizational feature--what were the clues in the segment? How is the conversation organized? Circle all that apply and explain what clues were in the message to justify your answer (respond in English) (NOT ALL APPLY):

   A. Public Service Announcement
   B. Compare-Contrast
   C. Interview
   D. Conversation

E.   News Item

Justification from the audio: _____

_____

_____

V.   Guessing Meaning from Context

Based on what you have heard, write what the following three words and/or expressions probably mean in English.

1.   "está sangrando por todas partes" _____

2.   "dejamos el hotel" _____

3.   "primeros auxilios" _____

VI. Inferences

"Listen between the lines" to select the best inference of the three listed below. Circle the best inference and provide evidence from the audio to support your selection (respond in Spanish).

A.   The woman who calls the operator is injured.

B.   The woman who calls the operator is able to give details of her whereabouts.

C.   The woman who calls the operator seems to be nervous as she is not able to provide details of her whereabouts.

Evidence from audio to support your answer:

_____

_____

_____

VII. Operator´s Purpose

Select the primary perspective or point of view you think the operator receiving the call adopted as she responded to the caller and justify your answer with information you heard in the segment (respond in English).

A. to persuade

B. to collect information

C. to inform

Justification from the audio:

_____

_____

_____

VIII. Comparing Cultural Perspectives

Answer the following question:

Based on what you have heard in the conversation, would you identify a similar/different procedure for reporting an emergency for a car accident in the U.S? (Respond in English)

_____

_____

_____

IX. Personal Reaction to the Message

Using specific information from the audio conversation, describe your personal reaction **in Spanish** to the emergency situation. Be sure to provide reasons that support your reaction.

_____

_____

_____

Interpretive Reading—"Caso clínico"

Adapted from the following Reading source url: Salud Play

https://www.salusplay.com/casos-clinicos-de-enfermeria/MQ_29_48_1258-001560

Sexo: Hombre **Edad**: 32 años **Profesión**: Cocinero **País**: España

Motivo de consulta: Paciente de 32 años trasladado al servicio de urgencias del Hospital Universitario de Quito tras sufrir accidente de tráfico con su moto, a espera de subir a planta y establecer cirugía. Presenta fractura de tibia y fíbula, hemorragia leve controlada y quemaduras por fricción.

Historial médico: Padece de hipertensión arterial y sobrepeso (1.75 m, 80 kg, IMC: 26.12). Alérgia: Nolotil [painkiller drug]. Sin intolerancias. Medicación para hipertensión arterial, analgésicos (en ocasiones). Fumador desde hace 5 años (10 cigarrillos/día). Consumo de alcohol moderado. Todas las vacunas al día. Padre y hermana hipertensos. Madre obesidad y diabetes mellitus tipo 2. Vive con sus padres, sin hijos y soltero.

REVISIÓN DE SISTEMAS Y ESTADO/CONDICIÓN (or) ESTADO FÍSICO Y MENTAL DEL PACIENTE

1.	**Respiración**: Sin alteraciones
2.	**Alimentación / Hidratación**: Sin alteraciones
3.	**Excreción**: Sin alteraciones
4.	**Movilidad / Postura**: Disminución de la movilidad debido a la fractura de tibia y fíbula (no puede caminar ni soportar peso), en la actualidad está en cama casi todo el tiempo hasta modificación de la situación.
5.	**Dormir / Descansar**: Sueño alterado debido al dolor agudo que presenta por la fractura aunque el analgésico sea administrado.
6.	**Vestirse / Desvestirse**: Alterada por fractura de la fíbula.
7.	**Temperatura corporal**: Sin alteraciones
8.	**Integridad piel y mucosas**: Alteraciones de la integridad cutánea con hemorragia controlada en heridas menores en miembros debido a fricción. Fractura cerrada (no sobresale ningún fragmento de hueso a través de la piel). Inflamación.
9.	**Evitar peligros**: Dolor intenso a pesar de la administración regular de analgésicos.
10.	**Estado de ánimo del paciente**: Irritabilidad, inquietud, preocupación por su pierna y su vehículo.
11.	**Comunicación / Relaciones sociales**: Preocupación.
12.	**Valores / Creencias**: Sin alteraciones
13.	**Autorrealización**: Adaptación difícil a su nueva situación debido a que es por lo general una persona activa.
14.	**Entretenimiento**: Sin alteraciones
15.	**Aprendizaje**: Sin alteraciones

I. Key Word Recognition

Find in the article the word/phrase in Spanish that best expresses the meaning of the following English words/expressions. Write the corresponding word(s) in the spaces provided:

1. floor (*of a building*) _____
2. suffer _____
3. overweight _____
4. (skin) burn _____
5. hospitalized _____
6. restlessness _____
7. worry _____
8. minor wounds _____
9. hemorrhage _____
10. single _____

II. Main Idea(s)

Using information from the clinical report, provide the main idea(s) of the reading in English.

_____

_____

_____

III. Supporting Details

1. Circle the letter of each detail that is mentioned in the article (not all are included!).
2. Write the letter of the detail next to where it appears in the text.
3. Write the information that is given in the article in the space provided next to the detail below.

    A. The age of the patient:

    _____

    B. Two parts of the body that he injured:

    _____

    C. Who smoked around the patient when he was little:

    _____

    D. Which member(s) of his family has hypertension:

    _____

    E. The patient's height and weight:

    _____

    F. Number of alcoholic drinks that the patient has per week:

    _____

    G. Which member(s) of his family has diabetes:

    _____

    H. The patient's temperature:

    _____

IV. Organizational Features

How is this text organized? Circle all that apply, explain why you selected each organizational feature, and identify the clues in the text (respond in English).

    A. Historical

    B. Description

    C. Compare/Contrast

    D. Pros and Cons

    E. Problem and Solution

Justification from the text:

_____

_____

_____

V. Guessing Meaning from Context

Based on the information provided in the article/clinical report, write what the following three words and/or expressions probably mean in English.

1. "cirugía" (see *Motivo de consulta* section) _____

2. "soportar peso" (see *Historial Médico* section) _____

3. "sobresale" (see 8. *Integridad piel y mucosas* section) _____

VI. Inferences

Read between the lines to answer the following questions, using information from the text. Please provide evidence in Spanish from the text to support your selection.

1. Why do you think the patient is worried?

Justification from the text:_____

_____

_____

2. What might be the effect of this patient's accident/hospital treatment?

Justification from the text:_____

_____

_____

3. Has the patient been a smoker all his adult life?

Justification from the text:_____

_____

_____

VII. Health Provider's Perspective

Select the perspective or point of view you think the authors(s) adopted as they wrote this article and justify your answer in English with information from the text.

    A. To inform

    B. To entertain

    C. To persuade

Justification from the text:_____

_____

VIII. Comparing Cultural Perspectives

Answer the following question in Spanish:

Using examples from the clinical note that you just read and any previous knowledge that you have, what are some similarities and/or dissimilarities in the type of information that you know to be normally collected in emergency rooms in the U.S.?

_____

_____

_____

_____

IX. Personal Reaction to the Text

Using specific information from the clinical note, describe and reflect on your personal reaction to the information provided **in Spanish**.

_____

_____

_____

_____

_____

_____

Interpersonal Speaking

Interview a family member or friend and ask them about a hypothetical or actual emergency care situation they experienced and how the situation was dealt with in the hospital. Make sure you ask questions that add details to the situation described. Upload the interview once you are done.

Presentational Speaking (video with pic)

Imagine that you work in a TV station and you have been tasked with the creation of a short 2-minutes video clip regarding the danger of cell phone use while driving by means of sharing a testimonial. Prepare a video clip with at least 3 images/pictures that describe the example of a distracted driving case and the hospitalization of the patient in the Urgent Care unit. Feel free to make up the case and the actors. You might create your own images or find them here: https://www.flickr.com/creativecommons/

Presentational Writing (description)

Imagine that you are the patient from the article you have read above (clinical note). After being hospitalized, you come back home and decide to email one friend/family member to describe what happened to you. Write a description of where you were, when you had the accident, who you were with, what happened on the road and then in the emergency room. You may want to provide details regarding your feelings as well and your actual emotional and physical state of being right after the accident, while being in the hospital, and finally now being home.

Introduction to Hispanic Heritage Month and History of Latin America (SPANISH)

Instructor: Tammy Lyons
Greensburg Salem High School,
Greensburg, PA
Languages and Levels Taught: Spanish
Levels IV, AP, 6, Independent Study 7,
FLES

IPA Theme: Introduction to Hispanic Heritage Month and
History of Latin America
Language: Spanish
IPA Level: Intermediate-High
Class Level/Size: Level IV+, 10-15 students

Standards Addressed:
Communication (Interpersonal, Interpretive, Presentational)
Cultures (Relating Cultural Practices to Perspectives; Relating
    Cultural Products to Perspectives)
Connections (Making Connections, Acquiring Information and
    Diverse Perspectives)
Comparisons (Cultural Comparisons)
Communities (School and Global Communities)

Task Overview
*How have some important events in Latin American
history impacted present-day culture in Latin America?*

In Spanish class you have been studying the colonization of Latin America, the poems *La United Fruit Co.*
and *Alturas de Machu Picchu* by Pablo Neruda, the
movie *También la lluvia*, and linguistic discrimination,
which all relate to the history and current culture in
Latin America. To help others empathize with the perspective of Latin Americans, you will write an article for
your high school Spanish Club literary magazine in
which you explain the perspective of a person from
Latin America with indigenous ancestry in relation to
the colonization of their homeland or you will write
a critique of the song and the corresponding video to
share at your next Spanish Club meeting. First you will
listen to the song "Latinoamérica" and watch the video.
Then you will have a conversation with a Spanish

speaker in class comparing and contrasting the colonization of Latin America with that of the United States
or you will discuss with a partner how the images in
the video relate directly or indirectly to the lyrics of the
song. Finally, you will write an article for the Spanish
Club literary magazine or you will write a critique of the
song and video.

Interpretive Task
You will listen to the song "Latinoamérica" by Calle 13 several times. You will also watch the video as many times as you
would like. As you listen and watch, you will answer several
questions about what you are hearing and seeing, to help you
interpret the cultural references in the lyrics and the video.

Interpersonal Task
After exploring the song "Latinoamérica" by Calle 13 in
class, you have an opportunity to have a conversation with a
Spanish speaker comparing and contrasting the colonization
of Latin America with that of the United States. During your
conversation, try to find as many differences and similarities
as possible.

Interpersonal Task (alternative for lower-level students)
After viewing the music video "Latinoamérica" by Calle 13
in class, discuss with a partner how the images in the video
relate directly or indirectly to the lyrics of the song. Be sure
to discuss at least 8-10 images or scenes from the video and
discuss how they relate to the overall meaning of the song.

Presentational Task
Based on your interpretation of the song, your discussion
with the Spanish speaker and what you have learned in class
about colonialism in Latin America, write an article for your
high school Spanish Club literary magazine in which you
explain the perspective of a person from Latin America with
indigenous ancestry in relation to the colonization of their
homeland. Your audience is a group of advanced-level students studying Spanish at your high school and the purpose
of the article is to provide an informed viewpoint about how
the indigenous people view/viewed the colonization of their
lands, in order to help others empathize with and understand the perspective of those who were colonized.

Presentational Task (alternative for lower-level students)
Based on your interpretation of the song, your discussion with your partner and what you have learned in class, write a critique of the song and the corresponding video to share at your next Spanish Club meeting. Try to persuade the listener to listen to the song and/or watch the video.

Instructions and Materials for the IPA

Spanish: Interpretive Task for Music Video "Latinoamérica" —Calle 13 https://www.youtube.com/watch?v=l-L0GV9bdjY (For song only, teachers can turn off screen.)

I. Key Word Recognition
As you watch the video, list 8 words, phrases or sentences that you hear that you think are important to understand the meaning of the song. Avoid listing words/phrases such as prepositions (*of, from, in, out,* etc.) and conjunctions (*and, but, or,* etc.), which do not carry much meaning. Then provide an English equivalent to the right of each word you listed.

_____   _____

_____   _____

_____   _____

_____   _____

II. Main Idea
Using information from the video, provide the main idea of the song in English.

_____

_____

_____

_____

III. Supporting Details
1. Circle the letter of each detail that is mentioned in the video (not all are included!).
2. Write the information that is given in the video in the space provided next to the detail below.
    A. An explanation by the singer of who he is:

    _____

    B. The history of the singer's homeland:

    _____

    C. Things that are not for sale:

    _____

    D. Specific events in Latin America history:

    _____

    E. What happened in Perú at Machu Picchu:

    _____

    F. Examples of landscapes in Latin America:

    _____

    G. What the singer's religion does for him:

    _____

    H. What the singer is proud of:

    _____

IV. Organizational Features

How is this video organized? Choose all that apply and explain briefly why you selected each organizational feature—what were the clues in the video?

    A. News item

    B. Music video

    C. Interview

    D. Documentary

    E. Commercial

Justification from the text: _____

_____

_____

_____

_____

V. Guessing Meaning from Context

Based on this music video, write what the following words/phrases probably mean in English:

1.   soy todas **las sobras** de lo que se robaron

    (0:35) _____

2.   mano de **obra campesina** para tu consumo

    (0:45)_ _____

3.   **un discurso** político pero sin saliva

    (1:02) _____

4.   y si **se derrumba** yo lo reconstruyo

    (4:23) _____

5.   Operación Cóndor **invadiendo mi nido**, perdono pero nunca olvido

    (4:31) _____

VI. Inferences

"View between the lines" to answer the following questions, using the lyrics as a basis for your responses. Answer in Spanish or English.

1. ¿Cómo se siente el cantante acerca de la historia de América Latina? Explica. (How does the singer feel about the history of Latin America. Justify your response.)

_____

_____

_____

_____

_____

2. ¿Qué está tratando de decir el cantante en el coro de la canción? No traduzcas el coro sino más bien explica el significado más profundo. (What is the singer trying to say in the chorus of the song? Do NOT provide a translation but rather, explain the deeper meaning of the chorus.)

_____

_____

_____

VII. Author's Purpose

Select the perspective or point of view you think the singer adopted as he created this song and justify your answer with information you heard in the video.

    A. to inform

    B. to make a political statement

    C. to persuade

Justification from the text:_____

_____

_____

_____

VIII. Comparing Cultural Perspectives

Answer the following questions **in Spanish**.

1. ¿Cómo relacionan las referencias históricas en la canción con lo que has estudiado de la historia de América Latina? (How do the historical references in the song relate to what you have studied about the history of Latin America?)

_____

_____

_____

_____

2. En tu opinión, ¿qué semejanzas y/o diferencias habría entre la perspectiva del cantante y la perspectiva de una persona indígena de una tribu de los Estados Unidos? (In your opinion, what similarities and/or differences would there be between the singer's perspective and the perspective of an indigenous person from a tribe in the United States?)

_____

_____

_____

_____

IX. Personal Reaction to the Lyrics

Using specific information from the music video, describe your personal reaction to the song **in Spanish**. Be sure to provide reasons to support your reaction.

1. ¿Cómo te hace sentir la canción? (How does the song make you feel?)

_____

_____

_____

_____

_____

2. ¿Cuáles tipos de imágenes se producen en tu mente cuando escuchas la canción? (What types of mental images are produced in your mind when you listen to the song?)

_____

_____

_____

_____

_____

Human Rights (SPANISH)

Instructor: Naysa Altmeyer
River Valley High School, Blairsville, PA
Languages and Levels Taught:
Spanish 1, 2, 3, FLES, Exploratory

IPA Theme: Human Rights
Language: Spanish
IPA Level: Intermediate High
Class Level/Size: Spanish 3 / 25 students

Standards Addressed:

Communication (Interpersonal, Interpretive, Presentational)
Cultures (Relating Cultural Practices to Perspectives, Relating Cultural Products to Perspectives)
Connections (Acquiring Information and Diverse Perspectives)
Communities (School and Global Communities)

Task Overview
What challenges do children face in Guatemala and how can we help?
In your Spanish class you have been studying a major problem occurring in Guatemala: child homelessness. To help the children who are living this crisis you are going to make a public service announcement to raise awareness within our school and community and fundraise to support these children. First, you will watch a news segment on Los Guajeros to understand the depth of this crisis. Then, you will place yourselves in the shoes of a guajero child by journaling from their perspective and interviewing a classmate. Finally, you will create a public service announcement explaining the crisis to your school and community and sell Guatemalan-made bracelets to give back to the cause and help ease the living situation of Guajeros.

Interpretive Task
Education and Awareness
After learning about the conditions in which some Guatemalan children are living, you want to further explore this humanitarian crisis. You will first watch a news article called "Los Ángeles de la Basura" to educate yourself on the daily dangers Guajeros face living in garbage dumps. Watch the news article and complete the accompanying comprehension activity.

Interpersonal Task
Building Empathy
Now that you have a deeper understanding of the Guajero crisis, you are going to turn this awareness into empathy by interviewing a classmate who will play the role of a news reporter who has been documenting the challenges facing the Guajero children.

Presentational Task
Making a Difference
Now that a strong foundation of awareness and empathy has been built, you and your classmates are going to create a public service announcement that shows the crisis in Guatemala and ask for the school and community's help in aiding these children by purchasing Guatemalan-made bracelets so the money can be donated to a Guajero-focused charity called www.safepassage.org

Spanish: Interpretive Task for "Los Ángeles de la Basura"
https://vimeo.com/472401771

I. Key Word Recognition

As you watch the video segment, jot down a list of 8 content words/phrases that you hear that convey meaning related to the video, such as key nouns and verbs. Avoid listing words/phrases such as prepositions (*of, from, in, out, etc.*) and conjunctions (*and, but, or etc.*), which do not carry much meaning. Then provide an English equivalent to the right of each word you listed.

_____   _____
_____   _____
_____   _____
_____   _____
_____   _____
_____   _____
_____   _____
_____   _____

II. Main Idea

Using information from the video you watched, provide the main idea in English.

_____
_____
_____

III. Supporting Details

Circle the letter of each detail that is mentioned in the video (not all are included!). Write the information that is given in the video in the space provided next to the detail below.

A. The amount of trash collected daily: _____
_____

B. Who is working in the dump: _____
_____

C. Who is not allowed access into the dump: _____
_____

D. What fathers working as trash collectors do to provide for their children: _____
_____

E. The deadly impact living and eating in the dump can have on children: _____
_____

F. How the extreme seasons in Guatemala affect people working in the dumps:_____
_____

G. Two steps the government is taking to support the children: _____
_____

H: Why no one speaks up about the situation to protect the children: _____
_____

IV. Organizational Features

How is this segment organized? Choose all that apply and explain briefly why you selected each organizational feature--what were the clues in the segment?

    A. a talk show
    B. a news report
    C. a commercial
    D. an anecdote
    E. a reality show

Justification from video: _____

_____

_____

V. Guessing Meaning from Context

Based on this video, write what the following three words/phrases probably mean in English:

    A. (:34) Es un lugar donde diariamente **arrojan** más de dos mil toneladas de basura _____
    B. (:40) Docenas de familias, con sus hijos, **sobreviven** entre desperdicios (basura) _____
    C. (1:15) Estas imágenes **muestran** una realidad que el gobierno trata de ocultar _____

VI. Inferences

"View between the lines" to answer the following questions, using information from the video. You may respond in Spanish or English.

    1. Describe the life of a child living in the dump. Be sure to use details from the video, both verbal and visual, to support your answer. _____

_____

_____

_____

    2. Why might it be beneficial for the government to NOT intervene on behalf of the children living in the dump?

_____

_____

_____

VII. Author's Perspective

Select the perspective(s) or point(s) of view you think the author adopted as they created this video and justify your answer with information you heard in the video. You may respond in Spanish or English.

This segment is trying to…

    A. persuade the listener to donate money to the guajeros in Guatemala
    B. raise awareness of the current guajero issue in Guatemala
    C. make fun of the Guatemalan government
    D. give the history of the guajero situation in Guatemala

Justification from segment: _____

_____

_____

_____

VIII. Comparing Cultural Perspectives

Answer the following questions in Spanish or English.

A.   What do the interviews and content of this video reveal about the Guatemalan government?

_____

_____

_____

B.   How might this situation be different if it were a child from the United States living in a dump?

_____

_____

_____

IX. Personal Reaction to the Video

Using specific information from the video, describe your personal reaction to the segment **in Spanish**. Be sure to provide reasons that support your reaction.

_____

_____

_____

Sample Integrated Performance Assessments: Advanced

Social Issues in Arabic-Speaking Countries (ARABIC)

Instructor: Dr. Myriam Abdel-Malek
University of Pittsburgh, PA
Languages and Levels Taught:
Arabic 1, 2, 3, 4, 6

IPA Theme: *Social Issues in Arabic*
Speaking Countries
Language: *Arabic*
IPA Level: *Advanced*
Class Level/Size: *Arabic 6 / 6 students*

Standards Addressed:
Communication (Interpersonal, Interpretive, Presentational)
Cultures (Relating Cultural Practices to Perspectives, Relating Cultural Products to Perspectives)
Connections (Making Connections, Acquiring Information and Diverse Perspectives)
Comparisons (Cultural Comparisons)
Communities (School and Global Communities)

> ***Task Overview***
> You are an advocate for social justice in Arabic speaking countries. Before leading a local social justice movement, you would like to learn more and inform other advocates like you about a prevalent social issue that faces the youth in one or more of the Arabic speaking countries.

Interpretive Task
To be an informed advocate for social justice, you would like to learn more about some of the prevalent social issues in Arabic speaking countries. To learn about one of these social issues, "youth unemployment" and its causes, read the article and answer the comprehension guide.

Interpersonal Task
You also want to learn about social issues from people living in Arabic speaking countries. Use the information you gathered through the interpretive task to form your questions

and have a conversation with a person living in one of the Arabic speaking countries about the social issues they face. Some of the questions you may ask:

1. What is the major social issue in your country that affects people and especially youth?

2. Why do you think it is a major social issue?

3. Would you give me a brief account on how this (mention the social issue) became a social issue?

4. What do you think will lead to change?

5. How can the youth be involved in a change?

Presentational Task
Using the information you learned from the text, from your conversation, and your own research, write an article to be published on a social justice website that highlights one or more social issues in the Arabic-speaking countries and the factors that are the cause of these issues. This article will help other advocates like you to be more informed.

The article you read for the interpretive task should be used as a model for writing the text for the presentational task. The following parts should be included in your article:

a. Start by stating/defining the social issue and give some factual information

b. Give a brief history of how this issue came to life

c. Give some factors that are/were the cause of this social issue

d. Give a solution that is culturally relevant to the issue

e. End by encouraging the youth to overcome this social issue

Instructions and Materials for the IPA
Text for the Interpretive Task is on the following page.

بطالة الشباب في الدول العربية

Author: Salam AL Mardi   سلام المزيدي

البطالة هي عدم توافر فرص عمل في أي من المجالات المختلفة رغم وجود الرغبة و الحاجة لذلك. وتعد البطالة أحد أهم المشاكل التي تواجه الشباب العربي في الآونة الأخيرة، و قد بدأت تأخذ منعطفا خطيرا من حيث انتشارها و تأثيرها سواء على الفرد أو على المجتمع. و تشير معظم التوقعات بأن نسبة البطالة في المنطقة العربية آخذة بالازدياد خاصة في فئة الشباب، فمثلا في دولة مثل الأردن بلغت نسبة البطالة بين الشباب 50% حسب دراسة حديثة أجراها البنك الدولي لعام 2020. ولا نستطيع أن ننكر وجود الكثير من الأسباب الداعمة للبطالة في المنطقة العربية والتي ينتج عنها الكثير من الآثار السلبية.

لنعد بالزمن قليلا إلى الوراء، لعام 2011، سنة ثورات الدول العربية أو ما يعرف "بالربيع العربي" عندما نزلت الشعوب العربية في عدة بلدان منها مصر، تونس، و سوريا و غيرها ليطالبوا بإسقاط أنظمتهم التي رأوا فيها فشلا ذريعا في تحقيق مستقبل أفضل لهم. فكان الشباب أول من نزل إلى الميادين يصرخ بشعاراته و يطالب برياح التغيير، ولكن رياح التغيير ما لبثت أن ذهبت بأحلامهم و طموحاتهم بعيدا، فوجد الشباب أنفسهم في حروب و مآسي، و مشاكل اجتماعية أكثر، و أنظمة حاكمة أصعب من ذي قبل. و من هنا يمكننا القول أن البطالة وضعت نفسها على طاولة مشاكل الشباب العربي، حيث أصبحت أعداد العاطلين عن العمل في ازدياد مستمر و مرجحة للارتفاع إلى 12.5% خلال العام 2021 أي أن تأثير الربيع العربي ما زال موجودا حتى بعد عقد من الزمن.

بعيدا عن الحروب و الثورات، فهناك عوامل أخرى أدت لازدياد نسبة البطالة بهذا الشكل المخيف، أحدها استمرار ميل معظم الشباب لتخصصات راكدة، و وظائف مشبعة فقط لإرضاء أهاليهم أو ليحصلوا على نظرة إيجابية من المجتمع، فأصبحنا نرى أطباء بدون عمل و مهندسين يعملون كسائقي سيارة أجرة لتوفير قوت يومهم. أو "ثقافة العيب" و هي ظاهرة يرى فيها الشخص أن وظيفة معينة لا تليق بمستواه أو نظرته عن نفسه، فيفضل البقاء بلا عمل.

مشكلة البطالة لا تأتي وحدها، إذ ينتج عنها عدة مشاكل اجتماعية أخرى. كالفقر مثلا، الذي تزداد معدلاته كل يوم. و في حالات قد تؤدي البطالة الى مشاكل النفسية كالإحساس بالفشل و أن ليس للشخص دورا بارزا في المجتمع.

بما أن البطالة مشكلة متشعبة و لها عدة أسباب و عادة ما تكون نتائجها طويلة الأمد، فإن حلها ليس سهلا و قد يأخذ وقتا طويلا، و يتطلب جهود و قرارات كبيرة من الدول، إلا أنه من الممكن اتخاذ بعض الخطوات التي قد تساعد الشباب على إيجاد فرص عمل تناسب مهاراتهم واهتماماتهم. مثل تشجيع المشاريع الفردية الصغيرة و دعمها، لأنها لا تدعم الشباب و حسب بل كل فئات المجتمع و أي شخص يرى في نفسه قدرة أو موهبة ما تساعده في فتح مشروع،كصناعة الاكسسوارات اليدوية والأطعمة مثلا.

خطوة أخرى يمكن للدول اتخاذها هي توعية الشباب أكثر بالتخصصات و الوظائف المطلوبة في سوق العمل قبل أن يختاروها، و بذلك يتجنبون اختيار الوظائف المشبعة، و يتجهون للتخصصات و الوظائف المطلوبة و التي لها مستقبل ناجح على المدى الطويل.

في الختام، فإن الدول العربية فيها ما يكفي من الثروة البشرية و خاصة الشباب ما يمكنها من الازدهار و التقدم، فالمجتمعات العربية مجتمعات فتية مليئة بالشباب القادر على العمل طالما أتيحت له الفرصة، لكنهم كأي من شباب هذا العصر يحتاجون إلى توعية و إرشاد بمجالات العمل المطلوبة، و هنا يأتي دور الدول في أن تركز على أبنائها و تفتح لهم المجال لأن يبدعوا و تستثمر في طاقتهم بما يحقق الفائدة لهم ولها. رغم كل ما مرت به الدول العربية و ما زالت تمر به، فإن شبابها لم يفقد الأمل يوما بعيش كريم و ما زال يتميز و يثبت نفسه كل يوم، و لن يتوقف عن ذلك أبدا، لأن في داخله أملا أن رياح التغيير ستأتي يوما و تجلب معها ما يستحقون من حياة كريمة و عيش حر.

IPA INTERPRETIVE READING COMPREHENSION GUIDE

I. Key Word Recognition

Find in the article the word/phrase in the target language that best expresses the meaning of each of the following English words/phrases:

1. Take a dangerous turn _____
2. Supportive reasons _____
3. Resulting in _____
4. A miserable fail _____
5. Phenomenon _____
6. Take some steps _____

7. Encourage _____
8. Raise awareness of the youth _____
9. Saturated jobs_____
10. Human capital _____

II. Main Idea(s)

Using information from the article, provide the main idea(s) of the article in English.

_____

_____

_____

III. Supporting Details

1. Circle the letter of each detail that is mentioned in the article (not all are included!).
2. Write the letter of the detail next to where it appears in the text.
3. Write the information that is given in the article in the space provided next to the detail below.

A. One of the issues that confronted the youth after the Arab Spring: _____

_____

B. One societal factor that contributes to unemployment: _____

_____

C. The jobs that the Arab youth avoid: _____

_____

D. One of the effects of unemployment on society: _____

_____

E. One reason for unemployment that is associated with youth's choices for jobs: _____

_____

F. The government's need to encourage youth to work by: _____

_____

G. The Arab countries have a valuable asset and that is: _____

_____

H. The driving force for the Arab youth is: _____

_____

IV. Organizational Features.

How is this text organized? Choose all that apply and explain briefly why you selected each organizational feature. What were the clues in the text?

A. Description
B. Problem and solution
C. Compare/contrast
D. Chronological order
E. Cause and effect

Justification from text: _____

_____

_____

V. Guessing Meaning from Context

Based on this passage, write what the following three words/expressions probably mean in English.

١. رياح التغيير _____

٢. البطالة وضعت نفسها على طاولة مشاكل الشباب العربي _____

٣. مشكلة متشعبة _____

VI. Inferences

"Read between the lines" to answer the following questions, using information from the text.

1. Why do you think the author is confident that the youth did not lose hope because of the social issues affecting them?

   _____

   _____

2. Why is it important that the youth overcome "ثقافة العيب"? _____

   _____

   _____

VII. Author's Perspective

Select the perspective or point of view you think the author adopted as they wrote this article and justify your answer with information from the text.

   A. Religious

   B. Factual

   C. Scientific

Justification from text **in Arabic:**

_____

_____

VIII. Comparing Cultural Perspectives

Answer the following questions **in Arabic:**

1. What are the cultural similarities and differences between the social issues the youth face in Arabic speaking countries and the social issues in your culture? _____

2. How do the youth's practices regarding job choices in the article reflect the target culture perspectives? _____

3. What did you learn about the target culture from this article? _____

IX. Personal Reaction to the Text

The author mentioned some of the social issues that are the cause of youth unemployment in Arabic speaking countries. How do you think these social issues affect the youth? Please respond **in Arabic.** _____

_____

_____

_____

Language and Racial Ideologies (Spanish)

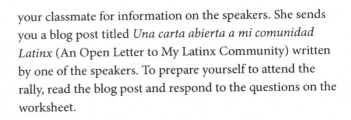

Instructor: Lauren Miranda
The Ohio State University, Columbus, OH
Languages and Levels Taught:
Spanish 1101 & 1102

IPA Theme: *Language and
Racial Ideologies*
Language: **Spanish**
IPA Level: *Advanced*
Class Level/Size: *University 2nd-year Spanish as a Heritage
Language Class/22 students*

Standards Addressed:

Communication (Interpersonal, Interpretive, Presentational)
*Cultures (Relating Cultural Practices to Perspectives, Relating
Cultural Products to Perspectives)*
Connections (Acquiring Information and Diverse Perspectives)

Task Overview

The next issue of *¿Qué Pasa? Ohio State* is looking for media content created by OSU students for a special online section called "*La lengua importa /* Language Matters." This will feature student perspectives on how language shapes our perception of the world around us. In keeping with the objectives of campus racial equity task forces and overall efforts to address racism both on campus and at large, this issue of *¿Qué Pasa? Ohio State* will focus on how language shapes our understanding of racialized peoples and conceptions of race in the Spanish-speaking community. In its call for submissions, *¿Qué Pasa? Ohio State* is asking students to create video blogs to make visible and educate the wider community about everyday language practices in Spanish that promote essentialized visions of Black and indigenous members of the Latinx community.

Interpretive Task

As part of your research for your video blog, one of your classmates suggests attending a human rights and racial equity rally on campus being held by local Latinx community organizers. Wanting to know more about the event, you ask your classmate for information on the speakers. She sends you a blog post titled *Una carta abierta a mi comunidad Latinx* (An Open Letter to My Latinx Community) written by one of the speakers. To prepare yourself to attend the rally, read the blog post and respond to the questions on the worksheet.

Interpersonal Task

Hearing first-hand accounts and testimonies is a powerful way of learning more about social justice topics. Recognizing this, you decide to incorporate knowledge from the lived experience of a community member into your video blog. You know this will engage your viewers by giving them insight into a personal account of how race and language plays out in your own community. To do this, you will conduct an interview in Spanish with either a family or a community member to learn about their experiences with and opinions on the topic of race in the Latinx community.

Presentational Task

¿Qué Pasa? Ohio State is looking for students to submit video blogs *en español* for a special online supplement to their upcoming issue. The call for submissions is looking for student vlogs that discuss the themes of race, identity, and language in the U.S. Latinx and greater Spanish-speaking community. As part of preparing material to discuss in your video blogs, you have already engaged in two types of research: (1) internet-based research, and (2) interview-based research, which you carried out with a Spanish-speaking member of your family or community.

Your final video blog will include the following content:

- An overview of your research findings obtained from the internet and from interviewees (3-4 minutes)
- Your reactions to and opinions on your findings (2-3 minutes)
- At least one suggestion for how to be an ally to BIPOC members of the Latinx community

Instructions and Materials for the IPA

Interpretive Task for "Una carta abierta a mi comunidad Latinx"
Link to the Authentic Text: <u>go.osu.edu/ipatexts</u>

Una carta abierta a mi comunidad Latinx. De Diana Mateo

POSTED BY AVA BENACH
JUNE 5, 2020

Questions? Call: 202 644 8600

SHARE THIS!

SHARE THIS!

¡Hola, amigos! Soy una de las paralegales de BC, Diana. Como una Latina profesional de inmigración, quería compartir algunas ideas con nuestros amigos y clientes de BC sobre algunos problemas preocupantes que he visto en nuestra comunidad latina, y sobre formas en que podemos ser mejores aliados para nuestros hermanos Negros. Las muertes de George Floyd, Ahmaud Arbery y Breonna Taylor son actos de asesinato horribles, y es parte de nuestra responsabilidad como inmigrantes de defender a nuestros hermanos Negros contra el genocidio de ellos en los Estados Unidos de la misma manera que nos enfrentamos al genocidio en la frontera.

I. Identifying Key Words

Find in the article the words in Spanish that best express the meaning of each of the following key words in English.

1. racism: _____
2. allies: _____
3. to erase: _____
4. erasure: _____
5. racism: _____
6. privilege: _____
7. (in)justice: _____
8. anti-Blackness: _____
9. white supremacy: _____
10. brutality: _____
11. stereotypes: _____
12. to perpetuate: _____
13. generalizations: _____
14. to reject: _____
15. to un-learn: _____

II. Main Idea

Using information from the blog, describe the main idea of the text in English.

_____
_____
_____
_____

III. Supporting Details

1. Circle the letter of each detail that is mentioned in the article (not all are included!)
2. Write the letter of the detail next to where it appears in the text.
3. Write the information that is given in the article in the space provided next to the detail below.

A. The author's profession: _____
_____

B. The specific event in 2020 that motivated Diana to write this blog: _____
_____

C. The author's experience at a Black Lives Matter rally:_____
_____

D. How Black men are stereotyped in the Latinx community:_____
_____

E. Data about immigration rates into the US:_____
_____

F. How indigenous communities face discrimination in the US: _____
_____

G. An experience that the Black community, non-Black Latinx community and immigrant community all share in common:
_____

H. An action that the Latinx community can take to combat anti-Blackness:_____
_____

IV. Organizational Features

How is this blog organized? Choose all that apply and briefly explain why you selected each organizational feature using details from the text.

- A. Chronological order
- B. Letter/message
- C. Compare/contrast
- D. Biography/autobiography
- E. Problem and solution

Justification from text: _____

_____

_____

_____

V. Guessing Meaning from Context

Based on this passage, write what the following three verbs probably mean in English.

A. Mi intención hoy es animar a nuestros amigos Latinos no Negros a poner fin a todo lo anti-Negro en nuestra comunidad, y comenzar a desmantelar la supremacía blanca. (paragraph 2)

Desmantelar - _____

B. Como parte de mis privilegios como una latina no Negra profesional, me comprometo a hacer lo mejor para mis hermanos Negros. (paragraph 13)

Comprometo - _____

C. Pero también tenemos que enfrentar el arduo trabajo que se necesita para asegurarnos de que nuestros amigos Negros puedan vivir sin miedo. (paragraph 15)

Enfrentar - _____

VI. Inferences

"Read between the lines" to answer the following questions, using information from the text.

A. Why does the author argue that it is important to have conversations about anti-Blackness in the Latinx community?

_____

_____

_____

B. Why do you think that there exist negative attitudes towards Blackness across communities?

_____

_____

_____

_____

VII. Author's Perspective

Choose the objectives you think motivated the author to write this text. Utilize information from the text to justify your response.

    A. To be comical

    B. To persuade her audience

    C. To advertise for a company

Justification from text: _____

_____

_____

VIII. Comparison – Cultural Perspectives

Respond to the following questions in Spanish.

A. In your opinion, is the attitude of the Latinx community towards the Black community as described by the author similar or different from the attitude of US society in general toward the Black community? Why do you think this?

_____

_____

_____

_____

_____

_____

B. Regarding anti-Blackness, what similarities or differences are there between what the author describes and what you observe in your own community (in your family, friend group, on campus, in your hometown)?

_____

_____

_____

_____

_____

_____

IX. Personal Reaction to the Text:

Using specific information from the text, describe your personal reaction to the blog. Provide reasons to support your reaction **in Spanish**.

_____

_____

_____

_____

_____

Chapter 7

Transforming the L2 Literature Course with IPAs

As seen in previous chapters, IPAs have been shown to benefit L2 instruction at all levels in both K-12 and postsecondary settings. One particular area in which IPAs can have a strong impact is in world languages literature courses. IPAs are uniquely positioned to help bridge the language-literature divide that exists in many undergraduate world language programs. This chapter situates IPAs in the world languages literature course context, presents a rationale for use of the IPA in this context, outlines IPA implementation from start to finish, and provides example literature-based IPA tasks at various levels of the ACTFL Scale. The chapter concludes with a look toward the future of IPAs in world languages literature courses.

The IPA and the Language-Literature Divide

Applied linguistics research in the last few decades has critically examined what is commonly referred to as the language-literature divide in undergraduate world languages programs. In typical undergraduate world language programs, the first two years of instruction are framed in a communicative approach in which there is systematic emphasis on the development of listening, speaking, reading, and writing skills, often of a transactional or daily-life nature. In the third year, there is a transition to content courses in literature, culture, and other topics, with an almost exclusive focus on the content itself, often at the expense of continued language skill development.

In short, the goals of the lower division and the upper division of undergraduate world language curricula tend to be at odds with each other. First and second-year courses tend to provide learners with little intellectual/analytical content in favor of functional language instruction. In spite of a principled focus on language development during the first two years of instruction, third and fourth-year courses are often populated with learners who are not yet at a proficiency level at which they are able to discuss and analyze

Dawn Smith-Sherwood, Ph.D., *Indiana University of Pennsylvania* and **Mark Darhower Ph.D.**, *North Carolina State University*

the abstract themes treated in literary pieces. Yet continued systematic development of language skills is typically not a priority in upper division courses such as those focused on literature. As Scott (2001) cogently stated, "I love French literature and I am implicitly participating in marginalizing its role by not exploring the link between language and literature, or more specifically, the link between theories in second language acquisition (SLA) and the teaching of literature" (p. 538).

For much of the twenty-first century to date, language and literature scholars have been working to mend the language-literature divide in world language instruction. Scott & Tucker, two researchers in the French language program at Vanderbilt University, found themselves in the unique position of needing each other's expertise—one as a supervisor of graduate teaching assistants and one as a literature professor. The wealth of knowledge and practical experience that they gained from their collaboration inspired them to dedicate an entire volume (2002) to language and literature pedagogy in which they sought to merge insights from the second language acquisition/applied linguistics realm with practices in teaching literature to undergraduates.

The 2007 MLA Report advocated "replacing the two-tiered language-literature structure with a broader and more coherent curriculum in which language, culture, and literature are taught as a continuous whole" (MLA Ad Hoc Committee on Foreign Languages, 2007, p. 3). The report urged constituents from both sides to bridge the divide, and researchers responded, developing studies, reporting findings, and offering practical solutions to help resolve the curricular bifurcation, "more an administrative construct than a pedagogically justified curriculum design" (Katz Bourns et al., 2020, p. 171). Conceptual frameworks, curricular models, and pedagogical strategies, both before and after the report, have attempted to redress the two-tier system. However, as Lomicka and Lord (2018) reported ten years later, "Progress has been made in the past decade, but there is undoubtedly still work to do to bring our language curricula in line with the ideals of the MLA report" (p. 119).

In their historical review of methods and approaches to teaching language and literature in the United States, Katz Bourns et al. (2020) declare, "Language pedagogy has always been linked to societal values, perceptions, and demands, and pedagogical changes reflect these external influences" (p. 19). The recent ascendance of assessment in higher education might be considered such an external influence. As Bernhardt (2008) asserts, "Large-scale assessment programs and the public's push for accountability are two of the most important developments in American education in a long time" (p. 19). When language and literature faculty were, in essence, "voluntold" to develop measurable student learning outcomes for their world languages programs and constituent courses for accreditation purposes, the assessment of those outcomes revealed the distance between what had become the traditional approach to professing literature and the linguistic development needs of world languages learners. A change in focus from content delivery to communicative competence, from teacher-centered to learner-centered classrooms, makes mending the language-literature divide not only aspirational but emergent. Bernhardt (2008) argued, however, that the new accountability era might usefully serve language and literature departments: "A systemic and systematic assessment program offers a powerful real and conceptual support structure for the bridge from language learning to literature learning that the profession has long sought" (p. 14).

In this context, the IPA serves as both a curricular construct and an assessment tool; it is based on the conceptual framework of the World-Readiness Standards for Learning Languages (National Standards Collaborative Board, 2015), promotes adaptable pedagogical strategies for instruction, and provides a systematic means to assess course and programmatic learning outcomes. The IPA emanates from the authentic text, and literature faculty in world languages departments are well-positioned to activate their area of expertise to increase learners' cultural competence as well as promote their developing linguistic proficiency at all levels of language study.

Findings on IPAS in Literature Courses

As seen in Chapter 3, the bulk of research on IPAs has been carried out in the K-12 and lower division undergraduate contexts. The undergraduate literature course is understudied to date, although some illuminating research findings have emerged in this context. Inspired by scholarship such as that of Scott & Tucker (2002) and later Donato & Brooks (2004) and Darhower (2014), Smith-Sherwood (2020; see also Smith-Sherwood & Rhodes, 2019), a literature professor, took interest in the IPA as a tool to help bridge the language-literature divide.

This review of findings on the use of IPAs in literature courses provides an overview of publications that examine such issues as the impact of IPAs on the presentational and interpersonal modes of communication; differentiation of IPA tasks by oral proficiency level; the co-constructed feedback loop during the IPA process in a literature course; and learner perceptions regarding IPA-informed literature instruction.

Presentational Mode

In the spirit of reintegrating language and literature, working across disciplinary boundaries of applied linguistics and literary studies (Scott & Tucker, 2002), Smith-Sherwood began implementing IPAs in her undergraduate Introduction to Hispanic Literature course and then paired first with a statistician at her institution and later with an applied linguist at another institution to formally investigate the effects of implementing this new tool in her course. In the first study, Smith-Sherwood initially implemented IPAs in her Introduction to Hispanic Literature course as part of her department's overarching effort to base courses in their curriculum on "what students *will be able to do* rather than what they will be *expected to know*" (Smith-Sherwood & Rhodes, 2019, p. 19). Prior to implementing IPAs in her course, Smith-Sherwood taught the course the "traditional" way in which "they read a literary work, answered questions regarding that literary work, took a quiz regarding that literary work, and later took an exam (including multiple choice, matching, and fill-in-the-blank activities) on multiple literary works" (p. 22). Smith-Sherwood described this approach as an opportunity to get the "right answers" and then reproduce those answers on the next homework assignments and quizzes. In other words, the class was based primarily on comprehension of texts and memorization of facts about the texts. The next time she taught the course, she employed an IPA-informed approach using the overarching theme of the family and having learners complete one thematic IPA cycle per genre—narrative, poetry, and drama. The IPA cycles included an interpretive reading, an interpersonal speaking, and a presentational writing task. Smith-Sherwood and Rhodes compared the results of each category of the writing rubric between the traditional (control) group and the subsequent IPA (treatment) group, as well as results in reading, writing, listening, and speaking confidence. The IPA group outperformed the traditional group in impact, comprehensibility, and language control, but not in language functions or text type. In regard to confidence, however, the IPA group outperformed the traditional group in all four categories. The researchers concluded that the combination of increased writing gains in some categories and confidence in all four language skills is promising for continued use of IPAs in the course in the future.

Smith-Sherwood (2020) subsequently authored a pedagogical piece in which she described the transformation that can take place when implementing an IPA-informed approach to teaching a canonical work such as Miguel de Unamuno's *San Manuel Bueno, mártir*. Her aim was to encourage literature instructors in world languages to "ensure that they are meeting students where they actually are linguistically and show them the way forward, so that students not only know about the challenging works of the literary canon but also learn how to engage with texts in meaningful ways that will additionally serve to develop their linguistic proficiency" (p. 207). To do this in her own literature class, Smith-Sherwood implemented full IPA cycles including interpretive, interpersonal, and presentational tasks with corresponding evaluation rubrics (Adair-Hauck et al., 2013) for each one. Her article highlighted the fact that IPA tasks "cannot be completed in a 'look back and lift off' manner" (p. 209), but rather require genuine interaction with the text, fellow classmates, and the teacher. Additionally, she noted that the IPA-informed approach is in consonance with backward design, which has gained prominence in world languages pedagogy.

Interpersonal Mode

The interpersonal mode of communication can easily take a back burner to interpretive and presentational communication in world languages literature courses. Darhower & Smith-Sherwood (2021) focused on the interpersonal mode of the IPA cycle that Smith-Sherwood had begun to implement (Smith-Sherwood, 2020; Smith-Sherwood & Rhodes, 2019). In this study, the researchers implemented full IPA cycles in Smith-Sherwood's Introduction to Hispanic Literature course, but the data analysis focused on the interpersonal mode. Study participants were placed in dyads such that each member had the same predetermined oral proficiency level as the other or was only one sublevel above or below on the ACTFL Scale. The participants completed four IPA cycles throughout the semester and two co-constructed feedback sessions (Adair Hauck et al., 2013) with the researchers. The interpersonal speaking tasks required learners to draw on literary concepts that they had learned in the course and to employ their critical thinking skills toward successful completion of the task. The tasks also contained a personalized component to stimulate learners' interest and engagement. The results showed that all fifteen learners were able to engage in interpersonal communication on a literary topic at their current oral proficiency level and in some cases beyond it. Additionally, every learner made gains in their performance from the beginning to the end of the semester, except for one learner who remained steady. The researchers considered this finding to be a positive response to previous research that had identified deficiencies in literature classroom discourse and called for strategies to make literature classroom discourse more meaningful and useful for learners as their speaking skills developed (Darhower 2014; Donato & Brooks 2004).

A fundamental research and pedagogical instrument in this study was the interpersonal speaking rubric used to evaluate the interpersonal speaking tasks. These were taken from the second edition of the IPA Manual (Adair-Hauck et al., 2013) and slightly adapted for the literary context. The rubric enabled the researchers to break down the interpersonal speaking construct into distinct measurable components and observe which categories were more susceptible to improvement. There was substantial improvement in four of the six assessment categories: language structures, communicative functions, negotiation strategies, and vocabulary use. The comprehensibility category remained consistent. Very little improvement was seen in text type (length and cohesion of utterances). Interestingly, the finding about text type corroborates previous research in which mean utterance lengths of learners (in teacher-centered class discourse) in a literature class was found to be 8-14 words (Darhower 2014), which rules out the likelihood that learners are engaging in discourse beyond the sentence level.

Another illuminating component of this study was the collection of learner perceptions data regarding their experience with the IPA-informed approach to their literature course. Half of the cohort expressed an increase in their interest in Hispanic literature, and the majority of learners felt that their interpretive reading (n = 9), interpersonal speaking (n = 12), and literary skills (n = 12) had increased. Also, the learners unanimously felt more motivated to improve their interpersonal speaking skills. Slightly more than half of the learners (N = 8) reported that they enjoyed the IPAs, yet two of the learners were neutral and five reported that they did not enjoy the IPAs. Additionally, eight of the learners found the IPAs to be stressful. If some of the same learners enjoyed the IPAs and found them stressful, this suggests that they likely took the assessments very seriously and enjoyed the challenge to their speaking skills. Learners who did not enjoy the IPAs and felt they were stressful may have been reacting to the novelty of having to demonstrate interpersonal speaking skills in a measured manner if they were not used to this approach. Further learner data in the affective realm would be useful for future IPA-centered research and pedagogy.

Feedback

Co-constructed feedback sessions held between the learners and the researchers in the Darhower & Smith-Sherwood (2021) study uncovered some interesting findings. The feedback sessions were held between the interpersonal speaking component of the first IPA cycle in the course and the interpersonal speaking component of the second IPA cycle, as well as between the second and third cycles. The sessions were approximately a half hour in length, conducted in the researcher-instructor's office with the researcher-proficien-cy tester participating via videoconference. A Likert scale questionnaire administered at the end of the study included several items related to the co-constructed feedback sessions. In the first sessions, the researchers and learners discussed the learners' performance on the first interpersonal IPA task. In the second session, they compared the learners' performance in the second IPA cycle to their performance in the first, looking for areas of improvement. All 14 participants who completed the questionnaire either agreed or strongly agreed that the feedback they had received was specific and individualized as well as supportive and non-judgmental, and that the feedback helped them to identify the strengths and weaknesses in their interpersonal speaking proficiency in Spanish.

Differentiation

During the oral proficiency assessment phase of the Darhower & Smith-Sherwood research project, the researchers discovered that among their fifteen learners there was a wide range of oral proficiency levels, from Novice-Mid to Advanced-Mid. While it is typical to have a range of levels in third-year undergraduate language and literature courses, this range was larger than usual. It is challenging to work with learners who at one end of the spectrum speak primarily at the memorized word and expression level and at the other end are able to carry out full narrations and descriptions in all major time frames in paragraph-length discourse. The researchers noticed a gap in the literature in that the IPAs described in the previous edition of the current manual all targeted learners of a single level. If such tasks were to be implemented in the course under study by Darhower and Smith-Sherwood, there would inevitably have been too much challenge for learners at the lower end and not enough challenge for learners at the upper end of the proficiency scale. The researchers thus implemented interpersonal IPA tasks oriented to the oral proficiency level of each learner (Novice, Intermediate, Advanced), and also used evaluation rubrics oriented to learners' proficiency levels. Each task presented the same general scenario but had two prompts: one pitched at the learner's current proficiency level and one pitched to the next higher level, much as Oral Proficiency Interviews do.

To explore the impact of differentiating IPA tasks and evaluation rubrics, the researchers compared each learner's grade on the rubric tailored to their oral proficiency level to the grade they would have received on a "one-size-fits-all" rubric targeted to the middle proficiency level of the class (Intermediate). For the nine Intermediate-level speakers, the grades would have been the same with either rubric. However, differences were apparent in the Novice-Mid learner, the Intermediate-High learner, and the four Advanced learners. The Novice-Mid learner scored approximately 12% higher on each differentiated Novice assessment rubric (72-88%) as compared to what the score would have been on an Intermediate rubric (60-76%). The Intermediate-High learner scored 84-94% on the Advanced rubric as compared to a hypothetical score of 100% on all but the first assessment (98%) using an Intermediate rubric. Similarly the Advanced learners scored primarily in the mid-70s to upper 80s range on the Advanced rubric, but would have scored 100% on the Intermediate rubric (likely without having to exert much effort.) The researchers concluded that differentiation of both the task and the rubric "met learners where they were," thus challenging all learners equally rather than challenging the Novice-Mid learner too much and not challenging the Intermediate and Advanced learners enough.

Learner perceptions data collected in the post-study questionnaire were also enlightening in terms of the effects of differentiation in the IPAs. For the Likert scale statement "Orienting the IPAs to a student's oral proficiency level is beneficial to learning," all learners agreed strongly or agreed, for a mean of 4.5. However, the statement "Orienting the evaluation rubrics to the student's oral proficiency level can be unfair to some students," generated ambivalent results. While the majority of the learners (N=8) disagreed or disagreed strongly, two of them were ambivalent, three agreed and one agreed strongly, for a mean of 2.64. This finding reflects the reality that grades can carry just as much weight as, if not more than, the learning process. It also presents an opportunity, however, to engage learners in a conversation about the relationship of assessment to individual development as opposed to a comparison to a one-size-fits-all norm.

The researchers further explored learner perceptions about differentiation by focusing on one learner who was below the middle oral proficiency level of the class (Intermediate), a Novice-Mid learner (NM1), and one learner who was above the Intermediate level, at the Advanced-Low level (AL1). NM1 strongly agreed that orienting the IPAs to the learner's oral proficiency was beneficial to learning, while AL1 agreed with the statement but not strongly. Regarding

the issue of fairness, however, the two learners deviated from each other. NM1 disagreed that orienting the IPA evaluation rubric to the learner's oral proficiency level could be unfair to some students, while AL1 agreed with the statement. Note that if a one-size-fits-all task and rubric had been used in the class, AL1 would have been challenged less and received a higher grade on the Intermediate rubric as opposed to the Advanced rubric. AL1 noted that "sometimes, grades, although not counted, were discouraging," yet recognized that "interpersonal tasks were challenging enough to leave room for improvement" and "interpersonal tasks really showed the areas I was lacking in." NM1 made an insightful comment regarding the fairness issue: "Everyone is different. Equal and fair are different in terms of evaluation. The necessary rubrics for each student help to more accurately assess the student."

As can be seen from this review of the small but growing body of research on IPAs in the literature course context, IPAs have great promise for reintegrating literary analysis and the systematic development of language proficiency. Differentiation in IPAs is a very young branch of research. More research into the effects of differentiation, as well as additional studies on changes in classroom activities and instructional approaches to complement an IPA-informed approach to literature instruction, would be a welcome addition to the literature.

A Model of IPA Implementation in the World Languages Literature Course

Unit Planning with Backward Design
Planning for IPA-informed instruction begins with the selection and organization of course content into units. The planning template provided in Chapter 4, based on the principles of backward design, is a useful tool for mapping out each unit of instruction in an IPA format. Such organization may also facilitate the implementation of a cumulative summative assessment and verification of meeting course-level student learning outcomes.

In the context of a literature course that engages learners with texts from different genres, time periods, literary movements, or national traditions, instructors may be guided by the Communication C of the World-Readiness Standards inherent in use of the IPA to create their unit plans. Beginning with creation of the summative assessment, that is, descriptions of the three communicative tasks (interpretive, interpersonal, presentational) individually and in overview, instructors may then design formative assessments and learning activities that will promote learner performances that meet expectations, provide the groundwork for answering essential questions posed by the unit's content, and determine what learners will understand, know, and be able to do as a result of the unit. Figure 7.1 provides a sample plan from a unit on narrative.

Pre-Assessment of Learner Proficiency

In order to prepare IPA activities that will ensure learner success, it is recommended that instructors determine the proficiency levels of the learners toward the beginning of the course. This accords with the suggestion that "Instructors will need to decide which level of the IPA would be most appropriate for their students" (Adair-Hauck & Troyan, 2013, p. 14). Instructors can gain a sense of their current students' levels in several ways. If learners happen to have a recent oral proficiency assessment for mid-program review or another purpose, that data might be available for consideration. If instructors are ACTFL-certified tester-raters or have access to a colleague who is a certified tester-rater, they might ask learners to participate in an Oral Proficiency Interview at the beginning of the term. Instructors without access to these resources have additional options. They can participate in professional development to build their knowledge of the ACTFL Proficiency Guidelines (ACTFL, 2012b) and their implementation. ACTFL offers an array of workshops conducted in locations throughout the United States. Insti-

Figure 7.1. Sample Unit Planning Template—Narrative

Stage 1—Desired Results	
Established Student Learning Outcomes (Course): • Discuss the works read in present, past, and future time frames and use connected paragraph-length discourse in Spanish • Identify the characteristics and theoretical concepts of narrative • Analyze selected narrative readings • Use technical vocabulary to discuss the selected readings • Demonstrate an understanding of the course materials by analyzing selected works	**Standards Addressed:** • Communication (interpretive, interpersonal, presentational) • Cultures (products, practices, perspectives) • Connections (history, sociology, economics)
Essential Questions: • -What are the essential elements of narrative? • -How does communication occur in a narrative? • -How are internal family dynamics impacted by external political/social/economic factors?	**Understandings:** Students will understand … • The importance of a narrator • The difference between a narrator and an author • The difference between a narratee and a reader • The elements of a story, its discourse features, and its theme
Key Cultural/Linguistic Knowledge: Students will know … • Family vocabulary in Spanish • History of (im/e) migration between Spain/ Spanish America/the U.S.	**Key Language Functions/Communicative Strategies:** Students will be able to … • Give commands to an individual or group using appropriate forms • Report conversation as indirect discourse • Perform tasks at current proficiency level

Stage 2–Assessment Evidence	
Summative IPA Overview— You have been studying family-themed short stories by authors from different times and places in the Spanish-speaking world. These readings have dealt with themes of (im/e) migration, parent-child relationships, change, and loss. Interpretive Mode— You will read an additional short story that portrays a parent-child relationship, as well as a journey, and complete a two-part (literal/figurative) comprehension guide based on the short story. Interpersonal Mode— You and your classmate have been asked by the campus Orientation Team to comment on a Spanish-language text that will be shared with incoming Latino students prior to Orientation and that they will be asked to discuss in their residence hall learning communities during pre-move-in weekend community-building programs. The Orientation Team is interested in the short story you have just read as a potential springboard for discussion. Presentational Mode– Relationship dynamics are often marked by misunderstandings. Using what you have learned in this unit, write a letter to the father from the first-person narrative perspective of the son. What happened prior to his injury? Did he ask for forgiveness? Did he lay blame? Be creative, but do not radically alter the essential points of the original story.	**Formative Assessment Evidence** Interpretive Mode Learning Task 5 Interpersonal Mode Learning Task 6 Presentational Mode Learning Task 7

Stage 3–Learning Plan

Learning Activities:

1. Introduce the genre (narrative) and the subtheme (nuclear family) of the unit.

2. Introduce the unit's essential questions and culminating tasks.

3. Students identify past time frame verbs and their aspect (preterit/imperfect) using the PACE method.

4. Students identify command forms, their types and formation, using the PACE method.

5. Students complete practice comprehension guides for three short stories.

6. Students participate in practice conversations in which they play the role of a character in the short story under study and work together to solve a problem related to the plot.

7. Students write practice narrations in which they change the narrator, change the time frame, and change the dialogue to indirect discourse for a short story under study.

8. Students complete the summative IPA interpretive task.

9. Instructor provides structured in-class feedback on the interpretive task.

10. Students complete the summative IPA interpersonal task.

11. Students participate with the instructor in co-constructed feedback on the interpersonal task.

12. Students complete the summative IPA presentational task.

13. Instructor provides structured in-class feedback on the presentational task.

14. Students revise the presentational task for submission to the editors of the department's student magazine.

tutions can also host these workshops for faculty and invited local teachers and colleagues from other institutions. On the basis of this training, instructors can develop a bank of questions to ask learners in less formal interviews in an attempt to determine learners' approximate proficiency levels. Figure 7.2 provides sample questions for levels from Intermediate to Advanced. Finally, instructors can seek formal training in the understanding and implementation of the ACTFL Guidelines as described later in this chapter.

Mixed-Readiness and Differentiation in Tasks and Evaluation Rubrics

As is often the case at the postsecondary level, instructors may find that learners' proficiency levels vary, perhaps dramatically. When there is a wide range of proficiency levels in the same class (such as from Novice-High to Advanced-Low, or even wider), instructors might consider adapting IPA tasks, as well as other classroom learning activities, to account for learners' mixed readiness. If the proficiency range is not as wide spread, then a one-size-fits-all approach may be adequate. Differentiated IPA tasks and evaluation rubrics would challenge all learners at their current level and beyond. Differentiation necessitates the elaboration of IPA tasks at different levels of the ACTFL Scale as well as the use of evaluation rubrics targeted to different levels of the scale. The interpersonal and presentational mode rubrics included in the appendices of the present volume, encompassing Novice-Mid to Advanced-Mid levels, can be helpful in achieving the goal of meeting learners where they are and assisting them in reaching higher levels of proficiency.

Instructors will need to decide how to pair learners for interpersonal tasks based on their proficiency levels. It is recommended that dyads be formed within the same sub-level or within adjacent sub-levels in order to permit each learner to participate more fully in completion of the interpersonal task. Dyads may be constant throughout the semester or varied from task to task. Each approach has potential advantages and disadvantages. One advantage to the constant dyad is that learners potentially develop a rapport and investment in one another's development. Possible disadvantages are that one or both learners may feel they are being held back by the other's performance, or the two learners might not be compatible in terms of personality. Instructors will need to negotiate learner dynamics on a case-by-case basis. Instructors will also need to decide if and when to move a learner

to a higher level during the semester, which could also have an impact on assigned dyads. As Rifkin (2003) notes, "after students have achieved Intermediate-level function, instructional objectives should shift to Advanced-level tasks and the discourse and interaction patterns must change" (p. 587).

Task Creation

Instructors will select an authentic literary text as the basis of each IPA, considering factors such as thematic context, linguistic level, and relevance of the tasks that interpretation of the text will generate. For example, in a course in which the overarching theme is "family," literary works that feature nuclear families, extended families, and "families by choice" might be considered. Instructors might begin each unit with a less challenging text and then select more complex texts for subsequent learning activities, returning to a mid-range difficulty text for the summative IPA. Instructors are encouraged to review "Factors to Consider When Selecting Authentic Texts for the Interpretive Tasks" in Chapter 4 for additional guidance.

The Interpretive Phase

Summative interpretive tasks can be created using the "IPA Interpretive Task Comprehension Guide: Template" (Appendix D-3) which includes assistive "Note to instructor" prompts for each major section. Instructors should consider how the elements they select for inclusion in the Literal Comprehension sections (Key Word Recognition, Main Ideas, Supporting Details, Organizational Features) will assist learners in successful completion of the Interpretive Comprehension sections (Guessing Meaning From Context, Inferences, Author's Perspective, Cultural Perspectives). The categories of Supporting Details and Organizational Features can be useful in querying learners' understanding of literary terms and concepts.

Ideally, Interpretive Phase tasks will be completed in the classroom setting in order to avoid the use of assistive technologies. For this reason, it may be necessary to use excerpts from novels, brief short stories, scenes from plays, and poems that are able to be interpreted in the context of one class setting. Another option is to complete the comprehension guide in two steps: Literal Comprehension on Day 1 and Interpretive Comprehension on Day 2.

Instructors provide feedback following the interpretive task, including individual comments on each learner's

Figure 7.2. Sample Interview Questions—Pre-Assessment of Learner Proficiency Level

Warm-up (to establish topics for the conversation)
- What classes do you take? What is your major?
- Do you have a job? What do you do at work?
- What do you like to do in your free time?
- Where do you work/live? What is it like? What do you do there?

Present narration (Intermediate)
- Tell me everything that you do in your daily routine from morning to evening.
- You said your favorite class is ___. Tell me more about it. What do you do in that class? What do you like so much about it?
- Tell me more about where you live (or your job). What do you like the most about it?

Ask questions (for Intermediate level-speakers)
- What questions do you have for me regarding my profession or my interests?

Role play for Intermediate (for students that you believe to be NH, IL, IM):
- Purpose is to demonstrate the ability to obtain information by asking questions.
- It is the first day of school and you start talking to the person sitting next to you in class. Ask the person several questions to get to know them better.

Past narration (Advanced)
- You said you like to travel and you have visited ___. Tell me about a memorable experience you had there with as many details as possible. Why was the experience memorable?
- You said that you work at ___. Tell me about something unexpected or unusual that happened at work or about some problem that you had to resolve. Give me all the details.

Detailed description (Advanced)
- You said that before you lived in ___ you lived in ___. Describe the similarities and differences between these two places.
- You said that you visited ___. I'd like you to think of a place that you really liked there and describe it to me in detail so that I can imagine what it is like.

Speak beyond the biographical (Advanced)
- Tell me about an interesting topic that you saw on the news or on social media.

Provide an opinion about an abstract topic and support the opinion (Superior)
- You mentioned that you saw a news story about cryptocurrency. Why in your opinion is it advisable to invest in cryptocurrencies? What would be some arguments against investing in cryptocurrencies?

Hypothesize in the abstract mode (Superior)
- In your opinion, what would the implications be if in the next few years the majority of banking and finance transactions were to be carried out using cryptocurrencies? How would society change for better or worse?

Role play for Advanced (for students that you believe to be IH, AL, AM):
- Purpose is to demonstrate the ability to get out of a complication.
- Your child has a major school project due in a few days and you realize they will not be able to complete it. Call the child's teacher, explain the problem in detail and propose some solutions to the problem.

Interpretive Mode Rubric (Appendix F-1) as well as global comments in class. See Figure 7.3 for a sample comprehension guide.

Interpersonal Phase
For the summative interpersonal task, instructors will create a situational prompt related to the authentic text from the interpretive phase. This prompt should involve some real-life situation that learners will work together to resolve. It will include performance subtasks, some geared to the learner's current proficiency level and some geared to the next level. Special attention should be paid to the Functions or Global Tasks that learners are able to perform at each proficiency level. Intermediate-level speakers, for example, should be able to ask and answer questions and handle uncomplicated situations, while Advanced-level speakers should be able to describe and narrate in all major time frames and handle situations that present a complication. Instructors should

Figure 7.3. Sample Interpretive Mode Task (Comprehension Guide)—Narrative

I. Key Words
In the short story, find the Spanish word or phrase that best expresses the meaning of each of the following words or phrases in English. *Mark your text with the corresponding number* and *write the words or phrases in Spanish* here:

1. It was one shadow only _____

2. Like a large round flame_____

3. They told us that Tonaya was just behind the mountain _____

4. Without releasing the load from his shoulders_____

5. He was speaking little. Less every time. _____

6. I will not leave you thrown here so that you are done for by whomever _____

7. I do it for your dead mother. _____

8. And on top of the dry sweat, he was sweating again. _____

9. I have cursed the blood that you have from me. _____

10. He unlaced the fingers with difficulty _____

II. Main Idea
After reading the short story, provide a one-sentence synopsis of its main idea in English here:

_____

_____

III. Supporting Details
Circle the letter of each detail that is included in the short story. (HINT: All are included!) Write the letter of the detail where it appears in the short story. Write the information that is given in the short story in Spanish below.
  A. The name of the town being searched for _____
  B. The name of the son_____
  C. The time of day _____
  D. The name of the father's best friend _____
  E. The cause of death of the mother _____

IV. Organizational Features

How is this short story organized? Choose one (1) from the options below and explain briefly providing examples from the text. You may use English or Spanish to provide your explanations.
1. Time of day
2. Light/dark
3. Journey

_____

_____

V. Guessing Meaning from Context

Based on the short story, <u>explain</u> what the underlined words/phrase means in English (do NOT merely translate!):

"He dicho: <<¡Que se le pudra en los riñones la sangre que yo le di!>>"
[HINT: pudrir=to rot; riñón=kidney]

_____

_____

VI. Inferences

"Read between the lines" to answer the following questions. Be sure to use information from the short story. Answer in English or in Spanish.

What do the narrator's comments regarding the quality of light, shadow, the moon, etc., signify in the context of the son's state of being? [HINT: How is a day like a life? How is a journey like a life?]

_____

_____

VII. Author's Perspective

Of the following possibilities, select the one (1) type of perspective or point of view you think the author most adopted as he wrote this short story and justify your answer with information from the text. You may respond in English or in Spanish.
A. Moral/Ethical
B. Analytical/Objective

_____

_____

VIII. Comparing Cultural Perspectives

Answer the following question in Spanish or in English.

Consider the way in which the father addresses his son. Which 'you' (tú, Ud.) does he use at first? How does that change throughout the story? Given what you know about Spanish-speaking cultural practices, why does this seem unusual? What does this suggest?

_____

_____

IX. Personal Reaction to the Text

Using specific information from the short story, describe your personal reaction to it in Spanish. Be sure to provide reasons for your reaction.

_____

_____

_____

Figure 7.4. Sample Interpersonal Mode Task—Narrative

You and your classmate have been asked by the university Orientation Team to suggest a Spanish-language text that will be shared with incoming Latino students prior to Orientation and that they will be asked to discuss in their residence hall learning communities during move-in weekend community-building programs. The Orientation Team is interested in "No oyes ladrar los perros" as a potential springboard for discussion.

Consider the themes associated with "No oyes ladrar los perros" in the context of life challenges of university students and other young adults. What does the story potentially offer to stimulate the students' thinking about their new living-learning context?

Novice
- To begin your discussion, generate a list of characters and themes associated with the story. (Novice)
- Ask each other at least two follow-up questions apiece regarding the items on your list. The questions might be about, for example, the plot, the setting, the use of irony, the type of ending (closed, open), the use of figurative language, or other literary devices (symbols, leitmotifs). (Intermediate)
- Sometimes family members or friends disappoint each other with their actions, words, or behaviors. Share with your partner a situation you know of in which this occurs. (Intermediate)

Intermediate
- To begin your discussion, identify relevant themes associated with the story. (Intermediate)
- Ask each other follow-up questions to establish the relevance. The questions might be about, for example, the plot, the setting, the use of irony, the type of ending (closed, open), the use of figurative language, or other literary devices (symbols, leitmotifs). (Intermediate)
- Sometimes family members or friends disappoint each other with their actions, words, or behaviors. Share with your partner a time when you experienced such a disappointment in the past or knew of somebody else who had. Tell in detail what the situation was, how it unfolded and how it ended. Then switch so that each of you shares a story. (Advanced)
- Finally, together decide whether or not "No oyes ladrar los perros" seems well-suited for the Orientation Team's purpose and explain why.

Advanced
- To begin your discussion, identify a relevant theme associated with the story and specifically how it was manifested in the story. Consider the impact of such aspects of the story as the plot, the setting, the use of irony, the type of ending (closed, open), the use of figurative language, or other literary devices (symbols, leitmotifs). (Advanced)
- Sometimes family members or friends disappoint each other with their actions, words, or behaviors. Share with your partner a time when you experienced such a disappointment in the past or knew of somebody else who had. Tell in detail what the situation was, how it unfolded and how it ended. Then switch so that each of you shares a story. (Advanced)
- The father in the story clearly has a dilemma involving his love for his deceased wife and for his son, who has done some very bad things.
  - One of you should take a stance regarding the dilemma (for example, fatherly love should or should not be unconditional) and justify the stance.
  - The other should present an opposite or alternative stance and justify it. (You might need to invent this if you happen to agree with the original stance presented!)
  - Hypothesize what the world would be like or what the ramifications would be if parents generally acted a certain way (for example, if their love were not unconditional and they judged their children's actions). (Superior)

review Appendix B, Inverted Pyramid Showing Major Levels of the ACTFL Rating Scale, and Appendix C, Assessment Criteria Used to Assess Proficiency in Speaking and consult the example IPAs in Chapter 6 for inspiration.

Instructors will need to determine how to record the learner-to-learner interactions, whether with digital recording devices or phone apps. It is essential to have a recording to return to, not only for the purpose of instructor assessment, but also for learner self-evaluation and subsequent co-constructed (instructor-learner) feedback sessions. These dynamics can be difficult to manage in the postsecondary setting, where instructors tend to have less autonomy over space and time. In order to maintain the spontaneity of the interpersonal phase, it is essential that the task be witnessed by the instructor. The task may quickly become more presentational in nature if vocabulary and grammar is researched, scripts are employed, and second and third takes are recorded. Figure 7.4 includes sample interpersonal tasks for Novice, Intermediate, and Advanced levels.

Co-Constructed Feedback

Following the interpersonal phase, instructors will meet with learners to review their performance. This work may occur in the context of class time, while other learners are engaged in a learning activity, or outside of class time, during instructor office hours. This work may also be completed individually or with learner dyads.

Prior to the feedback session, instructors should ask learners to rate their own performances using the same rubric that will be used for assigning a grade. During the feedback session, learners share their evaluation of each category with the instructor and listen together to brief samples of the recorded conversation. The instructor asks the learner to explain their evaluation using the rubric language, and assists the learner in understanding what goals have been achieved and what steps may be taken to improve the next performance. Learners should be reminded that movement from one proficiency level to the next requires "significant time over the course of multiple IPAs" (Adair-Hauck et al., 2013, p. 17). See Chapter 5 as well as Appendices H and I for more on co-constructed feedback sessions.

Presentational Phase

Presentational tasks may occur in written or spoken form. Instructors will create a presentational context that springs from the previous interpretive and interpersonal phases. Learners will incorporate the understanding gained from completing the interpretive and interpersonal phases in this culminating activity. The presentational phase is distinguished by the category of Impact: "Clarity, organization, and depth of presentation; degree to which presentation maintains attention and interest of audience" (Appendix F-3). As with the interpersonal phase, the task's performance parameters may be adjusted to account for learner proficiency levels. The presentational task should also ideally be completed within the class-time context, as with the interpretive and interpersonal phases. See Figure 7.5 for sample presentational tasks at the Novice, Intermediate, and Advanced levels.

Evaluation with Rubrics

Rubrics for each phase of the IPA should be shared and reviewed with learners prior to the first summative assessment. Indeed, rubrics may be used in conjunction with formative assessment and learning activities so that learners gain a better understanding of the performance features of each phase of the IPA

Transforming the Literature Class in Light of IPAs

The implementation of an IPA-informed approach in world language literature courses motivates a pedagogical transformation beyond the IPA cycles themselves. With additional emphasis placed on language skills development in literature courses, determinations need to be made regarding course content, particularly the number of literary readings that can be employed in the IPA-informed approach as opposed to a traditional approach. Also, classroom activities and discourse patterns outside of IPA cycles might need to be adapted to ensure a seamless connection between instruction and assessment. Finally, learners must be instructed on the objectives and procedures of the approach.

> The implementation of an IPA-informed approach in L2 literature courses motivates a pedagogical transformation beyond the IPA cycles themselves.

Figure 7.5. Sample Presentational Mode Task—Narrative

Novice
- Generate a list of emotions you feel. (Novice)
- Tell why you are writing the letter, perhaps explaining why your child/parent relationship is so complicated. (Intermediate)
- Ask your father three questions. (Intermediate)

Intermediate
- Tell why you are writing the letter, perhaps explaining why your child/parent relationship is so complicated. (Intermediate)
- Ask your father three questions. (Intermediate)
- Explain the events that led up to the moment prior to your injury. (Advanced)

Advanced
- Explain the events that led up to the moment prior to your injury. (Advanced)
- Provide a detailed description of how/why your relationship became so strained. (Advanced)
- Argue that a parent's love for their child should be unconditional. (Superior)

Selection of Course Content

In her 1995 article "Teaching Literature or Teaching Students?" Bernhardt asks, "Are we in our classrooms for the benefit of students as individuals, or are we there to ensure that certain bodies of work remain in the consciousness of literary scholarship?" (p. 6). In an IPA-informed curriculum, it may be necessary to reduce the breadth of literary content in each course in order to provide time for continued focus on the systematic development of communication skills. While traditional literature courses have long focused on interpretive reading of multiple texts and presentational writing of exam responses (short-answer and essay) and final papers (literary analysis), interpersonal speaking, including spontaneous negotiation of meaning to complete real-world tasks, has not been featured in literature courses based on a genre, time period, movement, or national tradition. The change in focus from what learners *know about* a text to what learners *know from working with* a text inevitably leads to a reduction in the number of primary texts treated in any given course.

> In an IPA-informed curriculum, it may be necessary to reduce the breadth of literary content in each course in order to provide time for continued focus on the systematic development of communication skills.

Classroom Activities and Interaction Patterns

Research in applied linguistics has explored the dynamics of classroom discourse in the undergraduate literature course context and has identified a number of ways in which such discourse might not be as useful as one would hope in propelling learners to higher levels of the ACTFL Scale. For classroom activities to be successful at moving learners up, they would need to require learners to produce abundant language during each class period, not just one-word or short phrase contributions, and they would need to orient such language toward particular levels of the scale. Learners who aspire to the Advanced level, for example, would need consistent practice in narrating and describing in all major time frames and in resolving complications. They would also need to discuss topics beyond the biographical, such as topics of conversation in their community and beyond, or in their literary readings. Finally, they would need to expand their speaking beyond discrete sentences to connected sentences and paragraph-length discourse.

Studies conducted by Donato & Brooks (2004) and later by Darhower (2014) analyzed the discourse in undergraduate world language literature classes from multiple perspectives: instructor and learner turn-taking, length of instructor and learner utterances, types of questions asked by instructors, and instructor and learner verb distribution. The findings were similar in both studies. While Donato & Brooks studied one Spanish literature class, Darhower studied three literature classes taught by three different instructors. Data for this study were drawn from video recordings of three 75-minute class sessions from each instructor's class. Instructor and learner conversation turns were nearly even in each course, primarily due to "IRE sequences" in which the instructor would ask a question, a learner would answer the question, and the instructor would give a brief evaluation of the response and then continue the cycle with further questions. The mean length of utterance for instructors in each class ranged from 48-59 words, whereas learner utterances were 8-14 words. The vast majority of instructor questions in each class targeted the Novice and Intermediate levels of the ACTFL Scale, as was evidenced by a verb distribution that was overwhelmingly present indicative at the expense of all other tenses and moods.

Research in the literature class context has also generated findings in terms of classroom discourse models that may promote success in literature learners, both in literary analysis and language skill development. Mantero (2002), for example, outlines a model of "text-centered talk" in which learners are engaged in dialogue with the teacher and with each other, and the teacher scaffolds learners as they construct their own interpretations of literary texts, rather than leading learners to the instructor's interpretation. In their 2016 book *A Multiliteracies Framework for Collegiate Foreign Language Teaching*, Paesani et al. (2016) outline three text-based discourse models and provide a detailed template for implementing and assessing text-based instruction. Also see Nance (2010) for a substantive discussion of pedagogical models for teaching L2 literature.

This research has important pedagogical implications. If literature courses are to not only focus on literary content but also on the systematic development of functional communicative ability, then some changes in classroom activities and discourse patterns, as well as assessment, are in order. Ideally, instructors would talk less and encourage learners to talk more. This would be brought about by placing more emphasis on group work as well as altering classroom discourse patterns. Instructors would also push learners to perform at higher proficiency levels by asking questions that incorporate the criteria of higher proficiency levels (that is, Advanced and Superior). For example, an Advanced question would require a complete paragraph description or narration as opposed to accepting one or two sentences or even less. Instructors would sometimes require responses in the past

time frame, even though it is a convention of literary studies to narrate plots in the historical present. Figure 7.6 includes sample questions that instructors might pose to learners of different proficiency levels.

Fostering Learner Dispositions

This change of perspective on the purpose and objectives of world language literature courses implies action not only on the part of instructors, but also on the part of learners. If instructors will need to embrace a depth-over-breadth approach to their course delivery, learners will need to embrace an active-over-passive approach to their course participation. Learners will need to resist their expectations of the traditional "banking model" (Freire, 2018) in which they receive deposits of information to file and store until they need to be withdrawn for display to the instructor.

Instructors will assist learners in becoming more active by clarifying the objectives, procedures, and expectations of an IPA-informed approach to studying literature. They will produce models for learners to emulate, permit practice for learners to negotiate, promote performance for learners to evaluate, and provide feedback for learners to assimilate.

> Instructors will assist learners in becoming more active by clarifying the objectives, procedures, and expectations of an IPA-informed approach to studying literature. They will produce models for learners to emulate, permit practice for learners to negotiate, promote performance for learners to evaluate, and provide feedback for learners to assimilate.

Research suggests that learners are motivated to perform at or above expectations when the evaluation process is made transparent and participatory. Results from an unpublished conference presentation detail the impact of the IPA on learner motivation in a postsecondary culture course, finding that "learners were significantly more motivated to learn Spanish after IPA assessment" (Adair-Hauck et al., 2009). As the presenters concluded, "In the IPA paradigm, the instructor becomes a facilitator or coach whose primary purpose is to assist the learners to improve their performance."

These findings, as well as those of Darhower &

Figure 7.6. Sample In-Class Questions to Target Higher Proficiency Levels

Original question and corresponding proficiency level	Enhanced question and corresponding proficiency level
What prize does Vargas Llosa deserve? (Novice)	Explain, with examples, the characteristics of Mario Vargas Llosa's writing that might make him worthy of a Nobel Prize in Literature. (Intermediate-Advanced)
Key words? Tell me some themes. (Novice)	Identify some themes that are found in this literary piece and discuss the importance of these themes. (Intermediate-Advanced)
What do the United States corporations symbolize? (Novice-Intermediate)	Describe, with examples, what United States corporations symbolize in the literary piece and what impact the corporations have on Latin American society. (Intermediate-Advanced)
What is a Trojan horse? (Novice-Intermediate)	Explain the origin of the expression "Trojan horse" and how this symbol applies to the current reading. (Intermediate-Advanced)
What is happening around them while they are talking? (Intermediate)	Describe the scene that surrounded the characters while they were talking. What kind of mood did the scene set and what impact did that mood have on the development of the story? (Advanced)
Why does he talk about the future in the poem? What is going to happen in the future? (Intermediate-Advanced)	Why do you think the character talks about the future in the poem? What do you think is going to happen in the future and what makes you think that? What if it does happen and what if it doesn't? (Advanced)
Is it easy for Pedro Tenorio to lie to the king? (Intermediate)	Explain the possible consequences for lying to the king. What do you think was going through Pedro Tenorio's mind as he contemplated lying to the king? (Advanced)
What options does Juan have at the end of the movie? (Intermediate)	What in your opinion are the options available to Juan at the end of the movie? Which option is best for him in your opinion and why is that better than the other options? How would his life and the lives of other characters in the story change if he chose that option? (Advanced-Superior)
What was Mrs. Trask's life like? (Intermediate-Advanced)	Describe with details from the text what Mrs. Trask's life was like. Do you think it was overall a good life or bad life? Why? (Advanced)
What do we know about Don Juan's past? (Intermediate-Advanced)	Describe Don Juan's past in detail according to the text. What were the experiences that shaped his personality? (Advanced)

Smith-Sherwood (2021, 2023) outlined above, suggest that learners in mixed-readiness contexts may also be motivated to aim for performances at or above the level of the majority of their classmates. Those whose current proficiency levels are below average may be motivated to continue to pursue coursework, study abroad, or complete certificates, minors, and majors rather than abandoning language study as they are guided by instructors to take targeted steps to perform at higher levels of proficiency. Those whose current proficiency levels lie above the class average, such as native and heritage speakers or those from high-performing high school programs, may also be motivated to reach even higher levels of proficiency than those prescribed by course or program objectives. Additional research is needed to confirm the positive impact of IPA-informed instruction, learning, and assessment on learners in mixed-readiness classrooms.

Looking Toward the Future

Professional Development
In order to implement IPAs successfully in their courses, instructors would be well advised to develop a solid understanding of the criteria of the ACTFL Scales in reading, writing, listening, and speaking. Some professional development may be necessary in that regard for practicing literature professors as well as future literature professors in graduate school programs.

The professional development of future foreign language and literature instructors begins in undergraduate programs for K-12 instructors and graduate programs for postsecondary instructors. In most undergraduate programs, students take a few courses in general education and at least one course in foreign language teaching methodology. In graduate programs in foreign languages and literatures, students typically take one required teaching methodology course to prepare them to teach first and second-year language courses in their graduate program and perhaps beyond. What is missing from both levels are courses in *teaching literature in foreign languages*. Indeed, an internet perusal of university graduate foreign language curricula failed to find such a course. Such a course would integrate methodology pertaining to language instruction with literature pedagogy in such a way that instructors would implement instruction that would focus on the systematic development of world language communication skills throughout the curriculum,

even in the so-called undergraduate upper division content courses.

For practicing language and literature instructors, the implementation of any new assessment program will likely necessitate professional development. As Bernhardt (2008) noted, "the professional development program behind performance assessment is the most important dimension of any language program. Adequate assessment needs instructors trained in both the practicalities and the theory of a particular assessment" (p. 16-17). The Stanford Language Center is a positive role model for this orientation to professional development, having attained at one point 98% of the language faculty with training in the ACTFL Oral Proficiency Guidelines and the World-Readiness Standards for Learning Languages. Professional development for literature instructors would focus on the specific criteria of the assessment system and the protocols for implementing it. In the United States, the principal language assessment system is the set of ACTFL Proficiency Scales for speaking, listening, reading, and writing (ACTFL 2012b), supported by the World-Readiness Standards for Learning Languages (National Standards Collaborative Board, 2015). Instructors who have experience with the European context might also be familiar with the Common European Framework of Reference (CEFR, Council of Europe, 2001).

Articulation between K-12 and college/university programs
Another important area of concern in the profession is articulation between world languages programs in secondary schools and those in college/university programs, as well as articulation between the lower division (first and second year) courses and upper division (third and fourth year) courses within undergraduate programs. As discussed earlier in this chapter, literary texts can and should be implemented at all levels of world language instruction. Incorporating texts from the beginning of instruction, with increasing levels of complexity throughout the undergraduate major, will arouse learners' analytical skills in earlier levels of instruction. Continuing to focus on developing language proficiency in upper level courses, along with literary analysis, brings the integration of language and literature full circle. The IPA is a unique pedagogical tool that can assist this endeavor.

IPAs can also facilitate the transition between high

school and college/university world language programs. The College Board's Advanced Placement courses in Language and Culture and Literature and Culture, for example, provide an instructional framework that meshes well with the IPA. Courses below that level can also incorporate IPAs, since IPAs can be designed for all proficiency levels. If high school students are already accustomed to IPAs and IPAs are used in their university world language classes, the transition will be much smoother for them.

Conclusion: The IPA as a Bridge Between Language and Literature

At "20 years and counting," IPAs have nearly reached their heyday in world language instruction. As world language programs struggle to prove their continued relevance in today's society, IPAs help to provide a seamless link between instruction and assessment, allowing learners to provide evidence of their growing world language proficiency and literary analysis skills. By linking instruction and assessment, the IPA can provide a model for an overall redesign of literature courses focused on the systematic development of functional communicative abilities as learners also build their literary analysis skills. In other words, the IPA is a concrete example of a construct that can be employed to truly bridge the language-literature divide that has frustrated researchers and practitioners for decades. Further research and more widespread implementation of IPAs in literature courses will strengthen the power of this transformative pedagogical tool.

> IPAs are a concrete example of a construct that can be employed to truly bridge the language-literature divide that has frustrated researchers and practitioners for decades.

Chapter 8

Voices from the Field: Washback of Twenty Years of Integrated Performance Assessment

As Chapter 3 shows, over the course of twenty years the IPA has had a clear impact on the field in terms of advancing the work of proficiency-oriented, standards-based instruction and assessment. In this chapter, different stakeholders share their experiences and further describe the influence of the IPA across the United States. Some describe IPA work in the states of Ohio and California, while others—some of whom have contributed their IPAs for this book—share the experiences they have had in incorporating the IPA in their districts, programs, and classrooms. Overall, the testimonials highlight that implementation of IPA has impacted their programs positively by encouraging instructors

- To use a backward design approach for planning, teaching, and assessment
- To shift to a performance and proficiency-based instructional approach to world language learning
- To increase meaningful target language input, as well as increase time for meaningful target language learner output
- To integrate more culturally rich authentic materials for instruction as well as assessment purposes
- To provide more robust feedback to learners.

Furthermore, the testimonials reveal that the IPA provides positive washback for the learners by

- Serving as a consciousness-raising tool to help learners focus more on proficiency levels rather than on grades
- Setting the learners up for success on ACTFL's Assessment of Performance toward Proficiency in Language
- Increasing many learners' proficiency so that they graduate from high school with the Seal of Biliteracy (Davin & Heineke, 2022).

Washback Effect: State Level

Washback Effect of the IPA in the State of Ohio

Kathleen Shelton and Ryan Wertz
World Language Consultants
Ohio Department of Education

In 2013, the Ohio Department of Education (ODE) launched its World Languages Model Curriculum, a state-mandated resource repository to support teachers in implementing the state standards. Included in the model curriculum are resources for instruction and assessment, whose foundational structure is based on the backward design process of identifying learning outcomes, determining evidence of learning, and planning learning experiences. The Integrated Performance Assessment (IPA) is the framework that Ohio chose to model what "evidence of learning" looks like for performance-based outcomes in the world language classroom.

Within the Ohio model curriculum are sample thematic units that demonstrate how to implement the backward design process when creating learning experiences. These units range from Novice-Low to Advanced-Low language proficiency and include an example IPA in each unit. Additionally, Ohio developed holistic rubrics aligned to the ACTFL proficiency sub-levels to use in conjunction with the IPA to explicitly clarify teacher and student understanding of proficiency and to guide the development of teacher-created IPAs. Additionally, Ohio created lists of authentic resources categorized by language and topic to further support the intercultural aspect of creating an IPA and using culture to drive language learning and instruction.

Using the online model curriculum resources, the ODE world language team continues to lead workshops to help Ohio K-12 world language teachers continue to shift to a proficiency-based instructional model. We have observed that the simplicity of the IPA framework makes it an accessible entry point for teachers to create performance-based assessments. The use of a thematic focus across modes and skills is already familiar to most teachers. However, the integrated component of the tasks that build upon each other based on an authentic resource can be a new and more challenging component for teachers and their students.

With intentional and scaffolded support from the ODE team, as well as the Ohio Foreign Language Association, many teachers in Ohio have transitioned to a more proficiency-based assessment format based on the IPA framework. This transition in assessment practices has led to a transformation in instructional practices as well, as formative assessments and learning experiences have become more performance- and proficiency-based to mirror the intercultural tasks in a summative IPA.

The change in student learning goals and outcomes for Ohio world language programs over the past decade can be evidenced in myriad ways:

- Teachers across languages can now collaborate on the base theme and format of their IPA, making adjustments as needed for language-specific intercultural outcomes and authentic resources.
- Teachers are able to use one authentic resource and IPA across several levels by adjusting the tasks and targeted outcomes based on the proficiency levels of their students.
- Teachers have greatly increased their use of authentic resources in curriculum and lesson design due to the inclusion of authentic resources in their IPAs.
- The IPA framework has given teachers a concrete structure to match the revised format of the Advanced Placement exams.
- With the implementation of the Seal of Biliteracy in Ohio, the IPA provides a similar format to the proficiency-based vendor assessments students have to take to earn the seal.
- Ohio's teacher evaluation system requires teachers to provide evidence of student learning aligned to Ohio's 2020 learning standards, which reflect the ACTFL proficiency levels. The IPA is recommended as one way to gather

high-quality student data aligned to the state standards.
- Numerous Ohio teachers now lead professional learning or create shared resources based on the IPA format.
- Teachers who have used the IPA format for years have begun to transition from using the IPA format in its exact design to integrating and elaborating on its format in project-based learning and other skill-specific assessments.

The IPA continues to serve not only as the foundation of assessment development in Ohio, but also as the impetus for teachers to develop richer learning experiences that strive for intercultural competence in relevant and current real-world contexts.

Washback Effect of the IPA in the State of California

Nicole Naditz, M.Ed., NBCT
Program Specialist, World Languages and Instructional Technology
San Juan Unified School District, CA
ACTFL 2015 National Language Teacher of the Year

As an assessment strategy, Integrated Performance Assessments (IPAs) are so important, and so impactful, that they are featured in the *World Languages Framework for California Public Schools, Kindergarten Through Grade Twelve* (2020), specifically in Chapter 10, Assessment of World Language Learning. The writers of our state framework recognized the critical role of authentic, contextualized, and meaningful assessment to document learners' progress and growth in proficiency and interculturality, and note that IPAs include all of those features. IPAs serve as models of effective student assessment in world language programs.

It may go without saying that in an IPA, each task is tied to learning targets, usually phrased as can-do statements. These learning targets that have been taught and practiced are also linked to essential questions that the students have been exploring over the course of the unit leading up to the assessment. Perhaps less obvious, but equally critical, is the fact that in an IPA the entire assessment and each task within it is contextualized in an authentic and plausible setting and demands from students meaningful, culturally appropriate and authentic language interpretation and use. Thus, IPAs stand in direct contrast to the discrete, decontextualized activities often used in traditional assessment activities, such as verb fill-in paragraphs. In addition—and one of my favorite aspects of an IPA—the tasks in an IPA support each other, so that as students move from one task to the next, the flow of tasks feels natural and each task they do fosters success in the next.

As a practitioner, I noticed something even more powerful about the impact of implementing the IPA: Designing and using IPAs as a summative assessment strategy demands more than a change in the assessment tasks provided to learners to demonstrate what they know and can do. For me, and for many teachers I have supported in California and beyond, moving to the use of IPAs resulted in equally powerful shifts in instructional practice to promote the language and cultural skills students would need in order to be successful. Essentially, IPAs require a transition away from grammar-centered approaches and toward a more culturally rich, meaningful communicative approach to instruction and practice so that learners can be successful in a culturally rich, meaningful communicative summative assessment.

The IPA has had a washback effect on the teaching of many instructors who have embraced it. Once we began implementing IPAs as the primary method of summative assessment, we designed input that was more contextualized and culturally rich and more concretely tied to the established learning targets. Similarly, we increased and modified learners' practice opportunities so that they had more opportunities for meaningful target-language use and interpretation leading up to the IPA. This means that learners had ongoing opportunities to use the targeted language and interculturality skills in context throughout the unit, rather than only during the official assessment tasks at the end of the unit.

An additional shift in our practice was the increase in the amount of authentic materials students interacted with and interpreted *throughout* the learning cycle, as they worked toward the IPA. Essentially, learners were practicing everything they would ultimately need for the IPA via micro-tasks throughout the unit of study, all tied to the established learning targets. Finally, teachers have increased the amount of actionable feedback to learners on their practice tasks. In this way, students have had substantial opportunities to receive and act on feedback across the modes of communication *before* being assessed with the IPA. This has meant that we—students and teachers—have evidence *before* the IPA that learners were ready to document their progress on the learning targets through an IPA.

In short, implementing IPAs has impacted the entire instructional cycle—from input to summative assessment—in positive and powerful ways for many California teachers and their learners. And unlike many grammar-focused assessments whose tasks do not represent authentic language use and that often seem to search for what students *do not* know, IPAs document and celebrate what learners *can* do.

Washback Effect: Voices of Instructors

University of Minnesota–Twin Cities

Elizabeth Lake
Senior Teaching Specialist, Department of Spanish & Portuguese Studies
Faculty Coordinator, College in the Schools

Dr. Helena Ruf
Director of Language Instruction,
Department of German, Nordic, Slavic and Dutch

Dr. Elizabeth Kautz
German Teaching Faculty,
Department of German, Nordic, Slavic and Dutch

After attending "The Un-test: Implementing Integrated Performance Assessments (IPAs)" presented by Francis Troyan at the University of Minnesota in 2015 and getting to know the IPA examples in *Implementing Integrated Performance Assessment* (Adair-Hauck et al., 2013), we began thinking about how this assessment model might be incorporated into college-level, multi-section intermediate German and Spanish courses.

In German, we already had several elements similar to an IPA in our assessment plan, but they were not connected to each other and used different rubrics. For presentational tasks and interpersonal role-plays, our practice was to use very simple rubrics with a few comments for quick assessment. When we introduced the new IPA rubrics, instructors initially struggled to adjust to the categories and detailed criteria they contained, but they soon did appreciate and adopt the new interpersonal and presentational assessments. The interpretive assessment model and rubric proved more challenging, however, as instructors were less familiar and comfortable with the subjective aspects of evaluating student responses to questions about the author's purpose, inferences, or cultural comparisons. We overcame that discomfort by collecting student samples that we could all evaluate together while discussing how we applied the rubric and thus establishing greater inter-rater reliability across the multiple sections taught by different instructors.

Once we began using the IPA to assess student's communication skills in all three modes, we realized our assessments and daily practice were no longer in alignment. We needed to use backward design to close the gaps. For example, instructors began to modify existing reading assignments by adding the types of tasks that structure the IPA interpretive guide, such as more genre analysis, identifying authorial purpose, and inferencing. After initial pushback, teachers started to teach differently in order to ensure that students were prepared for the assessments. In this way, we pleasantly discovered that by making IPAs our assessment model, we really did bring about desired changes both in the general curriculum and in the daily teaching done by instructors. The changes did not happen overnight, but the longer we had the IPAs—and subsequently also revised and improved them—the more we saw positive changes in daily instructional practices.

In Spanish, one of the principal challenges we faced in implementing an IPA in an intermediate-level course was time: How could we fit an IPA into an already fast-paced, content-heavy course, and how could we ensure a robust feedback loop? To address the former challenge, we dropped five formative assessments from the chapter during which we implemented the IPA. For the latter, we deployed technology and self-grading. We wrote an interpretive guide using the examples in *Implementing Integrated Performance Assessment* (Adair-Hauck et al., 2013) and designed an interpersonal task in which students recorded a conversation discussing green project ideas in our digital language lab, allowing us to collect the conversations during a single class period. For the presentational task, we had dyads present their project proposals and facilitate a Q&A about them in poster-style presentations, allowing us to complete the presentational mode in two 50-minute class periods.

Student surveys conducted during academic year 2016-17 showed that 80% of students agreed that their understanding of the chapter theme (environmental issues) was deepened as a result of the IPA activities:

> "I really liked the topic of the project, as well as how we applied it to our community. To be honest, it was kind of exciting and stimulating to see students' ideas."

However, students also reported wanting more feedback from their instructors:

> "I liked everything regarding the homework and project for the IPA, I only wish that the instructor feedback was more detailed..."

While the students wanted more feedback, instructors reported that the IPA grading could be onerous and time consuming. In response to instructor concerns about the grading load and to ensure that our students received robust feedback, students self-graded the interpretive guide. The self-grading session was conducted in English and allowed students to defend and support their interpretations and cultural comparisons. This adjustment led to one of the richest outcomes of the IPA. Typically, the day after the students completed the interpretive guide, they arrived to class absolutely convinced that they had done abysmally. With this new approach, they quickly saw how much they had understood from the text, as well as their ability to make insightful cultural comparisons about the issues mentioned in the article. Students' sense of achievement was underscored by having them picture themselves sitting at a café in Madrid reading the local paper and thinking, "Hmmm, that reminds me of a problem back home at the U of M." As with German, working with IPAs and the burgeoning conversations about multiliteracies pedagogy in our department have led Spanish and Portuguese instructors to revamp their classroom practice and incorporate more authentic texts that afford students opportunities to engage in deeper textual and cultural analysis by discussing genre, author purpose, audience, language use, and cultural comparisons.

In the years since first introducing IPAs, our assessments have undergone many changes. Some are still being used largely as they were first conceptualized, others have been put to the side as new curriculums were brought in, and still others have been reworked to fit changes in the curriculum. What has remained is the deep sense that the focus on backward design that an IPA requires has been transformational for our thinking and instruction. We now turn our attention to questions of how to create an IPA-like assessment that aligns with critical pedagogies such as multiliteracies or social justice pedagogy. In what ways might we need to adjust our IPAs to meet these goals? In some courses this work has already begun, and we look forward to embarking on this next stage of our journey with IPAs.

Egg Harbor Township School District, NJ

Dr. Michele J. Schreiner
Supervisor of ELL and
World Languages

The decision to implement Integrated Performance Assessments (IPAs) into the World Languages curriculum in Egg Harbor Township School District has had the most positive impact on our students' proficiency. That pivotal decision has positioned our students to be able to graduate from high school with the Seal of Biliteracy. Our students who study their language for a long sequence (6 or more years of the same language) routinely reach the Intermediate-Mid, Intermediate-High, or Advanced-Low proficiency level by their senior year of high school. This is possible because the students are accustomed to being assessed through IPAs. Right from their first experiences in language class, students use the language for communicative purposes. They read authentic texts and listen to authentic audio. They are in the habit of asking one another questions as part of every unit they study.

Teachers in the Egg Harbor Township School District work together in Professional Learning Communities (PLCs) to develop thematic units that are targeted to benchmark proficiency levels. Each thematic unit is written using a backward design format that incorporates authentic resources to develop students' proficiency in the three modes of communication: interpretive, interpersonal, and presentational. Learning objectives are presented as Can Do statements and summative assessments are IPAs.

As a result, students are very familiar with the concept of a performance assessment. They expect to use the target language in class and they understand that they will be assessed on their use of it. Many students come into high school planning to study their language for all four years so

that they can graduate with the Seal of Biliteracy. The use of IPAs on a regular basis sets them up for success on ACTFL's Assessment of Performance toward Proficiency in Languages (AAPPL). Student success on the Seal of Biliteracy assessment encourages other students to continue their language study so that they, too, can graduate with the Seal. This success has made such a positive impact the World Languages Department.

Ottoson Middle School, Arlington Public School, MA

Na Lu-Hogan
Chinese Middle School Instructor

I was hired by Arlington Public Schools (APS) in 2013 to teach high school and middle school Mandarin Chinese (Novice-Low to Intermediate-Mid). As a world language department, we started developing thematic units and IPAs the same year. I started implementing thematic units and IPAs with my students the following year. Over the course of 2013 to 2015, the APS World Language Department provided several training workshops on thematic units and IPAs from ACTFL. The process of developing thematic units and IPAs was bittersweet; I would spend hours on scouting the appropriate authentic materials for each unit. But the connections to the target language and culture that my students made through those materials were empowering. Each year, I would review a chosen piece of authentic material to see if it still best reflected the current culture and practice of the target language, Mandarin Chinese. If I could find a better authentic text, I would replace the original with it so that students have the most accurate access to the current use of the language and culture. Over the years, I have used a variety of websites as resources for finding authentic materials, including YouTube, hihilulu, Youku, and Yabla. When it comes to interpersonal assessments, I would distribute an iPad or an alternative device to pairs of students. The learners would then use Flipgrid to submit their work. To connect IPAs to the community, I would often have students review each others' work and provide feedback, using a list of questions designed by me as the guideline. This is the ninth year I have been implementing IPAs in my curriculum.

The impact of the thematic units and IPAs has been tremendous. My students converse exclusively in the target language well over 95% of the time. They discover Chinese culture that is embedded in those authentic materials by completing IPA tasks. They expand their perspectives through comparing and contrasting cultures. Furthermore, my favorite moments are catching students conversing and making jokes within and beyond the school setting, and hearing from parents that siblings having discreet conversations in Mandarin Chinese at home. I look forward to making more powerful impacts on students' language acquisition through the implementation of IPAs.

University of Pittsburgh, Pittsburgh, PA

Dr. Myriam Abdel-Malek
Arabic Instructor
Less-Commonly-Taught-Languages
Center

I was introduced to the Integrated Performance Assessment (IPA) in a foreign language testing and assessment course that was part of my Master of Arts in Education program at the University of Pittsburgh. Since I was simultaneously exploring the assessment of culture in another course, I decided to explore the possibility of assessing culture using the three modes of communication. The IPA seemed like a highly suitable tool, given its focus on the National Standards. During the semester following the assessment course, I was assigned to teach the "Readings in Arabic" course, a third year course at the university level. The course objective was to expose students to different genres of Arabic writing. I decided to use the IPA to explore the assessment of students' cultural competence. This required redesigning the course syllabus while at the same time meeting the course objective and my students' needs. Even though the aim of the course was third-year-level students, the students in the class were at different proficiency levels.

Before making any changes to the syllabus, I looked for a theme around which to develop a unit of study. Keeping in mind that it had to be interesting for my students and had to expose them to cultural aspects from Arab speaking countries, I chose the theme "Freedom of young men and women in the Arab world," which would take about four

weeks of class time. Coincidentally, I taught the course at the same time as the Arab Spring, which made it culturally and linguistically relevant and intriguing for my students.

The IPA impacted the way I approached designing the course. With the IPA in mind, thinking of what I wanted my students to achieve at the end of the unit of study was the first thing I addressed. This was aligned with the concept of backward design. Normally, I would have chosen different texts from different genres and planned my lessons and then decided on the objectives and the method of assessment. However, with the IPA in mind my objectives were clear:

1. Have students read and understand authentic texts around the theme of the topic and infer cultural aspects

2. Have students use interpersonal communication to express their understanding of the topic in a culturally appropriate manner

3. Have students prepare presentations related to the topic that showed their cultural understanding

The second step was designing the IPA. Knowing that I had students at different proficiency levels, I decided to assess them using the IPA Intermediate or Intermediate-High rubrics according to their levels. Here, the IPA allowed me to differentiate the assessment, thus meeting my students' needs. This would have been difficult otherwise. Moreover, the IPA rubrics allowed me to focus assessment specifically on students' cultural competence by adding two cultural categories on each of the rubrics. These components, in effect, assessed the extent to which students met the Cultures and Comparisons 4.2 standards in the context of this unit of study.

The third step was finding authentic reading texts that the students would work on in preparation for the IPA. Using the IPA influenced the choice of texts. Instead of looking for texts on different themes, using the IPA made the choice more focused. Thus it helped expose my students to different cultural perspectives on the same topic from a wide variety of authors and genres. Normally, I would have jumped from topic to topic and students would not have had the opportunity to expand their vocabulary and cultural understanding of one topic.

The fourth step was designing the in-class activities. With the IPA in mind and the choice of texts made, the activities fell naturally into place. Again, the IPA changed the way I looked at instructional activities. Knowing that students had to practice the three modes of communication and at the same time discover the authors' cultural perspectives, the choice of those activities was more focused. Moreover, the IPA impacted my feedback to my students. Previously, my feedback was focused on the correction of grammar and vocabulary. During the daily preparation for the IPA and the formative assessment linked to the IPA tasks, my feedback to my students was aimed at helping them improve their communication skills. Also, the IPA assessment-feedback cycle helped my students to prepare for each task.

In conclusion, the IPA impacted my syllabus design, allowed me to differentiate my assessment, and helped me give more focused feedback to my students. Because I am a firm believer that language and culture have to be taught as one entity, the IPA allowed me to address the culture goal and offered a tool with which to assess both language and culture through the three modes of communication. Overall, the experience with the IPA revealed that culture as language can be taught and assessed in relation to the context of a unit of study.

Edison Township School District, Edison, New Jersey

José Pan
Spanish High School Instructor

ACTFL's Integrated Performance Assessment (IPA) model has thoroughly transformed how World Language is taught in Edison. Prior to the implementation of the IPA model, instruction at Edison High School was based on the paradigm of teaching, testing, and hoping for the best. Accordingly, our department sought to improve on the preponderant simple, rote tasks that had no meaningful function or benefit when it came to real world communication. Our department's desire to make communication our fundamental goal drove us to start creating IPAs and implementing them in our curricula. While FLENJ (*Foreign Language Educators of New Jersey*) was not personally involved in our IPA training in Edison Schools, the organization did provide a lot of professional development workshops on the topic that

teachers from our department attended prior and during our transition over to use of the IPA model in our curricula.

Once we established curricular benchmarks, our next goal was to determine realistic expectations for students at each proficiency level. Defining expectations was the beginning of the transition toward eventually developing and incorporating IPAs into our elementary, middle, and high school curricula. A summative IPA is now the foundation of every thematic unit at every level of the World Language program in Edison. These IPAs enable our students to climb the proficiency scale by communicating authentically, as opposed to engaging in random and rote memorization of structures, grammatical points, and vocabulary.

Implementing IPAs in my classes has led to some planning changes in order to correctly implement the model. The biggest change was in the way we needed to think and plan using a backward design model. Prior to this, I never approached teaching a unit thinking about the end first in order to plan out lessons and assessments. It has completely changed the way I create curriculum units as well as teach them in class.

During the last several years, I have been using new tools to help with the implementation of the IPA in my classes. First and foremost, I use sites such as YouTube to find authentic video and audio selections to use in class for interpretive tasks. I have found it to be extremely useful and it is my go-to source for material I can incorporate in any of my classes. I have also found tools such as Audacity and Vocaroo extremely beneficial to help record interpersonal tasks. They have really helped cut down the time needed to obtain student speaking samples, and they offer the ability to have the recordings with me at all times to assess them and provide feedback whenever I have a free moment to do so.

One advantage of the IPA model is how well the thematic units created around each IPA lend themselves to the integration of culture, especially when teachers select solid, culturally valid interpretive selections as the centerpieces of each IPA. These units immerse students in the target cultures, helping them better appreciate the products, practices, and perspectives of people from outside the United States. The element of culture lends real-world meaning to the study of language. Presently, at Edison, all levels of Spanish, French, and Italian are anchored in IPA-driven thematic units.

Integrating the IPA into our curricula has been a challenging but rewarding process involving many hours of articulation, curriculum writing, benchmarking, IPA creation, and implementation. As a result of our adoption of the IPA model, students in Edison now engage in language learning at a much deeper level than they previously did, and consequently form more significant connections. Ultimately, they communicate more proficiently and enjoy mastering a second language.

South Carolina Virtual School Program

Dr. Tracy Seiler
President, South Carolina Classical Association
Latin Instructor, World Languages Team Leader

When the South Carolina State Department of Education implemented a state-wide assessment of world language programs at the high school level in 2007, the expectation was that all world language programs, including Latin, would be expected to utilize the Integrated Performance Assessment (IPA) model. Latin teachers across the state were terrified, and as President of the state classical association, I felt it was incumbent upon me to explore this concept. In addition, the high school at which I was then teaching was one of the first to be assessed, and as I looked over the IPA manual, I realized that Latin was not represented there and that we would need to develop a slightly different set of expectations for the three modes of communication.

Traditionally, Latin teachers were never trained to speak Latin, unless it was to recite a poem aloud in meter, so the interpersonal mode was a daunting task to most teachers in our state. Additionally, our aims are different from those of modern language teachers: Our primary goal is reading proficiency. However, recent developments in Latin pedagogy have challenged the idea that one does not converse in Latin. Cutting-edge college programs like that of Terence Tunberg at the University of Kentucky require conversational Latin, and summer immersion programs now abound.

With that in mind, we have revised our assumptions over the years. We now know that the practice of speaking and writing in Latin improves one's reading ability in the language, and to that end, I have designed my own courses here at the South Carolina Virtual School Program to include interpersonal communication using Twitter and Voicethread

in every lesson. Students are encouraged not to translate Latin into English, but to read texts for comprehension and discuss their ideas, sometimes in the target language. While most of my students' communication with me and their peers is asynchronous due to the online medium, I have had recent success using Skype for synchronous interpersonal communication in Latin, and much of it is voluntary on the part of the students.

As a result of using the language in this way, my students have become much better readers of Latin. In the years since I was introduced to the IPA model, I have come to realize that Latin is not so different after all, and that much of the IPA model can be used with very good results in the Latin classroom.

Providence Day School, Charlotte, NC

Mary Jo Adams
Lower School French and Spanish Teacher

Adopting integrated performance assessments (IPAs) has positively influenced our teaching and has completely changed the way we write curriculum, plan, teach, and assess. All of our lesson planning now starts with the end goal in mind, and that end goal is articulated by the final task requirements in each mode of communication. The ability to provide clear goals and Can Do statements has been invaluable to both our students and our teachers. The benefits of the IPA are numerous. Our teachers collaborate to create a shared common goal, we have greatly improved our student feedback loop, and we have seen a measurable improvement in our students' proficiency. In short, IPAs provide the context and framework to successfully guide our students on their path to proficiency and global competency.

In 2011, our school launched Phase 1 of a proficiency-based approach for our transitional kindergarten (TK)-5 elementary school language program. A lot of professional development and support went into this multi-phase, multi-year effort. Our goal was to begin purposeful language instruction in our Foreign Language in the Elementary Schools (FLES) program in order to build a foundation for continued world language learning throughout our students' elementary, middle school, and high school years. From the start, we were guided by the ACTFL Standards and Can Do statements, but were challenged to define and measure the proficiency destination that we were setting for our youngest learners.

In 2013, when *Implementing Integrated Performance Assessment* (Adair-Hauck et al., 2013) was published, a copy was purchased for each member of the department and our elementary level teachers made it their professional development goal to implement IPAs at the lower school level. Our goal of implementing IPAs led to a major paradigm shift in every aspect of our teaching process—the curriculum planning, the teaching, the assessment, and how we give student feedback.

Implementing IPAs focused our attention on teaching and assessing in the same manner. We "teach to the test" because the tests that we have created are task based, requiring our students to use the language they have learned in a meaningful way. The IPA destination guides our journey in all three modes, ensuring that our authentic and comprehensible input supports students' output and messaging.

As a result of establishing clear communicative goals for our units, we became more comfortable in reducing the amount of vocabulary we were presenting in order to focus time and practice on the language functions. At the same time, we improved upon how to incorporate authentic resources that were age and proficiency appropriate—seeing examples of how to adapt the task, rather than the text—whereas previously we had felt the need to create materials to fit our units, rather than scaffold our planning to prepare our students to get the most out of an authentic resource.

One of the most significant changes in using IPAs is our student feedback loop. No longer is our grading based on the quantity of vocabulary memorized, but rather on how well our students are able to use their language to complete a task. Our students now ask us, "Is this Novice-High?" rather than, "Is this an 'A'?" We then go on to coach them on how they can improve upon and level up their proficiency. Our older elementary students complete the feedback loop by adding their own reflections based on their performance.

IPAs are the beginning and the end. They launch our planning process and allow for so much creativity! We want our students to be able to exchange simple information, give opinions, and ask questions to obtain information. Knowing in advance the requirements of the end-of-unit tasks allows us to take our students on a trip with a clear understanding of the destination—and we have seen that a well planned trip encourages and motivates students to continue their language journey and adventure.

Glossary

Assessing Question: A question posed to determine the level at which the learner can perform without assistance.

Assisting Question: A question posed to support the learner in reaching a level of performance they cannot reach without assistance.

Authentic Assessment: Assessment that mirrors the tasks and challenges faced by individuals in the real world.

Authentic Materials/Texts: Oral, video, or printed materials/texts that have been produced by and for speakers of the target language and culture for non-instructional purposes, such as newspapers, magazines, books, television programs, radio broadcasts, websites.

Backward Design: An approach to the planning of instruction and learning that views the instructor as "designer" of assessment and instruction. In the approach, the designer (1) identifies desired results, (2) determines acceptable evidence, and (3) plans learning activities with the desired results and acceptable evidence in mind (Wiggins & McTighe, 2005).

Co-Constructive Approach to IPA Feedback: An approach to feedback recommended in the IPA Framework that involves the instructor and learner in a conversation about the learner's performance. The instructor and the learner review the learner's performance, rate the performance with the IPA rubrics, and engage in a discussion in which the two identify aspects of the learner's performance. Current performance is related to past performances. Likewise, goals are set for future learning. This approach to feedback is considered dialogic as opposed to monologic. In other words, the instructor and the learner are engaged in a dialogue regarding the learner's performance (Adair-Hauck & Troyan, 2013).

Cognitive Probes: Hints provided by the instructor that assist the learner in completing a task.

Comprehensibility: The degree to which a spoken or written message is understandable, on a continuum from only the instructor being able to understand it to speakers unaccustomed to interacting with language learners being able to understand it.

Concept Inferences: The interpretive process of figuring out an author's intent by "reading/listening between the lines."

Discourse: Use of either oral or written language in communication that goes beyond the sentence level to paragraphs and longer texts.

Domain: A feature or characteristic of a performance as defined in scoring rubrics.

Feedback: Information provided to learners about their strengths and areas that need improvement following or during a classroom activity or following an assessment. Feedback focuses on both meaning and linguistic accuracy.

Feedback Loop: A strategy by which the instructor provides learners with feedback on their performance after each of the three tasks in the IPA is completed, and before the next task is begun; this is an important feature of the IPA, which uses a cyclical approach to second language instruction and includes modeling, practicing, performing, and feedback phases.

Formative Instructional Practices (FIP): A framework for assessment and instruction from special education that guides instructors in enacting inclusive education in any content area using a set of key practices.

Impact: The degree to which a written or oral message maintains the attention of the reader or listener.

Information Gap: A type of paired activity in which one speaker has information that the other does not have and vice versa, creating a real need for them to provide and obtain information through negotiation of meaning.

Input: A visual, oral, or printed message in the target language that calls for interpretation or reaction.

Instructor: To be inclusive of world language teaching professionals across K-16 teaching contexts, the authors have used "instructor" instead of "teacher" throughout this book. However, in some cases, publications that are quoted or summarized required the use of "teacher" because a K-12 teacher was involved in a particular study or was the target audience of the publication. In other cases, it was the term used by the author of a particular section, such as in Chapters 5 and 8.

Integrated Performance Assessment (IPA): A theme-based assessment that features a series of tasks in the three modes of communication that support and build on one another. For example, a learner might read an authentic text on the importance of maintaining good health (interpretive communication), interview classmates on their views about good health (interpersonal communication), and create an oral public service announcement with tips on ways to stay healthy (presentational communication).

Integrative Assessment: Assessment that combines the three modes of communication in a way that normally occurs in real-world communication.

Language Control: A characteristic of speech or writing that refers to the degree of accuracy, form, and fluency.

Language Functions: Language tasks that the learner is able to handle in a consistent, comfortable, sustained, and spontaneous manner.

Learner: The authors have chosen to use "learner" throughout to focus on the identity of learners and the potential that they have as language users in learning contexts. However, in some cases, publications that are quoted or summarized required the use of "student" because it was the term used in the original publication. In other cases, it was the term used by the author of a particular section, such as in Chapter 8.

Interpretive Comprehension: The ability to go beyond the literal meaning of an oral or printed text to identify word inferences, concept inferences, author/cultural perspectives, and the organizing principle(s) of the text.

Literal Comprehension: The ability to identify key words, main ideas, and supporting details from an oral or printed text.

Modes of Communication: The three ways in which communication is characterized, emphasizing the context and purpose of communication:

> **Interpersonal:** Individuals exchange information and negotiate meaning orally, whether face-to-face, by telephone, or online, or in writing through personal notes, letters, texting, or social media.

> **Interpretive:** A reader or listener is engaged in understanding the meaning of oral, written, or other cultural texts (including film, radio, internet, television, newspapers, magazines, or literature) when the author of these texts is not present and meaning cannot be negotiated.

> **Presentational:** Individuals engage in one-way oral, written, or multimodal communication (such as reports, speeches, or articles) that presents information to an audience for interpretation with no possibility of negotiating meaning.

Multimodality: The view of language use that considers all modes of interaction—including text, visual, gestural, and others—as part of communicative and language learning processes.

Negotiation of Meaning: A form of interaction in which individuals work to understand each other and be understood through verbal or gestural requests for clarification, comprehension checking, and confirmation checking, such as "Could you repeat that?" "What do you mean by…?" "So you're saying…?"

Organizing Principle(s): The manner in which an oral or printed text is organized, such as chronological order, pros and cons, cause/effect, compare/contrast, story telling, problem and solution.

Proficiency: One's ability to use the language effectively and appropriately in real-life situations as measured by criteria including global tasks and functions, context/content, accuracy, and text type.

Proficiency-oriented Instruction: Instruction that focuses on the development of effective communication in all three communicative modes.

Responsive Assistance: The help that the instructor provides to learners to enable them to perform tasks that they may not yet have the knowledge or ability to do on their own. Also called Guided Assistance.

Rubrics: Written and shared criteria for judging performance that indicate the qualities by which levels of performance can be differentiated, and that anchor judgments about the degree of success on a learner assessment.

Scaffolding: The process by which an "expert" and a "novice" interact in a problem-solving task. The expert takes control of those portions of the task that are beyond the novice's current level of competence, thus allowing the novice to focus on the elements within their range of ability.

Target Culture: The culture of the people who speak the language being learned, including their perspectives, practices, and products.

Target Language: The world language being learned in the classroom.

Text Type: The type of text used in an interpretive task at each performance level (Novice, Intermediate, Advanced) that exemplifies a certain level of linguistic complexity and topic familiarity; also refers to the quantity and organization of language discourse used by a speaker or writer (from word to phrase to sentence to connected sentences to paragraph to extended discourse).

Washback Effect: The influence a test or assessment has on the learning environment. Aspects of the learning environment include approach to instruction, assessment, curricular materials, student perceptions of learning, and learner performance on the test or assessment.

Word Inferences: The interpretive process of figuring out the meaning of unfamiliar words by using the context.

Zone of Proximal Development (ZPD): A concept defined by Vygotsky (1978) as "the distance between the learner's actual developmental level as determined by independent problem-solving and the level of potential development as determined through problem-solving under adult guidance or in collaboration with more capable peers" (p. 86).

References

Abdel-Malek, M. (2019). Writing recounts of habitual events: Investigating a genre-based approach. *Foreign Language Annals*, 52, 373–387. https://doi.org/10.1111/flan.12383

Abdel-Malek, M. (2020). Empowering Arabic learners to make meaning: A genre-based approach. *System, 94*. https://doi.org/10.1016/j.system.2020.102329

Abraham, L. B., & Williams, L. (2009). The discussion forum as a component of a technology-enhanced integrated performance assessment. In L. B. Abraham & L. Williams (Eds.), *Electronic discourse in language learning and language teaching* (pp. 319–343). Benjamins.

Adair-Hauck, B. (2003). Providing responsive assistance using the IPA feedback loop. In E. W. Glisan, B. Adair-Hauck, K. Koda, P. Sandrock, & E. Swender (Eds.), *The ACTFL integrated performance manual* (pp. 11–15). ACTFL.

Adair-Hauck, B., Glisan, E., Koda, K., Swender, E., & Sandrock, P. (2006). The integrated performance assessment (IPA): Connecting assessment to instruction and learning. *Foreign Language Annals*, 39(3), 359–382. https://doi.org/10.1111/j.1944-9720.2006.tb02894.x

Adair-Hauck, B., Glisan, E. W., & Troyan, F. J. (2013). *Implementing integrated performance assessment.* ACTFL.

Adair-Hauck, B., & Troyan, F. J. (2013). A descriptive and co-constructive approach to integrated performance assessment feedback. *Foreign Language Annals*, 46, 23–44. https://doi.org/10.1111/flan.12017

Allen, E., Bernhardt, E. B., Berry, M. T., & Demel, M. (1988). Comprehension and text genre: An analysis of secondary foreign language readers. *The Modern Language Journal*, 72, 63–72. https://doi.org/10.1111/j.1540-4781.1988.tb04178.x

Altstaedter, L., & Krosl, M. (2018). Perceptions of integrated performance assessments among beginning Spanish college students: A preliminary study. *Journal of Foreign Language Teaching and Applied Linguistics*, 5(2), 99–113.

American Council on the Teaching of Foreign Languages (ACTFL). (1982). *ACTFL provisional proficiency guidelines.*

American Council on the Teaching of Foreign Languages (ACTFL). (1998). *ACTFL performance guidelines for K–12 learners.*

American Council on the Teaching of Foreign Languages (ACTFL). (2012a). *ACTFL performance descriptors for language learners.*

American Council on the Teaching of Foreign Languages (ACTFL). (2012b). *ACTFL proficiency guidelines–speaking, writing, listening and reading*, 3rd ed.

American Council on the Teaching of Foreign Languages (ACTFL). (2017). *2017 NCSSFL-ACTFL can-do statements.* https://www.actfl.org/resources/ncssfl-actfl-can-do-statements

Annenberg Learner. (n.d.). Assessment strategies. https://www.learner.org/series/teaching-foreign-languages-k-12-a-library-of-classroom-practices/overview-introduction-to-the-library/overview-assessment-strategies/

Anya, U. (2017). *Racialized identities in second language learning: Speaking blackness in Brazil*. Routledge. https://doi.org/10.4324/9781315682280

Anya, U., & Randolph, L. J. (Oct/Nov, 2019). Diversifying language educators and learners. *The Language Educator*. https://dev.aisa.africa/wp-content/uploads/resources/language/all-language/diversifying-language-educators-and-learners-250820.pdf

Bachman, L. F. (2007). What is the construct? The dialectic of abilities and contexts in defining constructs in language assessment. In J. Fox, M. Wesche, & D. Bayliss (Eds.), *What are we measuring? Language testing reconsidered*. University of Ottawa Press.

Ball, D. L., & Forzani, F. M. (2009). The work of teaching and the challenge for teacher education. *Journal of Teacher Education*, 60, 497–511. https://www.doi.org/10.1177/0022487109348479

Bellon, J. J., Bellon, E. C., & Blank, M. A. (1992). *Teaching from a research knowledge base: A development and renewal process*. Macmillan.

Bernhardt, E. B. (1991). A psycholinguistic perspective on second language literacy. *Association Internationale de Linguistique Apliquée Review, 8*, 31–44.

Bernhardt, E. B. (1995). Teaching literature or teaching students? *ADFL Bulletin*, 26(2), 5–6.

Bernhardt, E. B. (2005). Progress and procrastination in second language reading. *Annual Review of Applied Linguistics*, 25, 133–150. https://doi.org/10.1017/S0267190505000073

Bernhardt, E. B. (2008). Systemic and systematic assessment as a keystone for language and literature programs. *ADFL Bulletin, 40*(1), 14–19.

Black, P., & Wiliam, D. (1998). Inside the black box: Raising standards through classroom assessment. *Phi Delta Kappan, 80*(2), 139–148. https://doi.org/10.1177/003172171009200119

Blackwell, L. S., Trzesniewski, K. H., & Dweck, C. S. (2007). Implicit theories of intelligence predict achievement across an adolescent transition: A longitudinal study and an intervention. *Child Development*, 78, 246–263. https://doi.org/10.1111/j.1467-8624.2007.00995.x

California Department of Education. (2020). *World languages framework for California public schools, kindergarten through grade twelve*. https://www.cde.ca.gov/ci/fl/cf/

California State Board of Education. (2019). *World languages standards*. https://www.cde.ca.gov/be/st/ss/worldlanguage.asp

Chan, P. E., Konrad, M., Gonzalez, V., Peters, M. T., & Ressa, V. A. (2014). The critical role of feedback in formative instructional practices. *Intervention in School and Clinic, 50*(2), 96–104. https://doi.org/10.1177/1053451214536044

Council of Europe. (2001). *Common European framework of reference for languages: Learning, teaching, assessment.* https://rm.coe.int/1680459f97

Council of Europe. (2020). *CEFR Global Scale.* https://www.coe.int/en/web/common-european-framework-reference-languages/table-1-cefr-3.3-common-reference-levels-global-scale

Crane, C., & Malloy, M. (2021). The development of temporal-spatial meaning in personal recounts of beginning L2 writers of German. *System, 99.* https://doi.org/10.1016/j.system.2021.102498

Darhower, M. A. (2014). Literary discussions and advanced-superior speaking functions in the undergraduate language program. *Hispania, 97,* 396–412. https://doi.org/10.1353/hpn.2014.0081

Darhower, M. A., & Smith-Sherwood, D. (2021). Bridging the language and literature divide via Integrated Performance Assessment in an introductory Hispanic literature course. *Hispania, 104,* 395–413. https://doi.org/10.1353/hpn.2021.0093

Darhower, M. A., & Smith-Sherwood, D. (2023). Meeting them where they are: Using differentiated integrated performance assessments to build interpersonal speaking skills in the L2 literature class. In Echevarría, M. (Ed.) *Rehumanizing the language and literature curriculum,* (pp. 159-184). Peter Lang.

Davin, K. J., & Heineke, A. J. (2022). *Promoting multilingualism in schools: A framework for implementing the Seal of Biliteracy.* ACTFL.

Davin, K. J., Rampert, T., & Hammerand, A. (2014). Converting data to knowledge: One district's experience using large-scale proficiency assessment. *Foreign Language Annals, 47,* 241–260. https://www.doi.org/10.1111/flan.12081

Davin, K. J., Troyan, F. J., Donato, R., & Hellmann, A. (2011). Research on the integrated performance assessment in an early foreign language learning program. *Foreign Language Annals, 44,* 605–625. https://doi.org/10.1111/j.1944-9720.2011.01153.x

Deane, P. (2020). Building and justifying interpretations of texts: A key practice in the English language arts. *ETS Research Report Series ISSN 2330-8516.* Educational Testing Service. https://www.doi.org/10.1002/ets2.12304

Donato, R., & Brooks, F. B. (2004). Literary discussions and advanced speaking functions: Researching the (dis)connection. *Foreign Language Annals, 37,* 183–199. https://doi.org/10.1111/j.1944-9720.2004.tb02192.x

Donato, R., & Tucker, G. R. (2010). *A tale of two schools: Developing sustainable early foreign language programs.* Multilingual Matters.

Dristas, V. M., & Grisenti, G. (1995). Motivation: Does interest influence reading and speaking proficiency in second language acquisition? Unpublished manuscript.

Duff, P. (2003). Intertextuality and hybrid discourses: The infusion of pop culture in educational discourse. *Linguistics and Education, 14,* 231–276. https://doi.org/10.1016/j.linged.2004.02.005

Dweck, C. S. (2006). *Mindset: The new psychology of success.* Random House.

Dweck, C. S. (2007). Boosting achievement with messages that motivate. *Education Canada, 47*(2), 6–10.

Eddy, J., & Bustamante, C. (2020). Closing the pre- and in-service gap: Perceptions and implementation of the IPA during student teaching. *Foreign Language Annals, 53*, 634–656. https://doi.org/10.1111/flan.12481

Eigler, F. (2001). Designing a third-year German course for a content-oriented, task-based curriculum. *Die Unterrichtspraxis/Teaching German, 34*(2), 107–118.

Ennser-Kananen, J. (2016). A pedagogy of pain: New directions for world language education. *The Modern Language Journal, 100*, 556–64. https://doi.org/10.1111/modl.1_12337

Freire, P. (2018). *Pedagogy of the oppressed: 50th anniversary edition.* Bloomsbury Academic.

Fuchs, D., & Fuchs, L. S. (2006). Introduction to response-to-intervention: What, why, and how valid is it? *Reading Research Quarterly, 41*, 93–99. https://doi.org/10.1598/RRQ.41.1.4

Gacs, A., Goertler, S., & Spasova, S. (2020). Planned online language education versus crisis-prompted online language teaching: Lessons for the future. *Foreign Language Annals, 53*(2), 380–392. https://doi.org/10.1111/flan.12460

Galloway, V. (1998). Constructing cultural realities: "Facts" and frameworks of association. In J. Harper, M. Lively, & M. Williams (Eds.), *The coming of age of the profession* (pp. 129–140). Heinle & Heinle.

García, O. (2009). *Bilingual education in the 21st century: A global perspective.* Wiley Blackwell.

Gironzetti, E., & Lacorte, M. (Eds.). (2023). *The Routledge handbook of multiliteracies, multimodality and interdisciplinarity in Spanish language teaching.* Routledge.

Glisan, E.W. (2010). Envisioning the big picture of program design. *The Language Educator, 5*(4), 7.

Glisan, E. W., Adair-Hauck, B., Koda, K., Sandrock, S. P., & Swender, E. (2003). *ACTFL integrated performance assessment.* ACTFL.

Glisan, E. W., & Donato, R. (2017). *Enacting the work of language instruction: High-leverage teaching practices, vol. 1.* ACTFL.

Glisan, E. W., & Donato, R. (2021). *Enacting the work of language instruction: High-leverage teaching practices, vol. 2.* ACTFL.

Glisan, E. W., Uribe, D., & Adair-Hauck, B. (2007). Research on integrated performance assessment at the post-secondary level: Student performance across the modes of communication. *The Canadian Modern Language Review, 64*, 39–68. https://doi.org/10.3138/cmlr.64.1.039

Glynn, C., Wesely, P., & Wassell, B. (2018). *Words and actions: Teaching languages through the lens of social justice.* (2nd ed.). ACTFL.

Graham-Day, K. J., Fishley, K. M., Konrad, M., Peters, M. T., & Ressa, V. A. (2014). Formative instructional practices: How core content teachers can borrow ideas from IDEA. *Intervention in School and Clinic, 50*(2), 69–75. https://doi.org/10.1177/1053451214536041

Graham-Day, K. J., Kaplan, C. S., Irish, C., & Troyan, F. J. (2020). Inclusive assessment practices: Using formative instructional practices to support the needs of all students. In A. Howley, S. Kroeger, B. Hansen, & C. Faiella (Eds.), *Inclusive education: A systematic perspective,* (pp. 135–148). Information Age.

Gutiérrez, K., Buquesdano-López, P., & Alvarez, C. (1999). Building a culture of collaboration through hybrid language practices. *Theory into Practice, 38*(2), 87–93. https://doi.org/10.1080/00405849909543837

Hafner, C. A., Yee, W., & Ho, J. (2020). Assessing digital multimodal composing in second language writing: Towards a process-based model. *Journal of Second Language Writing, 47*, 1–14. https://doi.org/10.1016/j.jslw.2020.100710

Halverson, R., Pritchett, R. B., & Watson, J. G. (2007). *Formative feedback systems and the new instructional leadership* (WCER Working Paper No. 2007-3). University of Wisconsin–Madison, Wisconsin Center for Education Research. http://www.wcer.wisc.edu/publications/workingPapers/papers.php

Hamilton, L. (2003). Assessment as a policy tool. *Review of Research in Education, 27*, 25–68. https://doi.org/10.3102/0091732X027001025

Hammadou Sullivan, J. A. (2002). Advanced foreign language readers' inferencing. In J. A. Hammadou Sullivan (Ed.), *Literacy and the second language learner* (pp. 217–238). Information Age.

Hattie, J. (2008). *Visible learning: A synthesis of over 800 meta-analyses relating to achievement.* Routledge.

Hattie, J., & Clarke, S. (2019). *Visible learning: Feedback.* Routledge.

Hattie, J., & Timperley, H. (2007). *The power of feedback. Review of Educational Research, 77*, 81–112. https://doi.org/10.3102/003465430298487

Henshaw, F. G., & Hawkins, M. D. (2022). *Common ground: Second language acquisition theory goes to the classroom.* Hackett.

Herazo, J. D. (2020). Mediating spoken meaning-making in genre-based lessons: The role of metalinguistic concepts. *System, 96.* https://doi.org/10.1016/j.system.2020.102398

Kang, S. (2022). Integrated performance assessment and KSL. In A. S. Byon & D. O. Pyun (Eds.), *The Routledge handbook of Korean as a second language* (pp. 518–539). Routledge. https://doi.org/10.4324/9781003034704-31

Katz Bourns, S., Krueger, C., & Mills, N. (2020). *Perspectives on teaching language and content.* Yale University Press.

Kissau, S., & Adams. M. J. (2016). Instructional decision making and IPAs: Assessing the modes of communication. *Foreign Language Annals, 49*, 105–23. https://doi.org/10.1111/flan.12184

Kleinert, H. L., Cloyd, E., Rego, M., & Gibson, J. (2007). Students with disabilities: Yes, foreign language instruction is important. *Teaching Exceptional Children, 39*, 24–29. https://doi.org/10.1177/004005990703900304

Kluger, A. N., & DeNisi, A. (1996). The effects of feedback interventions on performance: A historical review, a meta-analysis, and a preliminary feedback intervention theory. *Psychological Bulletin, 119*, 254–284. https://doi.org/10.1037/0033-2909.119.2.254

Kress, G., & Van Leeuwen, T. (2001). *Multimodal discourse: The modes and media of contemporary communication.* Arnold Publishers.

Kress, G., & Van Leeuwen, T. (2021). *Reading images: The grammar of visual design.* Arnold Publishers.

Lave, J., & Wenger, E. (1991). *Situated learning: Legitimate peripheral participation.* Cambridge University Press.

Lee, J. F., & Butler, Y. G. (2020). Reconceptualizing language assessment literacy: Where are language learners? *TESOL Quarterly, 54*, 1098–1111. https://doi.org/10.1002/tesq.576

Lee, J. F., & VanPatten, B. (1995). *Making communicative language teaching happen* (2nd ed.). McGraw-Hill.

Leung, C., Davison, C., East, M., Evans, M., Green, A., Hamp-Lyons, L., Liu, L., & Purpura, J. E. (2018). Using assessment to promote learning: Clarifying constructs, theories, and practices. In J. McE. Davis, J. M. Norris, M. E. Malone, T. McKay, & Y. A. Son (Eds.), *Useful assessment and evaluation in language education*, 75–91. Georgetown University Press.

Liskin-Gasparro, J. E. (1984). The ACTFL proficiency guidelines: A historical perspective. In T. V. Higgs (Ed.), *Teaching for proficiency: The organizing principle.* ACTFL.

Liskin-Gasparro, J. E. (2003). The ACTFL proficiency guidelines and the oral proficiency interview: A brief history and analysis of their survival. *Foreign Language Annals, 36*, 483–490. https://doi.org/10.1111/j.1944-9720.2003.tb02137.x

Lomicka, L., & Lord, G. (2018). Ten years after the MLA report: What has changed in foreign language departments? *ADFL Bulletin, 44*(2), 116–120. https://doi.org/10.1632/adfl.44.2.116

Lou, N. M., & Noels, K. (2019). Promoting growth in foreign and second language education: A research agenda for mindsets in language learning and teaching. *System, 86.* https://doi.org/10.1016/j.system.2019.102126

Loyola, S. W. (2014, June 18). Authentic activities for the world language classroom. Edutopia Teaching Strategies. https://www.edutopia.org/blog/authentic-activities-world-language-classroom-sarah-loyola

Mahoney, K. (2017). *The assessment of emergent bilinguals: Supporting English learners.* Multilingual Matters.

Malone, M. E. (2013). The essentials of assessment literacy: Contrasts between testers and users. *Language Testing, 30*, 329–344. https://doi.org/10.1177/0265532213480129

Mantero, M. (2002). *The reasons we speak: Cognition and discourse in the second language classroom.* Bergin & Garvey.

Martel, J. (2018). Postsecondary students' and instructors' evaluative comments about ACTFL's integrated performance assessment. *Journal of Applied Language Learning, 28*(1), 1–18.

Martel, J. (2019). Washback of ACTFL's integrated performance assessment in an intensive summer language program at the tertiary level. *Language Education & Assessment, 2*(2), 57–69. https://doi.org/10.29140/lea.v2n2.105

Martel, J. (2021). Designing interpretive communication activities in Canvas. *The French Review, 94*(3), 63–67. https://doi.org/10.1353/tfr.2021.0009

Martel, J. (2022). *Moving beyond the grammatical syllabus: Practical strategies for content-based curriculum design.* Routledge.

Martel, J., & Bailey, K. M. (2016). Exploring the trajectory of an educational innovation: Instructors' attitudes toward IPA implementation in a postsecondary intensive summer language program. *Foreign Language Annals, 49,* 530–543. https://doi.org/10.1111/flan.12210

Martin-Jones, M., & Jones, K. E. (2001). *Multilingual literacies: Reading and writing different worlds.* John Benjamins.

McLeskey, J., & Brownell, M. (2015). High-leverage practices and teacher preparation in special education (Document No. PR-1). http://ceedar.education.ufl.edu/wp-content/uploads/2016/05/High-Leverage-Practices-and-Teacher-Preparation-in-Special-Education.pdf

McNamara, T. (2001). Language assessment as social practice: Challenges for research. *Language Testing, 18,* 334–399. https://doi.org/10.1177/026553220101800402

Miranda, L., & Troyan, F. J. (2022). Interrogating racial ideologies: Enabling antiracist world language learning via IPA. *The Language Educator, 17*(1), 22–26.

MLA Ad Hoc Committee on Foreign Languages. (2007). *Foreign languages and higher education: New structures for a changed world.* Modern Language Association.

Moje, E. B., Afflerbach, P., Enciso, P., & Lesaux, N. K. (2020). *Handbook of reading research* (vol. V). Routledge.

Muñoz, A. P., & Álvarez, M. E. (2010). Washback of an oral assessment system in the EFL classroom. *Language Testing, 27*(1), 33–49. https://doi.org/10.1177/0265532209347148

Nance, K. (2010). *Teaching literature in the languages: Expanding the literary circle through student engagement.* Prentice Hall.

National Council on Education Standards and Testing. (1992). *Raising standards for American education.* https://eric.ed.gov/?id=ED338721

National Standards Collaborative Board. (2015). *World-readiness standards for learning languages,* 4th ed. ACTFL.

National Standards in Foreign Language Education Project (NSFLEP). (1996, 1999, 2006). *Standards for foreign language learning in the 21st century (SFLL).* Allen Press.

New York State Education Department. (2021). *New York State learning standards for world languages.* http://www.nysed.gov/common/nysed/files/programs/world-languages/nys-learning-standards-for-world-languages-2021.pdf

Oguro, Y. (2008). *Presentation of culture in English-as-a-foreign-language reading textbooks in Japan.* Unpublished doctoral dissertation, Virginia Tech, Blacksburg, VA.

Ohio Department of Education. (2020). *Ohio's learning standards for world languages and cultures.* https://education.ohio.gov/Topics/Learning-in-Ohio/Foreign-Language

Ohio Department of Education. (2021). *OTES 2.0 for world languages and cultures.* http://education.ohio.gov/Topics/Learning-in-Ohio/Foreign-Language/OTES-Guidance-for-World-Languages

Paesani, K., & Allen, H. (2012). Beyond the language-content divide: Research on advanced foreign language instruction at the postsecondary level. *Foreign Language Annals, 45*(S1), S54–S75. https://doi.org/10.1111/j.1944-9720.2012.01179.x

Paesani, K., Allen, H., & Dupuy, B. (2016). *A multiliteracies framework for collegiate foreign language teaching.* Pearson.

Phillips, J. K. (2006). Assessment now and into the future. In A. L. Heining-Boynton (Ed.), *2005-2015: Realizing our vision of languages for all* (pp. 75–103). Pearson.

President's Commission on Foreign Language and International Studies. (1979). *Strength through wisdom: A critique of U.S. capability.* https://doi.org/10.1111/j.1540-4781.1980.tb05167.x

Pryor, J., & Torrance, H. (2000). Questioning the three bears: The social construction of classroom assessment. In A. Filer (Ed.), *Assessment: Social practice and social product* (pp. 110–128). Oxford: Routledge.

Resnick, L. B., & Resnick, D. P. (1992). Assessing the thinking curriculum: New tools for educational reform. In B. R. Gifford & M. C. O'Connor (Eds.), *Changing assessment: Alternative views of aptitude, achievement, and instruction* (pp. 37–75). Kluwer.

Rifkin, B. (2003). Oral proficiency learning outcomes and curricular design. *Foreign Language Annals, 36*, 582–588. https://doi.org/10.1111/j.1944-9720.2003.tb02148.x

Rogoff, B. (1990). *Apprenticeship in learning.* Oxford University Press.

Rogoff, B. (1994). Developing understanding of the idea of communities of learning. *Mind, Culture, and Activity, 1*, 209–229.

Rogoff, B. (2003). *The cultural nature of human development.* Oxford University Press.

Russell, V., & Murphy-Judy, K. (2020). *Teaching language online: A guide to designing, developing, and delivering online, blended, and flipped language courses.* Routledge. https://doi.org/10.4324/9780429426483

Ryshina-Pankova, M. V. (2016). Scaffolding advanced literacy in the foreign language classroom: Implementing a genre-driven content-based approach. In L. Cammarata (Ed.), *Content-based foreign language teaching: Curriculum and pedagogy for developing advanced thinking and literacy skills* (pp. 51–76). Routledge.

Sadler, D. R. (1989). Formative assessment and the design of instructional systems. *Instructional Science, 18*, 199–144. https://doi.org/10.1007/BF00117714

Sandrock, P. (2010). *The keys to assessing language performance.* ACTFL.

Sapienza, B., Donato, R., & Tucker, G. R. (2006, October). Learning a second language: A district-wide foreign language program reaches the middle school. *The Language Educator, 1*, 24–27.

Schmitt, N., Jiang, X., & Grabe, W. (2011). The percentage of words known in a text and reading comprehension. *The Modern Language Journal, 95*, 26–43. https://doi.org/10.1111/j.1540-4781.2011.01146.x

Scott, V. (2001). An applied linguist in the literature classroom. *The French Review, 74*(3), 538–549.

Scott, V., & Tucker, H. (Eds.). (2002). *SLA and the literature classroom: Fostering dialogues.* Heinle.

Sedor, N. (2020). Investigating the integrated performance assessment (IPA) in university classrooms (Publication No. 27995891) [Doctoral dissertation, State University of New York at Buffalo]. ProQuest Dissertations Publishing.

Shepard, L. A. (2000). The role of assessment in a learning culture. *Educational Researcher, 29*(7), 4–14. https://doi.org/10.3102/0013189X029007004

Shepard, L. A. (2003). Reconsidering large-scale assessment to heighten its relevance to learning. In J. M. Atkin & J. E. Coffey (Eds.), *Everyday assessment in the science classroom: Science educators' essay collection* (pp. 121–146). National Science Teachers Association Press.

Shin, D.-S., Cimasko, T., & Yi, Y. (2020). Development of metalanguage for multimodal composing: A case study of an L2 writer's design of multimedia texts. *Journal of Second Language Writing, 47*, 1–14. https://doi.org/10.1016/j.jslw.2020.100714

Shrum, J. L., & Glisan, E. W. (2016). *Teacher's handbook: Contextualized language instruction* (5th ed.). Heinle Cengage Learning.

Smith-Sherwood, D. (2020). Unamuno's *San Manuel Bueno, Mártir*: An integrated performance assessment approach. In Álvarez-Castro, L. (Ed.), *Approaches to teaching the works of Miguel de Unamuno* (pp. 206–212). Modern Language Association.

Smith-Sherwood, D., & Rhodes, S. (2019). Introduction to Hispanic literatures and the impact of IPA-informed instruction on student writing proficiency in the presentational mode: Findings from a pilot SoTL study. *MIFLC Review, 19*, 13–56.

Stiggins, R., Arter, J., Chappuis, J., & Chappuis, S. (2007). *Classroom assessment for student learning: Doing it right—using it well.* Pearson Prentice Hall.

Sultana, N. (2018). Investigating the relationship between washback and curriculum alignment: A literature review. *Canadian Journal for New Scholars in Education, 9*(2), 151–158.

Supovitz, J. A., & Klein, V. (2003). *Mapping a course for improved student learning: How innovative schools systematically use student performance data to guide improvement.* Consortium for Policy Research in Education, University of Pennsylvania.

Swaffar, J., Arens, K., & Byrnes, H. (1991). *Reading for meaning.* Prentice Hall.

Swanson, P., & Goulette, E. (2018). The criticality of the integrated performance assessment in the world language edTPA. In P. Swanson & S. Hildebrandt (Eds.), *Researching edTPA promises and problems: Perspectives from English as an additional language* (pp. 201–220). Information Age.

Tedick, D., & Cammarata, L. (2012). Content and language integration in K–12 contexts: Student outcomes, teacher practices, and stakeholder perspectives. *Foreign Language Annals, 45*(S1), S28–S53. https://doi.org/10.1111/j.1944-9720.2012.01178.x

Tedick, D., & Walker, C. (1994). Second language teacher education: The problems that plague us. *Modern Language Journal, 78*(3), 300–312. https://doi.org/10.1111/j.1540-4781.1994.tb02044.x

Tharp, R. G., & Gallimore, R. (1988). *Rousing minds to life: Teaching, learning and schooling in social context.* Cambridge University Press.

Thoms, J. J. (2012). Classroom discourse in foreign language classrooms: A review of the literature. *Foreign Language Annals, 45*(S1), S8–S27. https://doi.org/10.1111/j.1944-9720.2012.01177.x

Troyan, F. J. (2008). Being authentic: Assessing standards-based tasks in a content-based curriculum. *The Language Educator, 3*(4), 52–54.

Troyan, F. J. (Ed.). (2021). *Genre in world language education: Contextualized assessment and learning.* Routledge. https://doi.org/10.4324/9780429321009

Troyan, F., Davin, K., & Donato, R. (2013). Exploring a practice-based approach to foreign language teacher preparation: A work in progress. *Canadian Modern Language Review, 69*(2), 154–180. https://doi.org/10.3138/cmlr.1523

Tunstall, P., & Gipps, C. (1996). Teacher feedback to young children in formative assessment: A typology. *British Educational Research Journal, 22,* 389–404. https://doi.org/10.1080/0141192960220402

Vygotsky, L. (1978). *Mind in society.* Harvard University Press.

Waltz, J. (1996). The classroom dynamics of information-gap activities. *Foreign Language Annals, 29,* 481–494. https://doi.org/10.1111/j.1944-9720.1996.tb01259.x

Warner, C., & Dupuy, B. (2018). Moving toward multiliteracies in foreign language teaching: Past and present perspectives… and beyond. *Foreign Language Annals, 51,* 116–128. https://doi.org/10.1111/flan.12316

Wassell, B., & Glynn, C. (Eds.). (2022). *Transforming world language teaching and teacher education for equity and justice: Pushing boundaries in US contexts.* Multilingual Matters.

Watzinger-Tharp, J., Tharp, D. S., & Rubio, F. (2021). Sustaining dual language immersion: Partner language outcomes in a statewide program. *The Modern Language Journal, 105,* 194–217. https://www.doi.org/10.1111/modl.12694

Wiggins, G. (1993). *Assessing student performance.* Jossey-Bass.

Wiggins, G. (1998). *Educative assessment.* Jossey-Bass.

Wiggins, G. (2012). *Seven keys to effective feedback.* Association for Supervision and Curriculum Development. https://www.ascd.org/el/articles/seven-keys-to-effective-feedback

Wiggins, G., & McTighe, J. (2005). *Understanding by design.* Association for Supervision and Curriculum Development.

Wight, M. C. S. (2015). Students with learning disabilities in the foreign language learning environment and the practice of exemption. *Foreign Language Annals, 48,* 39–55. https://doi.org/10.1111/flan.12122

Young, D. J. (1999). Linguistic simplification of SL reading material: Effective instructional practice? *The Modern Language Journal, 83,* 350–366. https://doi.org/10.1111/0026-7902.00027

Zapata, G. C. (2016). University students' perceptions of integrated performance assessment and the connection between classroom learning and assessment. *Foreign Language Annals, 49*, 93–104. https://doi.org/10.1111/flan.12176

Zapata, G. C. (2018a). A match made in heaven: An introduction to 'Learning by Design' and its role in heritage language education. In G. C. Zapata & M. Lacorte (Eds.), *Multiliteracies pedagogy and language learning: Teaching Spanish to heritage speakers* (pp. 1–26). Palgrave Macmillan.

Zapata, G. C. (2018b). The role of digital Learning by Design instructional materials in the development of Spanish heritage learners' literacy skills. In G. Zapata & M. Lacorte (Eds.), *Multiliteracies pedagogy and language learning: Teaching Spanish to heritage speakers* (pp. 67–106). Palgrave Macmillan.

Zapata, G. C., & Lacorte, M. (Eds.). (2018). *Multiliteracies pedagogy and language learning: Teaching Spanish to heritage speakers*. Palgrave Macmillan.

Zapata, G. C., & Ribota, A. (2021). Open educational resources in heritage and L2 Spanish classrooms: Design, development and implementation. In C. S. Blythe & J. J. Thoms (Eds.), *Open education in second language learning and teaching* (pp. 35–56). Multilingual Matters.

Zhang, X. (Under review). Motivational dynamics of intermediate Chinese learners in a COVID-induced remote IPA-informed CSL Curriculum: A case study from a CDST lens. *Chinese Journal for Applied Linguistics*.

Zwiers, J. (2013). *Building academic language: Essential practices for content classrooms, grades 5–12*. John Wiley & Sons.

Appendix A
World-Readiness Standards for Learning Languages

GOAL AREAS	STANDARDS		
COMMUNICATION Communicate effectively in more than one language in order to function in a variety of situations and for multiple purposes	**Interpersonal Communication:** Learners interact and negotiate meaning in spoken, signed, or written conversations to share information, reactions, feelings, and opinions.	**Interpretive Communication:** Learners understand, interpret, and analyze what is heard, read, or viewed on a variety of topics.	**Presentational Communication:** Learners present information, concepts, and ideas to inform, explain, persuade, and narrate on a variety of topics using appropriate media and adapting to various audiences of listeners, readers, or viewers.
CULTURES Interact with cultural competence and understanding	**Relating Cultural Practices to Perspectives:** Learners use the language to investigate, explain, and reflect on the relationship between the practices and perspectives of the cultures studied.	**Relating Cultural Products to Perspectives:** Learners use the language to investigate, explain, and reflect on the relationship between the products and perspectives of the cultures studied.	
CONNECTIONS Connect with other disciplines and acquire information and diverse perspectives in order to use the language to function in academic and career-related situations	**Making Connections:** Learners build, reinforce, and expand their knowledge of other disciplines while using the language to develop critical thinking and to solve problems creatively.	**Acquiring Information and Diverse Perspectives:** Learners access and evaluate information and diverse perspectives that are available through the language and its cultures.	
COMPARISONS Develop insight into the nature of language and culture in order to interact with cultural competence	**Language Comparisons:** Learners use the language to investigate, explain, and reflect on the nature of language through comparisons of the language studied and their own.	**Cultural Comparisons:** Learners use the language to investigate, explain, and reflect on the concept of culture through comparisons of the cultures studied and their own.	
COMMUNITIES Communicate and interact with cultural competence in order to participate in multilingual communities at home and around the world	**School and Global Communities:** Learners use the language both within and beyond the classroom to interact and collaborate in their community and the globalized world.	**Lifelong Learning:** Learners set goals and reflect on their progress in using languages for enjoyment, enrichment, and advancement.	

Appendix B
ACTFL Proficiency Levels

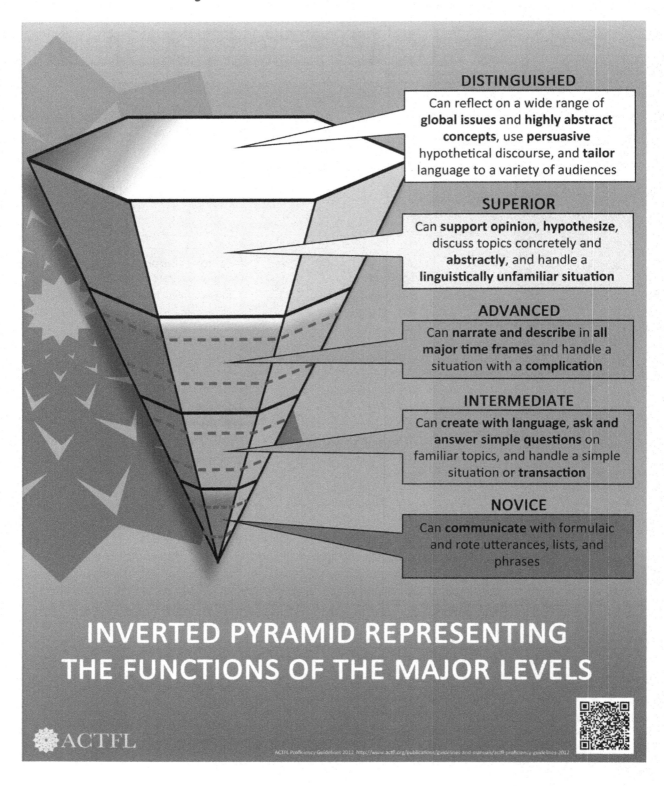

Appendix C
Assessment Criteria—ACTFL Proficiency Guidelines, Speaking

Proficiency Level	Global Tasks and Functions	Context/Content	Accuracy	Text Type
Superior	Discuss topics extensively, support options and hypothesize. Deal with a linguistically unfamiliar situation.	Most formal and informal settings from concrete to abstract perspectives. *Wide range of general interest topics and some special fields of interest and expertise.*	No pattern of error in basic structures. Errors virtually never interfere with communication or distract from the message.	Extended discourse
Advanced	Narrate and describe in major time frames and deal effectively with an unanticipated complication.	Most informal and some formal settings. *Topics of personal and general current interest.*	Can be understood without difficulty by speakers unaccustomed to dealing with sympathetic listeners.	Paragraphs
Intermediate	Create with language, initiate, maintain, and bring to a close simple conversations by asking and responding to simple questions.	Some informal settings and a limited number of transactional situations. *Predictable, familiar topics related to daily activities.*	Can be understood with some repetition, by speakers accustomed to interacting with language learners (sympathetic listener).	Discrete sentences
Novice	Communicate minimally with formulaic and rote utterances, lists, and phrases.	Most common informal settings. *Most common aspects of daily life*	May be difficult to understand, even for speakers accustomed to interacting with language learners.	Individual words and phrases

Source:
https://www.actfl.org/assessment-research-and-development/actfl-assessments/actfl-postsecondary-assessments/oral-proficiency-interview-opi

Appendix D-1
Interpretive Viewing Comprehension Guide: Template

I. Key Word Recognition

As you watch the video segment, jot down a list of 5 content words/phrases that you hear that convey meaning related to the text, such as key nouns and verbs. Avoid listing words/phrases such as prepositions (*of, from, in, out*) and conjunctions (*and, but, or*), which do not carry much meaning. Then provide an English equivalent to the right of each word you listed.

[Note to instructor: Score this section in terms of content words provided such as nouns and verbs. You could ask for up to 8 words/phrases depending on the length of the video.]

_____   _____
_____   _____
_____   _____
_____   _____
_____   _____

II. Main Idea(s)

Using information from the video you watched, provide the main idea(s) of it in English.

_____
_____
_____
_____
_____

III. Supporting Details

1. Circle the letter of each detail that is mentioned in the video (not all are included!).
2. Write the information that is given in the video in the space provided next to the detail below.

*[Note to instructor: Provide 5 correct details that support the main idea(s) and 3 distracters. **Elicit 2 details from the images and other visual support provided in the video.**]*

    A. XXXXX _____
    B. XXXXX _____
    C. XXXXX _____
    D. XXXXX _____
    E. XXXXX _____
    F. XXXXX _____
    G. XXXXX _____
    H. XXXXX _____

IV. Organizational Features

How is this video organized? Choose all that apply and explain briefly why you selected each organizational feature—what were the clues in the video?

[Note to instructor: Provide 2 correct answers and 3 distracters. Possible options may include public service announcement, conversation, interview, music video, story, commercial, news item, documentary, film segment.]

    A. XXXXX

    B. XXXXX

    C. XXXXX

    D. XXXXX

    E. XXXXX

Justification from text: _____

_____

_____

V. Guessing Meaning from Context

Based on this video, write what the following three words/expressions probably mean in English.

[Note to instructor: Provide 3 words that the learner may not be likely to know but should be able to understand from the context. Provide the entire phrase in which the word/expression appears, as well as a way to identify it such as whether it occurs at the beginning, after a particular pause, or near the end; or whether it is mentioned by a particular person who is speaking.]

    A. XXXXXXXX _____

    B. XXXXXXXX _____

    C. XXXXXXXX _____

VI. Inferences

"View between the lines" to answer the following questions, using information from the video.

[Note to instructor: For Intermediate-High and Advanced learners, create questions that require learners to infer meaning by listening between the lines. Write 2 open-ended questions such as "Why do you think that…?"; "Why does the author say that…?"; "Why is it important that..?; What might be the effect of….?", which require inferencing on the part of the learner. Questions may be in the target language. Specify which language learners are expected to use and indicate that they must use information from the video in their responses. Note that some adaptations to this task may be necessary for lower-level learners, who may need more guidance in using inferencing skills. For Novice-level learners, you might give them a statement and ask them to list any evidence from the video that would help them to determine whether it is true or false, drawing on inferencing skills. For Intermediate-level learners, you could give them 3 inferences and ask them to select the best inference of the 3 by providing evidence from the video to support their selection, drawing on inferencing skills.]

    A. _____

    B. _____

VII. Author's Perspective

Select the perspective or point of view you think the author(s) adopted as they created this video and justify your answer with information you heard in the video.

[Note to instructor: Provide 1 correct answer and 2 distracters. Possible options may include clinical/scientific, moral/religious, humanistic, factual, historical, comic, other. Specify which language learners are expected to use in their justifications.]

    A. XXX

    B. XXX

    C. XXX

Justification from text: _____

_____

_____

VIII.   Comparing Cultural Perspectives

Answer the following questions:

[Note to instructor: Below are some possible types of questions, which may be written in the target language. Be sure to make reference to cultural products, practices, and perspectives in some of your questions. Specify which language learners are expected to use.]

    A.   What are the cultural similarities and differences between XXX and XXX? _____

        _____

    B.   How do the practices/products in the video reflect the target culture perspectives? _____

        _____

    C.   What did you learn about the target culture from this video? _____

        _____

    D.   How would this video have been different if it were created for a U.S. audience?_____

        _____

IX. Personal Reaction to the Text

Using specific information from the text, describe your personal reaction to the video using the target language. Be sure to provide reasons that support your reaction.

[Note to instructor: This last section is designed to elicit a personal reaction from the learner in the target language. This can be a bridge to the interpersonal task that will follow. However, this reaction is not assessed on the interpretive rubric.]

_____

_____

_____

_____

Appendix D-2
Interpretive Listening Comprehension Guide: Template

I. Key Word Recognition

As you listen to the recorded segment, jot down a list of 5 content words/phrases that you hear that convey meaning related to the text, such as key nouns and verbs. Avoid listing words/phrases such as prepositions (*of, from, in, out*) and conjunctions (*and, but, or*), which do not carry much meaning. Then provide an English equivalent to the right of each word you listed. *[Note to instructor: Score this section in terms of content words provided such as nouns and verbs. You could ask for up to 8 words/phrases depending on the length of the segment.]*

_____   _____

_____   _____

_____   _____

_____   _____

_____   _____

II. Main Idea(s)

Using information from the segment you heard, provide the main idea(s) of it in English.

_____

_____

_____

_____

_____

III. Supporting Details

1. Circle the letter of each detail that is mentioned in the segment (not all are included!).
2. Write the information that is given in the segment in the space provided next to the detail below.

[Note to instructor: Provide 5 correct details that support the main idea(s) and 3 distracters.]

A. XXXXX _____

B. XXXXX _____

C. XXXXX _____

D. XXXXX _____

E. XXXXX _____

F. XXXXX _____

G. XXXXX _____

H. XXXXX _____

IV. Organizational Features

How is this segment organized? Based on the purpose of this segment, identify the organizational structure. Choose all that apply and explain briefly why you selected each organizational feature—what were the clues in the segment?

[Note to instructor: Provide 2 correct answers and 3 distracters. Possible options may include public service announcement, conversation, interview, song, story, advertisement/commercial, news item.]

    A. XXXXX

    B. XXXXX

    C. XXXXX

    D. XXXXX

    E. XXXXX

Justification from text: _____

_____

_____

V. Guessing Meaning from Context

Based on this segment, write what the following three words/expressions probably mean in English.

[Note to instructor: Provide 3 words that the learner may not be likely to know but should be able to understand from the context. Provide the entire phrase in which the word/expression occurs, as well as a way to identify it such as whether it occurs at the beginning, after a particular pause, or near the end; or whether it is mentioned by a particular person who is speaking.]

    A. XXXXXXXX _____

    B. XXXXXXXX _____

    C. XXXXXXXX _____

VI. Inferences

"Listen between the lines" to answer the following questions, using information from the segment.

[Note to instructor: For Intermediate-High and Advanced learners, create questions that require learners to infer meaning by listening between the lines. Write 2 open-ended questions such as "Why do you think that?"; "Why does the author say that…?"; "Why is it important that…?; What might be the effect of…?", which require inferencing on the part of the learner. Questions may be in the target language. Specify which language learners are expected to use and indicate that they must use information from the segment in their responses. Note that some adaptations to this task may be necessary for lower-level learners, who may need more guidance in using inferencing skills. For Novice-level learners, you might give them a statement and ask them to list any evidence from the segment that would help them to determine whether it is true or false, drawing on inferencing skills. For Intermediate-level learners, you could give them 3 inferences and ask them to select the best inference of the 3 by providing evidence from the segment to support their selection, drawing on inferencing skills.]

    A. _____

_____

    B. _____

_____

VII. Author's Perspective

Select the perspective or point of view you think the author(s) adopted as they created this segment and justify your answer with information you heard in the segment.

[Note to instructor: Provide 1 correct answer and 2 distracters. Possible options may include clinical/scientific, moral/religious, humanistic, factual, historical, comic, or other. Specify which language learners are expected to use in their justifications.]

    A. XXX

    B. XXX

    C. XXX

Justification from text: _____

_____

_____

VIII. Comparing Cultural Perspectives

Answer the following questions:

[Note to instructor: Below are some possible types of questions, which may be written in the target language. Be sure to make reference to cultural products, practices, and perspectives in some of your questions. Specify which language learners are expected to use

    A. What are the cultural similarities and differences between XXX and XXX? _____

    _____

    B. How do the practices/products in the segment reflect the target culture perspectives? _____

    _____

    C. What did you learn about the target culture from this segment? _____

    _____

    D. How would this segment have been different if it were created for a U.S. audience? _____

    _____

IX. Personal Reaction to the Text

Using specific information from the text, describe your personal reaction to the segment using the target language. Be sure to provide reasons that support your reaction.

[Note to instructor: This last section is designed to elicit a personal reaction from the learner in the target language. This can be a bridge to the interpersonal task that will follow. However, this reaction is not assessed on the interpretive rubric.]

_____

_____

_____

_____

Appendix D-3
Interpretive Reading Comprehension Guide: Template

I. Key Word Recognition

Find in the article the word/phrase in the target language that best expresses the meaning of each of the following English words/phrases:

[Note to instructor: Select 8-10 content words/phrases that convey meaning related to the text, such as key nouns and verbs, as opposed to words/phrases that carry little meaning such as prepositions (of, from, in, out) and conjunctions (and, but, or). Alternative format: Ask students to provide 8-10 words that relate to a specific topic or content area addressed in the text, such as nutrition.]

_____   _____

_____   _____

_____   _____

_____   _____

II. Main Idea(s)

Using information from the article, provide the main idea(s) of the article in English.

_____

_____

_____

_____

III. Supporting Details

1. Circle the letter of each detail that is mentioned in the article (not all are included!).
2. Write the letter of the detail next to where it appears in the text.
3. Write the information that is given in the article in the space provided next to the detail below.

[Note to instructor: Provide 5 correct details that support the main idea(s) and 3 distracters.

If the reading has images or other visual support, elicit 2 details from these visuals.]

A. XXXXX _____

B. XXXXX _____

C. XXXXX _____

D. XXXXX _____

E. XXXXX _____

F. XXXXX _____

G. XXXXX _____

H. XXXXX _____

IV. Organizational Features

How is this text organized? Choose all that apply and explain briefly why you selected each organizational feature—what were the clues in the text?

[Note to instructor: Provide 2 correct answers and 3 distracters. Possible options may include chronological, pros and cons, cause/ effect, compare/contrast, biography/autobiography, storytelling, description, problem and solution.]

    A. XXXXX

    B. XXXXX

    C. XXXXX

    D. XXXXX

    E. XXXXX

Justification from text: _____

_____

_____

V. Guessing Meaning from Context

Based on this text, write what the following three words/expressions probably mean in English.

[Note to instructor: Provide 3 words that the learner may not be likely to know but should be able to understand from the context. Provide the entire phrase in which the word/expression appears, as well as a way to find it in the text such as the number/line of the paragraph in which it appears.]

    A. XXXXXXX _____

    B. XXXXXXX _____

    C. XXXXXXX _____

VI. Inferences

"Read between the lines" to answer the following questions, using information from the text.

[Note to instructor: For Intermediate-High and Advanced learners, create questions that require learners to infer meaning by reading between the lines. Write 2 open-ended questions such as "Why do you think that...?"; "Why does the author say that...?"; "Why is it important that..?; What might be the effect of....?", which require inferencing on the part of the learner. Questions may be in the target language. Specify which language the learners are expected to use and indicate that they must use information from the text in their responses. Note that some adaptations to this task may be necessary for lower-level learners, who may need more guidance in using inferencing skills. For Novice-level learners, you might give them a statement and ask them to list any evidence from the text that would help them to determine whether it is true or false, drawing on inferencing skills. For Intermediate-level learners, you could give them 3 inferences and ask them to select the best inference of the 3 by providing evidence from the text to support their selection, drawing on inferencing skills.]

    A. _____

    _____

    B. _____

    _____

VII. Author's Perspective

Select the perspective or point of view you think the author(s) adopted as they wrote this article and justify your answer with information from the text.

[Note to instructor: Provide 1 correct answer and 2 distracters. Possible options may include clinical/scientific, moral/religious, humanistic, factual, historical, comic, or other. Specify which language learners are expected to use in their justifications.]

    A. XXX

    B. XXX

    C. XXX

Justification from text: _____

_____

_____

VIII. Comparing Cultural Perspectives

Answer the following questions:

[Note to instructor: Below are some possible types of questions, which may be written in the target language. Be sure to make reference to cultural products, practices, and perspectives in some of your questions. Specify which language learners are expected to use].

    A. What are the cultural similarities and differences between XXX and XXX? _____

    B. How do the practices/products in the article reflect the target culture perspectives? _____

    C. What did you learn about the target culture from this article? _____

    D. How would this article have been different if it were written for a U.S. audience? _____

IX. Personal Reaction to the Text

Using specific information from the text, describe your personal reaction to the article, using the target language. Be sure to provide reasons that support your reaction.

[Note to instructor: This last section is designed to elicit a personal reaction from the learner in the target language. This can be a bridge to the interpersonal task that will follow. However, this reaction is not assessed on the interpretive rubric.]

_____

_____

_____

_____

Appendix E
Interpretive Task Comprehension Guide for the Video "El acoso escolar contado por estudiantes" from *El País*

IPA on Social Media and Bullying, Intermediate Level
Created by Jesse Carnevali, Franklin Regional Sr. High School, Murrysville, PA

Spanish Interpretive Task for the Video: El acoso escolar contado por estudiantes - El País
https://www.youtube.com/watch?v=mDF0KQ1Gaqs

Note: This is set up as a template for learners to enter responses online, but it can also be used to elicit paper-and-pencil responses.

I. Key Word Recognition.
As you watch the video segment, jot down a list of 8 content words/phrases that you hear that convey meaning related to the text, such as key nouns and verbs. Avoid listing words/phrases such as prepositions (*of, from, in, out, etc.*) and conjunctions (*and, but, or, etc.*), which do not carry much meaning. Then provide an English equivalent to the right of each word you listed.

Content word/phrase	English equivalent

II. Main Idea(s)
Using information from the video you watched, provide the main idea(s) of it in English.

III. Supporting Details
1. Highlight/bold the letter of each detail that is mentioned in the video (not all are included!).
2. Type the information that is given in the video in the text box provided below each detail that you identify. You may respond in Spanish or English.
   A. la violencia como solución para combatir el acoso *[violence as a solution to combat bullying]*

B.   las influencias de las redes sociales sobre el acoso [social media influences on bullying]

C.   unas soluciones posibles de reducir el acoso [some possible solutions to reduce bullying]

D.   el papel (el rol) de la familia en el acoso *[the family's role on bullying]*

E.   las opiniones y voces de los bravucones *[the opinions and voices of the bullies]*

F.   la importancia de una voz activa *[the importance of an active voice]*

G.   las razones por las que ocurre el acoso*[reasons why bullying exists]*

H.   los diversos tipos de acoso *[the various types of bullying]*

IV. Organizational Features

How is this video organized? Choose all that apply and explain briefly why you selected each organizational feature—what were the clues in the video? You may respond in English.

   A.   Public Service Announcement
   B.   Documentary
   C.   Group Discussion
   D.   Commercial
   E.   News Item

Justification from text:

V. Guessing Meaning from Context

Based on this video, write what the following three words/expressions probably mean in English.

la clave (00:20)	
pegar (2:16)	
la asimetría (3:48)	

VI. Inferences

Below are three possible inferences from the video. Choose which one you think is the best and provide evidence from the video (in Spanish or English) to support your choice.

1. Una voz activa es la forma más eficaz de reducir el acoso escolar. *[An active voice is the most effective way to reduce school bullying.]*
2. Un grupo mediador es la forma más eficaz de reducir el acoso escolar. *[A mediating group is the most effective way to reduce school bullying.]*
3. Identificar y ayudar a los estudiantes más vulnerables es la forma más eficaz de reducir el acoso escolar. *[Identifying and helping the most vulnerable students is the most effective way to reduce school bullying.]*

VII. Author's Perspective

Select the perspective or point of view you think the author adopted in this video and justify your answer with information you heard in the video in English.

    A. clinical/scientific

    B. humanistic

    C. historical

Justification from text:

VIII. Comparing Cultural Perspectives.

Answer the following question in Spanish:

En este video, escuchaste las opiniones y las experiencias de unos estudiantes hispanohablantes de varias culturas. Pensando en la cultura (los productos, las prácticas, y las perspectivas), responde a la siguiente pregunta en español:

Después de ver este video, ¿crees que cada cultura tiene su propia perspectiva cultural sobre el acoso o no? Explica por qué sí o no, incorporando unas prácticas culturales para justificar tu opinión. *[After viewing this video, do you think that each culture has a different cultural perspective of bullying or not? Explain why yes or no, incorporating some cultural practices to justify your opinion.]*

IX. Personal Reaction to the Text.

Using specific information from the text, describe your personal reaction to the video in Spanish. Be sure to provide reasons that support your reaction.

Appendix F-1
Integrated Performance Assessment Rubric for Interpretive Reading/Listening/Viewing: A Continuum of Performance

The Interpretive Rubric is designed to show the continuum of performance for both literal comprehension and interpretation of text for language learners regardless of language level.

See the Rubric Score Conversion Chart at the end of this Appendix and Chapter 2 of this manual for suggestions on how to use this rubric to assign a percentage or grade

Integrated Performance Assessment Rubric for Interpretive Reading/Listening/Viewing: A Continuum of Performance

CRITERIA	EXCEEDS EXPECTATIONS Accomplished 4 points	MEETS EXPECTATIONS		DOES NOT MEET EXPECTATIONS Limited 1 point
		Strong 3 points	Minimal 2 points	
LITERAL COMPREHENSION OF TEXT				
Key word recognition	Identifies all key words appropriately within the context of the text.	Identifies majority of key words appropriately within the context of the text.	Identifies half of key words appropriately within the context of the text.	Identifies a few key words appropriately within the context of the text.
Main idea detection	Identifies the complete main idea(s) of the text.	Identifies the key parts of the main idea(s) of the text but misses some elements.	Identifies some part of the main idea(s) of the text.	May identify some ideas from the text but they do not represent the main idea(s).
Supporting detail detection	Identifies all supporting details in the text and accurately provides information from the text to explain these details.	Identifies the majority of supporting details in the text and provides information from the text to explain some of these details.	Identifies some supporting details in the text and may provide limited information from the text to explain these details. Or identifies the majority of supporting details but is unable to provide information from the text to explain these details.	Identifies a few supporting details in the text but may be unable to provide information from the text to explain these details.
INTERPRETATION OF TEXT				
Organizational features	Identifies the organizational feature(s) of the text and provides an appropriate rationale.	Identifies the organizational feature(s) of the text; rationale misses some key points.	Identifies in part the organizational feature(s) of the text; rationale may miss some key points. Or identifies the organizational feature(s) but rationale is not provided.	Attempts to identify the organizational feature(s) of the text but is not successful.

Integrated Performance Assessment Rubric for Interpretive Reading/Listening/Viewing: A Continuum of Performance

CRITERIA	EXCEEDS EXPECTATIONS Accomplished 4 points	MEETS EXPECTATIONS		DOES NOT MEET EXPECTATIONS Limited 1 point
		Strong 3 points	Minimal 2 points	
INTERPRETATION OF TEXT				
Guessing meaning from context	Infers meaning of unfamiliar words and phrases in the text. Inferences are accurate.	Infers meaning of unfamiliar words and phrases in the text. Most of the inferences are plausible, although some may not be accurate.	Infers meaning of unfamiliar words and phrases in the text. Most of the inferences are plausible, although many are not accurate.	Inferences of meanings of unfamiliar words and phrases are largely inaccurate or lacking.
Inferences (reading/ listening/ viewing between the lines)	Infers and interprets the text's meaning in a highly plausible manner. Justification is detailed and illustrates depth of inferencing.	Infers and interprets the text's meaning in a partially complete and/or partially plausible manner. Justification includes a few details to support inferencing.	Makes a few plausible inferences regarding the text's meaning. Justification illustrates lack of details to support inferencing.	Inferences and interpretations of the text's meaning are largely incomplete and/or not plausible.
Author's perspective	Identifies the author's perspective and provides a detailed justification.	Identifies the author's perspective and provides a justification.	Identifies the author's perspective but justification is either inappropriate or incomplete.	Attempts to identify the author's perspective. Justification may be lacking or inappropriate.
Cultural perspectives	Identifies cultural perspectives/ norms accurately. Provides a detailed connection of cultural products/ practices to perspectives.	Identifies some cultural perspectives/ norms accurately. Connects cultural products/practices to perspectives.	Identifies some cultural perspectives/norms accurately. Provides a minimal connection of cultural products/practices to perspectives.	Identification of cultural perspectives/norms is mostly superficial or lacking, and/ or connection of cultural practices/ products to perspectives is superficial or lacking.

Evidence of strengths: _____
_____
_____

Examples of where you could improve:_____
_____
_____

Other comments: _____
_____
_____

Interpretive Rubric Score Conversion Chart: Assigning Percentages and Grades	
Raw Rubric Score	Grade Conversion by Percentage
32	100
31	98
30	97
29	95
28	94
27	92
26	90
25	89
24	87
23	85
22	84
21	82
20	81
19	79
18	77
17	76
16	74
15	72
14	71
13	69
12	68
11	66
10	64
9	63
8	61
7	59
6	58
5	56
4	55
3	53
2	51
1	50

Note: A zero (0) for a given criterion would be given only if the learner had no performance that corresponded to that criterion.

These conversions are based upon this rubric formula:
(Total points x 52)/32 + 48 = _____%.
Lowest passing score: 60%;
to use a different passing score, go to http://www.roobrix.com

Appendix F-2
Integrated Performance Assessment Rubric for Interpersonal Mode

The IPA Interpersonal rubrics are based on the criteria associated with the major levels as described in the ACTFL Proficiency Guidelines (ACTFL, 2012b) and are aligned with the ranges of the ACTFL Performance Descriptors for Language Learners (ACTFL, 2012a).

Notes:

1. Performance on an IPA task at a particular proficiency level does NOT provide evidence of a learner's overall level of proficiency. Proficiency ratings for speaking can only be determined through an official ACTFL Oral Proficiency Interview (OPI).

2. For the last criterion, Intercultural Communication: Interact, the 2017 NCSSFL-ACTFL Can-Do Statements use the phrase "interact with others in and from another culture." This criterion has been changed in this IPA text to "interaction with others" to make it more inclusive and address intercultural communication in all interactions.

3. See the Rubric Score Conversion Chart at the end of this Appendix and Chapter 2 of this manual for suggestions on how to use this rubric to assign a percentage or grade.

Integrated Performance Assessment Interpersonal Mode Rubric: Novice-High Learner

CRITERIA	EXCEEDS EXPECTATIONS Intermediate-Low 4 points	MEETS EXPECTATIONS		DOES NOT MEET EXPECTATIONS Novice-Low 1 point
		STRONG Novice-High 3 points	MINIMAL Novice-Mid 2 points	
Language Functions Language tasks the speaker is able to handle in a consistent, comfortable, sustained, and spontaneous manner	Expresses personal meaning, creating with language in the present time frame by combining and recombining known language and what is heard from other speakers. Successfully handles a number of uncomplicated communicative tasks in straightforward social situations, primarily in concrete exchanges and topics necessary for survival in target-language cultures.	Uses mostly memorized language with some attempts to express personal meaning. Relies heavily on learned phrases or recombinations of these and what is heard from other speakers. Handles a limited number of uncomplicated communicative tasks involving topics related to basic personal information and some activities, preferences, and immediate needs.	Uses memorized and familiar language only.	Has no real functional ability. May be able to exchange greetings, give personal identity, and name a number of familiar objects from the immediate environment.

| CRITERIA | EXCEEDS EXPECTATIONS Intermediate-Low 4 points | MEETS EXPECTATIONS | | DOES NOT MEET EXPECTATIONS Novice-Low 1 point |
		STRONG Novice-High 3 points	MINIMAL Novice-Mid 2 points	
Text Type Quantity and organization of language discourse, on a continuum from words to phrases to sentences to connected sentences to paragraphs to extended discourse	Uses short and discrete sentences.	Uses short, sometimes incomplete sentences and memorized phrases.	Uses isolated words and memorized phrases.	Uses isolated words.
Communication Strategies Quality of engagement and interactivity in the conversation; how the learner participates in the conversation and advances it; how the learner uses strategies for negotiating meaning in the face of communication breakdown	Responds to direct questions and requests for information. Asks a few appropriate questions but is primarily reactive. Frequently tries to reformulate and self-correct.	Responds to simple, direct questions and requests for information. Asks a few formulaic questions but is primarily reactive. May clarify by repeating and/or substituting different words.	Responds to a limited number of formulaic questions. May use repetition or resort to the first language.	Is unable to participate in a true conversational exchange.
Comprehensibility Types of listeners who can understand the learner's language, on a continuum from sympathetic listeners used to the speech of language learners to target language speakers unaccustomed to such speech	Is generally understood by those accustomed to interacting with language learners, although repetition or rephrasing may be required.	Is understood with occasional difficulty by those accustomed to interacting with language learners, although repetition or rephrasing may be required.	May be understood with difficulty by those accustomed to interacting with language learners.	Most of what is said may be unintelligible or understood only with repetition.

CRITERIA	EXCEEDS EXPECTATIONS Intermediate-Low 4 points	MEETS EXPECTATIONS		DOES NOT MEET EXPECTATIONS Novice-Low 1 point
		STRONG Novice-High 3 points	MINIMAL Novice-Mid 2 points	
Language Control Degree of grammatical accuracy, appropriate vocabulary use, and fluency	Demonstrates some accuracy when producing simple sentences in the present time frame. Pronunciation, vocabulary, and syntax are strongly influenced by the first language. Maintains the functions of the Intermediate level, although just barely.	Demonstrates some accuracy with memorized language and stock phrases. Pronunciation, vocabulary, and syntax are strongly influenced by the first language. Accuracy decreases when attempting to handle topics and perform functions pertaining to the Intermediate level.	Accuracy is limited to memorized words. Accuracy may decrease when attempting to communicate beyond the word level.	Has little accuracy even with memorized words.
Intercultural Communication: Interact Degree and quality of use of cultural norms appropriate for interpersonal interaction	Uses some culturally appropriate expressions and some learned behaviors in everyday situations with others.	Uses some culturally appropriate expressions and some rehearsed behaviors in everyday situations with others.	Uses some culturally appropriate memorized expressions in everyday situations with others.	May use a few culturally appropriate memorized expressions in everyday situations with others.

Evidence of strengths: _____

_____

_____

Examples of where you could improve:_____

_____

_____

Other comments: _____

_____

_____

Integrated Performance Assessment Interpersonal Mode Rubric: Intermediate Learner

CRITERIA	EXCEEDS EXPECTATIONS Intermediate-High 4 points	MEETS EXPECTATIONS		DOES NOT MEET EXPECTATIONS Novice-High 1 point
		STRONG Intermediate-Mid 3 points	MINIMAL Intermediate-Low 2 points	
Language Functions Language tasks the speaker is able to handle in a consistent, comfortable, sustained, and spontaneous manner	Successfully handles uncomplicated tasks and social situations requiring exchange of basic information related to work, school, recreation, particular interests, and areas of competence. Narrates and describes in the major time frames of present, past, and future, although not consistently.	Expresses personal meaning by creating with language in mostly the present time frame, in part by combining and recombining known language and conversational input. Successfully handles a variety of uncomplicated communicative tasks in straightforward social situations, primarily in predictable and concrete exchanges necessary for survival in target-language cultures. These exchanges include personal information related to self, family, home, daily activities, interests, and personal preferences, as well as physical and social needs such as food, shopping, and travel.	Expresses personal meaning, creating with language in the present time frame by combining and recombining known language and what is heard from other speakers. Successfully handles a number of uncomplicated communicative tasks in straightforward social situations, primarily in concrete exchanges and topics necessary for survival in target-language cultures.	Uses mostly memorized language with some attempts to express personal meaning. Relies heavily on learned phrases or recombinations of these and what is heard from other speakers. Handles a limited number of uncomplicated communicative tasks involving topics related to basic personal information and some activities, preferences, and immediate needs.

| CRITERIA | EXCEEDS EXPECTATIONS Intermediate-High 4 points | MEETS EXPECTATIONS | | DOES NOT MEET EXPECTATIONS Novice-High 1 point |
		STRONG Intermediate-Mid 3 points	MINIMAL Intermediate-Low 2 points	
Text Type Quantity and organization of language discourse, on a continuum from words to phrases to sentences to connected sentences to paragraphs to extended discourse	Uses mostly connected sentences, with some paragraph-length discourse, but not consistently.	Uses sentences and strings of sentences, with some complex sentences (dependent clauses).	Uses short and discrete sentences.	Uses short, sometimes incomplete sentences and memorized phrases.
Communication Strategies Quality of engagement and interactivity in the conversation; how the learner participates in the conversation and advances it; how the learner uses strategies for negotiating meaning in the face of communication breakdown	Converses with ease and confidence when dealing with routine tasks and social situations of the Intermediate level. May clarify by paraphrasing.	Responds to direct questions and requests for information. Asks a variety of questions to obtain simple information but tends to function reactively. May clarify by reformulating and self-correcting speech.	Responds to direct questions and requests for information. Asks a few appropriate questions but is primarily reactive. Frequently tries to reformulate and self-correct.	Responds to simple, direct questions and requests for information. Asks a few formulaic questions but is primarily reactive. May clarify by repeating and/or substituting different words.
Comprehensibility Types of listeners who can understand the learner's language, on a continuum from sympathetic listeners used to the speech of language learners to target language speakers unaccustomed to such speech	Is generally understood by those unaccustomed to interacting with language learners, although interference from another language may be evident and gaps in communication may occur.	Is generally understood by those accustomed to interacting with language learners.	Is generally understood by those accustomed to interacting with language learners, although repetition or rephrasing may be required.	Is understood with occasional difficulty by those accustomed to interacting with language learners, although repetition or rephrasing may be required.

CRITERIA	EXCEEDS EXPECTATIONS Intermediate-High 4 points	MEETS EXPECTATIONS		DOES NOT MEET EXPECTATIONS Novice-High 1 point
		STRONG Intermediate-Mid 3 points	MINIMAL Intermediate-Low 2 points	
Language Control Degree of grammatical accuracy, appropriate vocabulary use, and fluency	Demonstrates significant quantity and quality of Intermediate-level language. When attempting to perform Advanced-level tasks, there is breakdown in one or more of the following areas: the ability to narrate and describe in the major time frames of present, past, and future; use of paragraph-length discourse; fluency; breadth of vocabulary.	Demonstrates significant quantity and quality of Intermediate-level language when performing Intermediate-level tasks, mostly in the present time frame. Accuracy and/or fluency decreases when attempting to perform functions or handle topics at the Advanced level.	Demonstrates some accuracy when producing simple sentences in the present time frame. Pronunciation, vocabulary, and syntax are strongly influenced by the first language. Maintains the functions of the Intermediate level, although just barely.	Demonstrates some accuracy with memorized language and stock phrases. Pronunciation, vocabulary, and syntax are strongly influenced by the first language. Accuracy decreases when attempting to handle topics and perform functions pertaining to the Intermediate level.
Intercultural Communication: Interact Degree and quality of use of cultural norms appropriate for interpersonal interaction	Communicates with others in familiar and some unfamiliar situations, using culturally appropriate expressions and learned behaviors. May show some ability to converse comfortably with others, although not consistently.	Communicates with others in familiar situations such as self, family, home, school, or survival situations, using culturally appropriate expressions and learned behaviors.	Uses some culturally appropriate expressions and some learned behaviors in everyday situations with others.	Uses some culturally appropriate expressions and some rehearsed behaviors in everyday situations with others.

Evidence of strengths: _____

_____

_____

Examples of where you could improve: _____

_____

_____

Other comments: _____

_____

_____

Integrated Performance Assessment Interpersonal Mode Rubric: Intermediate-High Learner

CRITERIA	EXCEEDS EXPECTATIONS Advanced-Low 4 points	MEETS EXPECTATIONS		DOES NOT MEET EXPECTATIONS Intermediate-Low 1 point
		STRONG Intermediate-High 3 points	MINIMAL Intermediate-Mid 2 points	
Language Functions Language tasks the speaker is able to handle in a consistent, comfortable, sustained, and spontaneous manner	Participates in most informal and some formal conversations on topics related to school, home, and leisure activities. Can speak about some topics related to employment, current events, and matters of public interest. Consistently narrates and describes in the major time frames of present, past, and future. Can handle appropriately the linguistic challenges presented by a complication or an unexpected turn of events.	Successfully handles uncomplicated tasks and social situations requiring exchange of basic information related to work, school, recreation, particular interests, and areas of competence. Narrates and describes in the major time frames of present, past, and future, although not consistently.	Expresses personal meaning by creating with language in mostly the present time frame, in part by combining and recombining known language and conversational input. Successfully handles a variety of uncomplicated communicative tasks in straightforward social situations, primarily in predictable and concrete exchanges necessary for survival in target-language cultures. These exchanges include personal information related to self, family, home, daily activities, interests, and personal preferences, as well as physical and social needs such as food, shopping, and travel.	Expresses personal meaning, creating with language in the present time frame by combining and recombining known language and what is heard from other speakers. Successfully handles a number of uncomplicated communicative tasks in straightforward social situations, primarily in concrete exchanges and topics necessary for survival in target-language cultures.
Text Type Quantity and organization of language discourse, on a continuum from words to phrases to sentences to connected sentences to paragraphs to extended discourse	Uses connected discourse of paragraph length, but responses are not longer than a single paragraph. Discourse tends to reflect the oral paragraph structure of the first language rather than that of the target language.	Uses mostly connected sentences, with some paragraph-length discourse, but not consistently.	Uses sentences and strings of sentences, with some complex sentences (dependent clauses).	Uses short and discrete sentences.

| CRITERIA | EXCEEDS EXPECTATIONS
Advanced-Low
4 points | MEETS EXPECTATIONS | | DOES NOT MEET EXPECTATIONS
Intermediate-Low
1 point |
		STRONG Intermediate-High 3 points	MINIMAL Intermediate-Mid 2 points	
Communication Strategies Quality of engagement and interactivity in the conversation; how the learner participates in the conversation and advances it; how the learner uses strategies for negotiating meaning in the face of communication breakdown	Engages in conversation in a participatory manner. May use communicative strategies such as rephrasing and circumlocution.	Converses with ease and confidence when dealing with routine tasks and social situations of the Intermediate level. May clarify by paraphrasing.	Responds to direct questions and requests for information. Asks a variety of questions to obtain simple information but tends to function reactively. May clarify by reformulating and self-correcting speech.	Responds to direct questions and requests for information. Asks a few appropriate questions but is primarily reactive. Frequently tries to reformulate and self-correct.
Comprehensibility Types of listeners who can understand the learner's language, on a continuum from sympathetic listeners used to the speech of language learners to target language speakers unaccustomed to such speech	Is understood by target language speakers, even those unaccustomed to interacting with language learners, although this may require some repetition or restatement.	Is generally understood by those unaccustomed to interacting with language learners, although interference from another language may be evident and a pattern of gaps in communication may occur.	Is generally understood by those accustomed to interacting with language learners.	Is generally understood by those accustomed to interacting with language learners, although repetition or rephrasing may be required.
Language Control Degree of grammatical accuracy, appropriate vocabulary use, and fluency	Performs Advanced-level tasks, albeit with minimal fluency and some control of aspect in narrating in the major time frames of present, past, and future. Vocabulary may lack specificity. Narration and description tend to be handled separately rather than interwoven.	Demonstrates significant quantity and quality of Intermediate-level language. When attempting to perform Advanced-level tasks, there is breakdown in one or more of the following areas: the ability to narrate and describe in the major time frames of present, past, and future; use of paragraph-length discourse; fluency; breadth of vocabulary.	Demonstrates significant quantity and quality of Intermediate-level language when performing Intermediate-level tasks in mostly the present time frame. Accuracy and/or fluency decreases when attempting to perform functions or handle topics at the Advanced level.	Demonstrates some accuracy when producing simple sentences in the present time frame. Pronunciation, vocabulary, and syntax are strongly influenced by the first language. Maintains the functions of the Intermediate level, although just barely.

CRITERIA	EXCEEDS EXPECTATIONS Advanced-Low 4 points	MEETS EXPECTATIONS		DOES NOT MEET EXPECTATIONS Intermediate-Low 1 point
		STRONG Intermediate-High 3 points	MINIMAL Intermediate-Mid 2 points	
Intercultural Communication: Interact Degree and quality of use of cultural norms appropriate for interpersonal interaction	Converses comfortably with others in familiar and some unfamiliar situations, using culturally appropriate expressions and learned behaviors. May avoid some social blunders.	Communicates with others in familiar and some unfamiliar situations, using culturally appropriate expressions and learned behaviors. May show some ability to converse comfortably with others, although not consistently.	Communicates with others in familiar situations such as self, family, home, school, and survival situations, using culturally appropriate expressions and learned behaviors.	Uses some culturally appropriate expressions and some learned behaviors in everyday situations with others.

Evidence of strengths: _____
_____
_____

Examples of where you could improve: _____
_____
_____

Other comments: _____
_____
_____

Integrated Performance Assessment Interpersonal Mode Rubric: Advanced Learner

CRITERIA	EXCEEDS EXPECTATIONS Advanced-High 4 points	MEETS EXPECTATIONS		DOES NOT MEET EXPECTATIONS Intermediate-High 1 point
		STRONG Advanced-Mid 3 points	MINIMAL Advanced-Low 2 points	
Language Functions Language tasks the speaker is able to handle in a consistent, comfortable, sustained, and spontaneous manner	Can discuss some topics abstractly, especially those related to particular interests and expertise. Narrates and describes fully and accurately in the major time frames of present, past, and future. May provide a structured argument to support opinions and may construct hypotheses.	Participates actively in most informal and some formal conversations on a variety of concrete topics relating to work, school, home, and leisure activities, as well as topics relating to events of current, public, and personal interest or individual relevance. Narrates and describes in the major time frames of present, past, and future by providing a full account. Can handle successfully and with relative ease the linguistic challenges presented by a complication or an unexpected turn of events.	Participates in most informal and some formal conversations on topics related to school, home, and leisure activities. Can speak about some topics related to employment, current events, and matters of public interest. Consistently narrates and describes in the major time frames of present, past, and future. Can handle appropriately the linguistic challenges presented by a complication or an unexpected turn of events.	Successfully handles uncomplicated tasks and social situations requiring exchange of basic information related to work, school, recreation, particular interests, and areas of competence. Narrates and describes in the major time frames of present, past, and future, although not consistently.
Text Type Quantity and organization of language discourse, on a continuum from words to phrases to sentences to connected sentences to paragraphs to extended discourse	Uses paragraph-length discourse and some extended discourse.	Uses connected, paragraph-length discourse. Discourse may still reflect the oral paragraph structure of the first language rather than that of the target language.	Uses connected discourse of paragraph length, but responses are not longer than a single paragraph. Discourse tends to reflect the oral paragraph structure of the first language rather than that of the target language.	Uses mostly connected sentences, with some paragraph-length discourse, but not consistently.

CRITERIA	EXCEEDS EXPECTATIONS Advanced-High 4 points	MEETS EXPECTATIONS		DOES NOT MEET EXPECTATIONS Intermediate-High 1 point
		STRONG Advanced-Mid 3 points	MINIMAL Advanced-Low 2 points	
Communication Strategies Quality of engagement and interactivity in the conversation; how the learner participates in the conversation and advances it; how the learner uses strategies for negotiating meaning in the face of communication breakdown	Converses with linguistic ease, confidence, and competence. Demonstrates confident use of communicative strategies such as paraphrasing, circumlocution, and illustration.	Converses with linguistic ease and confidence. Uses communicative strategies such as rephrasing and circumlocution.	Engages in conversation in a participatory manner. May use communicative strategies such as rephrasing and circumlocution.	Converses with ease and confidence when dealing with routine tasks and social situations of the Intermediate level. May clarify by paraphrasing.
Comprehensibility Types of listeners who can understand the learner's language, on a continuum from sympathetic listeners used to the speech of language learners to target language speakers unaccustomed to such speech	Is readily understood by target language speakers unaccustomed to interacting with language learners.	Is generally understood by target language speakers unaccustomed to interacting with language learners.	Is understood by target language speakers, even those unaccustomed to interacting with language learners, although this may require some repetition or restatement.	Is generally understood by those unaccustomed to interacting with language learners, although interference from another language may be evident and a pattern of gaps in communication may occur.
Language Control Degree of grammatical accuracy, appropriate vocabulary use, and fluency	Demonstrates full control of aspect in narrating in the major time frames of present, past, and future time. Uses precise vocabulary and intonation and often shows great fluency and ease of speech. Accuracy may break down when attempting to perform the complex tasks associated with the Superior level over a variety of topics.	Demonstrates good control of aspect in narrating in the major time frames of present, past, and future. Has substantial fluency and extensive vocabulary. Narration and description tend to be combined and interwoven. The quality and/or quantity of speech generally declines when attempting to perform functions or handle topics associated with the Superior level.	Performs Advanced-level tasks, albeit with minimal fluency and some control of aspect in narrating in the major time frames of present, past, and future. Vocabulary may lack specificity. Narration and description tend to be handled separately rather than interwoven.	Demonstrates significant quantity and quality of Intermediate-level language. When attempting to perform Advanced-level tasks, there is breakdown in one or more of the following areas: the ability to narrate and describe in the major time frames of present, past, and future; use of paragraph-length discourse; fluency; breadth of vocabulary.

CRITERIA	EXCEEDS EXPECTATIONS Advanced-High 4 points	MEETS EXPECTATIONS		DOES NOT MEET EXPECTATIONS Intermediate-High 1 point
		STRONG Advanced-Mid 3 points	MINIMAL Advanced-Low 2 points	
Intercultural Communication: Interact Degree and quality of use of cultural norms appropriate for interpersonal interaction	Converses comfortably with others, including in some complex situations. Adheres to basic social and professional norms and etiquette, reads non-verbal cues, and adjusts behavior accordingly, although not consistently.	Converses comfortably with others in familiar and some unfamiliar situations, using culturally appropriate language and behaviors and avoiding major social blunders.	Converses comfortably with others in familiar and some unfamiliar situations, using culturally appropriate expressions and learned behaviors. May avoid some social blunders.	Communicates with others in familiar and some unfamiliar situations, using culturally appropriate expressions and learned behaviors. May show some ability to converse comfortably with others, although not consistently.

Evidence of strengths: _____
_____
_____

Examples of where you could improve:_____
_____
_____

Other comments: _____
_____
_____

Interpersonal Rubric Score Conversion Chart: Assigning Percentages and Grades	
Raw Rubric Score	Grade Conversion by Percentage
24	100
23	98
22	96
21	94
20	91
19	89
18	87
17	85
16	83
15	81
14	78
13	76
12	74
11	72
10	70
9	68
8	65
7	63
6	61
5	59
4	57
3	55
2	52
1	50

Note: A zero (0) for a given criterion would be given only if the learner had no performance that corresponded to that criterion.

These conversions are based upon this rubric formula:
(Total points x 52)/24 + 48 = _____%.
Lowest passing score: 60%; to use a different passing score, go to http://www.roobrix.com

Appendix F-3
Integrated Performance Assessment Rubrics for Presentational Mode

The IPA Presentational rubrics are based on the criteria associated with the major levels as described in the ACTFL Proficiency Guidelines (ACTFL, 2012b) and are aligned with the ranges of the ACTFL Performance Descriptors for Language Learners (ACTFL, 2012a).

Notes:

1. The rubric for each IPA level is divided into two sections. In the top section, containing the criteria of Language Functions, Text Type, Comprehensibility, and Language Control, the descriptors on the continuum from Does Not Meet Expectations to Exceeds Expectations correspond to the proficiency levels indicated at the top of each column. In the lower section, containing the criteria of Intercultural Communication: Present, Impact of Written/Oral Presentation, and Impact of Multimodal Presentation, the descriptors correspond only to the Exceeds, Meets, Does Not Meet Expectations continuum. Therefore, the descriptors across the performance continuum for these criteria are the same regardless of the IPA level.

2. Performance on an IPA task at a particular proficiency level does not provide evidence of a learner's overall level of proficiency. Proficiency ratings can only be determined through an official ACTFL Oral Proficiency Interview (OPI) for speaking and an official ACTFL Writing Proficiency Test (WPT) for writing.

3. See the Rubric Score Conversion Chart at the end of this Appendix and Chapter 2 of this manual for suggestions on how to use this rubric to assign a percentage or grade.

Integrated Performance Assessment Presentational Mode Rubric: Novice-High Learner

CRITERIA	EXCEEDS EXPECTATIONS Intermediate-Low 4 points	MEETS EXPECTATIONS		DOES NOT MEET EXPECTATIONS Novice-Low 1 point
		STRONG Novice-High 3 points	MINIMAL Novice-Mid 2 points	
LANGUAGE PROFICIENCY/PERFORMANCE CRITERIA				
Language Functions Language tasks the speaker/writer is able to handle in a consistent, comfortable, sustained, and spontaneous manner	Expresses personal meaning, creating with language in the present time frame by combining and re-combining known language. Successfully handles a number of uncomplicated communicative tasks and topics necessary for survival in target-language cultures.	Uses mostly memorized language with some attempts to express personal meaning. Relies heavily on learned phrases or recombinations of these. Handles a limited number of uncomplicated communicative tasks involving topics related to basic personal information and some activities, preferences, and immediate needs.	Uses memorized and familiar language only.	Has no real functional ability. May be able to exchange greetings, give personal identity, and name a number of familiar objects from the immediate environment.

CRITERIA	EXCEEDS EXPECTATIONS Intermediate-Low 4 points	MEETS EXPECTATIONS		DOES NOT MEET EXPECTATIONS Novice-Low 1 point
		STRONG Novice-High 3 points	MINIMAL Novice-Mid 2 points	
Text Type Quantity and organization of language discourse on a continuum from words to phrases to sentences to connected sentences to paragraphs to extended discourse	Uses short and discrete sentences.	Uses short, sometimes incomplete sentences and memorized phrases.	Uses isolated words and memorized phrases.	Uses isolated words.
Comprehensibility Types of listeners/readers who can understand the learner's language, on a continuum from sympathetic interlocutors accustomed to the speech/writing of language learners to target language speakers unaccustomed to the speech/writing of such learners	Is generally understood by those accustomed to the speech/writing of language learners, although additional effort may be required.	Is understood with occasional difficulty by those accustomed to the speech/writing of language learners, although additional effort may be required.	May be understood with difficulty by those accustomed to the speech/writing of language learners.	Most of spoken/written language may be unintelligible or understood only with additional effort.
Language Control Degree of grammatical accuracy, appropriate vocabulary use, and fluency	Demonstrates some accuracy when producing simple sentences in the present time frame. Pronunciation, vocabulary, and syntax are strongly influenced by the first language. Maintains the functions of the Intermediate level, although just barely.	Demonstrates some accuracy with memorized language and stock phrases. Pronunciation, vocabulary, and syntax are strongly influenced by the first language. Accuracy decreases when attempting to handle topics and perform functions pertaining to the Intermediate level.	Accuracy is limited to memorized words. Accuracy may decrease when attempting to communicate beyond the word level.	Has little accuracy even with memorized words.

CRITERIA	EXCEEDS EXPECTATIONS Intermediate-Low 4 points	MEETS EXPECTATIONS		DOES NOT MEET EXPECTATIONS Novice-Low 1 point
		STRONG Novice-High 3 points	MINIMAL Novice-Mid 2 points	
INTERCULTURAL COMMUNICATION AND IMPACT CRITERIA				
Intercultural Communication: Present Learner's ability to investigate cultural products and practices and connect them to cultural perspectives appropriately in a presentation	Presentation appropriately includes cultural products and practices and integrates them with cultural perspectives.	Presentation appropriately includes some cultural products and/or practices and connects them to at least one cultural perspective.	Presentation appropriately includes some cultural products and/or practices.	Presentation includes a few cultural products and/or practices.
Impact of Written/Oral Presentation Clarity, organization, and depth of the written/oral presentation; the degree to which the presentation maintains the audience's attention and interest	Presented in a clear and organized manner. Presentation maintains audience interest through organization of the written/oral text, some details, and an unexpected feature.	Presented in a clear and organized manner. Presentation maintains audience interest through organization of the written/oral text and some details.	Presented in a clear, mostly organized manner. Some effort to maintain audience interest through organization of the written/oral text and/or a few details.	Presentation may be either unclear or unorganized. Minimal to no effort to maintain audience interest.
Impact of Multimodal Presentation Clarity, organization, and depth of the presentation; the degree to which the presentation maintains the audience's attention and interest; and the use of multimodal design (such as video, pictures, objects, graphs, diagrams, tables)	Presented in a clear and organized manner. Presentation maintains audience interest through organization, some details, and an unexpected feature. Integrates appropriate multimedia that heighten the effectiveness of the message conveyed in the presentation.	Presented in a clear and organized manner. Presentation maintains audience interest through organization and some details. Integrates appropriate multimedia that support the message conveyed in the presentation.	Presented in a clear, mostly organized manner. Some effort to maintain audience interest through organization and/or a few details. Integrates at least one example of appropriate multimedia that provides some support of the message conveyed in the presentation.	Presentation may be either unclear or unorganized. Minimal to no effort to maintain audience interest. May include one example of visual support.

The leftmost column for the last two rows is labeled vertically: **SELECT BY PRESENTATION TYPE**

Evidence of strengths: _____

_____

_____

Examples of where you could improve: _____

_____

_____

Other comments: _____

_____

_____

Integrated Performance Assessment Presentational Mode Rubric: Intermediate Learner

CRITERIA	EXCEEDS EXPECTATIONS Intermediate-High 4 points	MEETS EXPECTATIONS		DOES NOT MEET EXPECTATIONS Novice-High 1 point
		STRONG Intermediate-Mid 3 points	MINIMAL Intermediate-Low 2 points	
LANGUAGE PROFICIENCY/PERFORMANCE CRITERIA				
Language Functions Language tasks the speaker/writer is able to handle in a consistent, comfortable, sustained, and spontaneous manner	Successfully handles uncomplicated tasks requiring basic information related to work, school, recreation, particular interests, and areas of competence. Narrates and describes in the major time frames of present, past, and future, although not consistently.	Expresses personal meaning by creating with language in mostly the present time frame, in part by combining and recombining known language. Successfully handles a variety of uncomplicated communicative tasks and topics necessary for survival in target-language cultures. These tasks include personal information related to self, family, home, daily activities, interests, and personal preferences, as well as physical and social needs such as food, shopping, and travel.	Expresses personal meaning, creating with language in the present time frame by combining and recombining known language. Successfully handles a number of uncomplicated communicative tasks and topics necessary for survival in target-language cultures.	Uses mostly memorized language with some attempts to express personal meaning. Relies heavily on learned phrases or recombinations of these. Handles a limited number of uncomplicated communicative tasks involving topics related to basic personal information and some activities, preferences, and immediate needs.

CRITERIA	EXCEEDS EXPECTATIONS Intermediate-High 4 points	MEETS EXPECTATIONS STRONG Intermediate-Mid 3 points	MINIMAL Intermediate-Low 2 points	DOES NOT MEET EXPECTATIONS Novice-High 1 point
Text Type Quantity and organization of language discourse on a continuum from words to phrases to sentences to connected sentences to paragraphs to extended discourse	Uses mostly connected sentences, with some paragraph-length discourse, but not consistently.	Uses sentences and strings of sentences, with some complex sentences (dependent clauses).	Uses short and discrete sentences.	Uses short, sometimes incomplete sentences and memorized phrases.
Comprehensibility Types of listeners/readers who can understand the learner's language, on a continuum from sympathetic interlocutors accustomed to the speech/writing of language learners to target language speakers unaccustomed to the speech/writing of such learners	Is generally understood by those unaccustomed to the speech/writing of language learners, although interference from another language may be evident and gaps in communication may occur.	Is generally understood by those accustomed to the speech/writing of language learners.	Is generally understood by those accustomed to the speech/writing of language learners, although additional effort may be required.	Is understood with occasional difficulty by those accustomed to the speech/writing of language learners, although additional effort may be required.
Language Control Degree of grammatical accuracy, appropriate vocabulary use, and fluency	Demonstrates significant quantity and quality of Intermediate-level language. When attempting to perform Advanced-level tasks, there is breakdown in one or more of the following areas: the ability to narrate and describe in the major time frames of present, past, and future; use of paragraph-length discourse; fluency; breadth of vocabulary.	Demonstrates significant quantity and quality of Intermediate-level language when performing Intermediate-level tasks in mostly the present time frame. Accuracy and/or fluency decreases when attempting to perform functions or handle topics at the Advanced level.	Demonstrates some accuracy when producing simple sentences in the present time frame. Pronunciation, vocabulary, and syntax are strongly influenced by the first language. Maintains the functions of the Intermediate level, although just barely.	Demonstrates some accuracy with memorized language and stock phrases. Pronunciation, vocabulary, and syntax are strongly influenced by the first language. Accuracy decreases when attempting to handle topics and perform functions pertaining to the Intermediate level.

CRITERIA	EXCEEDS EXPECTATIONS Intermediate-High 4 points	MEETS EXPECTATIONS		DOES NOT MEET EXPECTATIONS Novice-High 1 point
		STRONG Intermediate-Mid 3 points	MINIMAL Intermediate-Low 2 points	
INTERCULTURAL COMMUNICATION AND IMPACT CRITERIA				
Intercultural Communication: Present Learner's ability to investigate products and practices and connect them to cultural perspectives appropriately in a presentation	Presentation appropriately includes cultural products and practices and integrates them with cultural perspectives.	Presentation appropriately includes some cultural products and/or practices and connects them to at least one cultural perspective.	Presentation appropriately includes some cultural products and/or practices.	Presentation includes a few cultural products and/or practices.
Impact of Written/Oral Presentation Clarity, organization, and depth of the written/oral presentation; the degree to which the presentation maintains the audience's attention and interest	Presented in a clear and organized manner. Presentation maintains audience interest through organization of the written/oral text, some details, and an unexpected feature.	Presented in a clear and organized manner. Presentation maintains audience interest through organization of the written/oral text and some details.	Presented in a clear, mostly organized manner. Some effort to maintain audience interest through organization of the written/oral text and/or a few details.	Presentation may be either unclear or unorganized. Minimal to no effort to maintain audience interest.
Impact of Multimodal Presentation Clarity, organization, and depth of the presentation; the degree to which the presentation maintains the audience's attention and interest; and the use of multimodal design (such as video, pictures, objects, graphs, diagrams, tables)	Presented in a clear and organized manner. Presentation maintains audience interest through organization, some details, and an unexpected feature. Integrates appropriate multimedia that heighten the effectiveness of the message conveyed in the presentation.	Presented in a clear and organized manner. Presentation maintains audience interest through organization and some details. Integrates appropriate multimedia that support the message conveyed in the presentation.	Presented in a clear, mostly organized manner. Some effort to maintain audience interest through organization and/or a few details. Integrates at least one example of appropriate multimedia that provides some support of the message conveyed in the presentation.	Presentation may be either unclear or unorganized. Minimal to no effort to maintain audience interest. May include one example of visual support.

SELECT BY PRESENTATION TYPE

Evidence of strengths: _____

_____

_____

Examples of where you could improve:_____

_____

_____

Other comments: _____

_____

_____

Integrated Performance Assessment Presentational Mode Rubric: Intermediate-High Learner

CRITERIA	EXCEEDS EXPECTATIONS Advanced-Low 4 points	MEETS EXPECTATIONS STRONG Intermediate-High 3 points	MEETS EXPECTATIONS MINIMAL Intermediate-Mid 2 points	DOES NOT MEET EXPECTATIONS Intermediate-Low 1 point
LANGUAGE PROFICIENCY/PERFORMANCE CRITERIA				
Language Functions Language tasks the speaker/writer is able to handle in a consistent, comfortable, sustained, and spontaneous manner	Can communicate on familiar topics and some topics related to employment, current events, and matters of public interest. Consistently narrates and describes in the major time frames of present, past, and future. Can handle appropriately the linguistic challenges presented by a complication or an unexpected turn of events.	Successfully handles uncomplicated tasks requiring basic information related to work, school, recreation, particular interests, and areas of competence. Narrates and describes in the major time frames of present, past, and future, although not consistently.	Expresses personal meaning by creating with language in mostly the present time frame, in part by combining and recombining known language. Successfully handles a variety of uncomplicated communicative tasks and topics necessary for survival in target-language cultures. These tasks include personal information related to self, family, home, daily activities, interests, and personal preferences, as well as physical and social needs such as food, shopping, and travel.	Expresses personal meaning, creating with language in the present time frame by combining and recombining known language. Successfully handles a number of uncomplicated communicative tasks and topics necessary for survival in target-language cultures.

CRITERIA	EXCEEDS EXPECTATIONS Advanced-Low 4 points	MEETS EXPECTATIONS		DOES NOT MEET EXPECTATIONS Intermediate-Low 1 point
		STRONG Intermediate-High 3 points	MINIMAL Intermediate-Mid 2 points	
Text Type Quantity and organization of language discourse on a continuum from words to phrases to sentences to connected sentences to paragraphs to extended discourse	Uses connected discourse of paragraph length, but responses may not be substantive. Discourse tends to reflect the oral/written paragraph structure of the first language rather than that of the target language.	Uses mostly connected sentences, with some paragraph-length discourse, but not consistently.	Uses sentences and strings of sentences, with some complex sentences (dependent clauses).	Uses short and discrete sentences.
Comprehensibility Types of listeners/readers who can understand the learner's language, on a continuum from sympathetic interlocutors accustomed to the speech/writing of language learners to target language speakers unaccustomed to the speech/writing of such learners	Is understood by target language speakers, even those unaccustomed to the speech/writing of language learners, although this may require some additional effort.	Is generally understood by those unaccustomed to the speech/writing of language learners, although interference from another language may be evident and a pattern of gaps in communication may occur.	Is generally understood by those accustomed to the speech/writing of language learners.	Is generally understood by those accustomed to the speech/writing of language learners, although additional effort may be required.
Language Control Degree of grammatical accuracy, appropriate vocabulary use, and fluency	Performs Advanced-level tasks, albeit with minimal fluency and some control of aspect in narrating in the major time frames of present, past and future. Vocabulary may lack specificity. Narration and description tend to be handled separately rather than interwoven.	Demonstrates significant quantity and quality of Intermediate-level language. When attempting to perform Advanced-level tasks, there is breakdown in one or more of the following areas: the ability to narrate and describe in the major time frames of present, past, and future; use of paragraph-length discourse; fluency; breadth of vocabulary.	Demonstrates significant quantity and quality of Intermediate-level language when performing Intermediate-level tasks in mostly the present time frame. Accuracy and/or fluency decreases when attempting to perform functions or handle topics at the Advanced level.	Demonstrates some accuracy when producing simple sentences in the present time frame. Pronunciation, vocabulary, and syntax are strongly influenced by the first language. Maintains the functions of the Intermediate level, although just barely.

CRITERIA	EXCEEDS EXPECTATIONS Advanced-Low 4 points	MEETS EXPECTATIONS		DOES NOT MEET EXPECTATIONS Intermediate-Low 1 point
		STRONG Intermediate-High 3 points	MINIMAL Intermediate-Mid 2 points	
INTERCULTURAL COMMUNICATION AND IMPACT CRITERIA				
Intercultural Communication: Present Learner's ability to investigate products and practices and connect them to cultural perspectives appropriately in a presentation	Presentation appropriately includes cultural products and practices and integrates them with cultural perspectives.	Presentation appropriately includes some cultural products and/or practices and connects them to at least one cultural perspective.	Presentation appropriately includes some cultural products and/or practices.	Presentation includes a few cultural products and/or practices.
SELECT BY PRESENTATION TYPE — **Impact of Written/Oral Presentation** Clarity, organization, and depth of the written/oral presentation; the degree to which the presentation maintains the audience's attention and interest	Presented in a clear and organized manner. Presentation maintains audience interest through organization of the written/oral text, some details, and an unexpected feature.	Presented in a clear and organized manner. Presentation maintains audience interest through organization of the written/oral text and some details.	Presented in a clear, mostly organized manner. Some effort to maintain audience interest through organization of the written/oral text and/or a few details.	Presentation may be either unclear or unorganized. Minimal to no effort to maintain audience interest.
Impact of Multimodal Presentation Clarity, organization, and depth of the presentation; the degree to which the presentation maintains the audience's attention and interest; and the use of multimodal design (such as video, pictures, objects, graphs, diagrams, tables)	Presented in a clear and organized manner. Presentation maintains audience interest through organization, some details, and an unexpected feature. Integrates appropriate multimedia that heighten the effectiveness of the message conveyed in the presentation.	Presented in a clear and organized manner. Presentation maintains audience interest through organization and some details. Integrates appropriate multimedia that support the message conveyed in the presentation.	Presented in a clear, mostly organized manner. Some effort to maintain audience interest through organization and/or a few details. Integrates at least one example of appropriate multimedia that provides some support of the message conveyed in the presentation.	Presentation may be either unclear or unorganized. Minimal to no effort to maintain audience interest. May include one example of visual support.

Evidence of strengths: _____
_____
_____

Examples of where you could improve:_____
_____
_____

Other comments: _____
_____
_____

Integrated Performance Assessment Presentational Mode Rubric: Advanced Learner

CRITERIA	EXCEEDS EXPECTATIONS Advanced-High 4 points	MEETS EXPECTATIONS		DOES NOT MEET EXPECTATIONS Intermediate-High 1 point
		STRONG Advanced-Mid 3 points	MINIMAL Advanced-Low 2 points	
LANGUAGE PROFICIENCY/PERFORMANCE CRITERIA				
Language Functions Language tasks the speaker/writer is able to handle in a consistent, comfortable, sustained, and spontaneous manner	Can communicate on some abstract topics, especially those related to particular interests and expertise. Narrates and describes fully and accurately in the major time frames of present, past, and future. May provide a structured argument to support opinions and may construct hypotheses.	Can communicate on a variety of concrete topics relating to work, school, home, and leisure activities, as well as topics relating to events of current, public, and personal interest or individual relevance. Narrates and describes in the major time frames of present, past, and future by providing a full account. Can handle successfully and with relative ease the linguistic challenges presented by a complication or an unexpected turn of events.	Can communicate on familiar topics and some topics related to employment, current events, and matters of public interest. Consistently narrates and describes in the major time frames of present, past, and future. Can handle appropriately the linguistic challenges presented by a complication or an unexpected turn of events.	Successfully handles uncomplicated tasks requiring basic information related to work, school, recreation, particular interests, and areas of competence. Narrates and describes in the major time frames of present, past, and future, although not consistently.

CRITERIA	EXCEEDS EXPECTATIONS Advanced-High 4 points	MEETS EXPECTATIONS		DOES NOT MEET EXPECTATIONS Intermediate-High 1 point
		STRONG Advanced-Mid 3 points	MINIMAL Advanced-Low 2 points	
Text Type Quantity and organization of language discourse on a continuum from words to phrases to sentences to connected sentences to paragraphs to extended discourse	Uses paragraph-length discourse and some extended discourse.	Uses connected, paragraph-length discourse. Discourse may still reflect the oral/written paragraph structure of the first language rather than that of the target language.	Uses connected discourse of paragraph length, but responses may not be substantive. Discourse tends to reflect the oral/written paragraph structure of the first language rather than that of the target language.	Uses mostly connected sentences, with some paragraph-length discourse, but not consistently.
Comprehensibility Types of listeners/readers who can understand the learner's language, on a continuum from sympathetic interlocutors accustomed to the speech/writing of language learners to target language speakers unaccustomed to the speech/writing of such learners	Is readily understood by target language speakers unaccustomed to the speech/writing of language learners.	Is generally understood by target language speakers unaccustomed to the speech/writing of language learners.	Is understood by target language speakers, even those unaccustomed to the speech/writing of language learners, although this may require some additional effort.	Is generally understood by those unaccustomed to the speech/writing of language learners, although interference from another language may be evident and a pattern of gaps in communication may occur.
Language Control Degree of grammatical accuracy, appropriate vocabulary use, and fluency	Demonstrates full control of aspect in narrating in the major time frames of present, past, and future. Uses precise vocabulary and intonation and often shows great fluency and ease of speech. Accuracy may break down when attempting to perform the complex tasks associated with the Superior level over a variety of topics.	Demonstrates good control of aspect in narrating in the major time frames of present, past, and future. Has substantial fluency and extensive vocabulary. Narration and description tend to be combined and interwoven. The quality and/or quantity of speech generally declines when attempting to perform functions or handle topics associated with the Superior level.	Performs Advanced-level tasks, albeit with minimal fluency and some control of aspect in narrating in the major time frames of present, past, and future. Vocabulary may lack specificity. Narration and description tend to be handled separately rather than interwoven.	Demonstrates significant quantity and quality of Intermediate-level language. When attempting to perform Advanced-level tasks, there is breakdown in one or more of the following areas: the ability to narrate and describe in the major time frames of present, past, and future; use of paragraph-length discourse; fluency; breadth of vocabulary.

| CRITERIA | EXCEEDS EXPECTATIONS Advanced-High 4 points | MEETS EXPECTATIONS | | DOES NOT MEET EXPECTATIONS Intermediate-High 1 point |
		STRONG Advanced-Mid 3 points	MINIMAL Advanced-Low 2 points	
INTERCULTURAL COMMUNICATION AND IMPACT CRITERIA				
Intercultural Communication: Present Learner's ability to investigate products and practices and connect them to cultural perspectives appropriately in a presentation	Presentation appropriately includes cultural products and practices and integrates them with cultural perspectives.	Presentation appropriately includes some cultural products and/or practices and connects them to at least one cultural perspective.	Presentation appropriately includes some cultural products and/or practices.	Presentation includes a few cultural products and/or practices.
Impact of Written/Oral Presentation Clarity, organization, and depth of the written/oral presentation; the degree to which the presentation maintains the audience's attention and interest	Presented in a clear and organized manner. Presentation maintains audience interest through organization of the written/oral text, some details, and an unexpected feature.	Presented in a clear and organized manner. Presentation maintains audience interest through organization of the written/oral text and some details.	Presented in a clear, mostly organized manner. Some effort to maintain audience interest through organization of the written/oral text and/or a few details.	Presentation may be either unclear or unorganized. Minimal to no effort to maintain audience interest.
Impact of Multimodal Presentation Clarity, orga-nization, and depth of the presentation; the degree to which the presentation maintains the audience's attention and interest; and the use of multimodal design (such as video, pictures, objects, graphs, diagrams, tables)	Presented in a clear and organized manner. Presentation maintains audience interest through organization, some details, and an unexpected feature. Integrates appropriate multimedia that heighten the effectiveness of the message conveyed in the presentation.	Presented in a clear and organized manner. Presentation maintains audience interest through organization and some details. Integrates appropriate multimedia that support the message conveyed in the presentation.	Presented in a clear, mostly organized manner. Some effort to maintain audience interest through organization and/or a few details. Integrates at least one example of appropriate multimedia that provides some support of the message conveyed in the presentation.	Presentation may be either unclear or unorganized. Minimal to no effort to maintain audience interest. May include one example of visual support.

The left side of the table is labeled vertically: **SELECT BY PRESENTATION TYPE**

Evidence of strengths: _____
_____
_____

Examples of where you could improve:_____
_____
_____

Other comments: _____
_____
_____

Presentational Rubric Score Conversion Chart: Assigning Percentages and Grades	
Raw Rubric Score	Grade Conversion by Percentage
24	100
23	98
22	96
21	94
20	91
19	89
18	87
17	85
16	83
15	81
14	78
13	76
12	74
11	72
10	70
9	68
8	65
7	63
6	61
5	59
4	57
3	55
2	52
1	50

Note: A zero (0) for a given criterion would be given only if the learner had no performance that corresponded to that criterion.

These conversions are based upon this rubric formula:
(Total points x 52)/24 + 48 = _____%.
Lowest passing score: 60%; to use a different passing score, go to http://www.roobrix.com

Appendix G
Tus hábitos tecnológicos - Los móviles y las redes sociales (Learning activity from Unit on Social Media & Bullying by Jesse Carnevali)

¿Con qué frecuencia usas tu móvil?

 -nunca

 -menos de una hora

 -1-2 horas al día

 -2-3 horas al día

 -3-4 horas al día

 -más de 4 horas al día

¿Para qué usas tu móvil? ¿Qué te gusta hacer con tu móvil?

_____

_____

¿Con qué frecuencia usas las redes sociales?

 -siempre (todos los días)

 -cinco a seis días a la semana

 -tres a cuatro días a la semana

 -uno o dos días a la semana

 -nunca (no uso las redes sociales)

Identifica las redes sociales que usas:

 -Instagram

 -Facebook

 -Tiktok

 -Twitter

 -YouTube

 -Snapchat

 -Otras no mencionadas →

 -¡Ningunas!

Cuando usas las redes sociales, ¿qué haces? ¿Haces cosas diferentes con las redes sociales diferentes?

_____

_____

_____

¿Crees que las redes sociales son necesarias?

   -Sí

   -No

¿Qué haces con más frecuencia?

   -Hablar con familia y amigos por mi móvil (mensajes de texto, las redes sociales, etc.)

   -Hablar con familia y amigos en persona

¿Es posible vivir una vida feliz e interesante sin los móviles y las redes sociales?

   -Sí

   -No

Appendix H

Feedback Loop: Key Features of the Cyclical Approach Explicit vs Co-Constructive Feedback for the Interpretive Mode

by Bonnie Adair-Hauck, Ph.D.

The feedback loop is an excellent opportunity to assist the students' understanding of the interpretive text before they go to the next phase of the IPA. Additionally, if the teacher provides responsive assistance during the feedback loop, the students can gain a better understanding of **how to improve their performance on the next IPA.**

After the teacher has corrected the students' responses for the interpretive tasks, s/he is equipped with a comprehensive understanding of which tasks the *students can perform on their own,* and which tasks are challenging and require *responsive assistance on the part of the teacher.* For example, after correcting the interpretive responses, the teacher notices that many of the students did well on two sections of intermediate level tasks: main idea and supporting details. However, the students did not perform nearly as well on the "guessing meaning from context" tasks. Enlightened with this critical information, the teacher has a rich opportunity to work within the students' *zone of proximal development during the feedback loop.* Recall that learners bring two levels of cognitive development when faced with problem-solving tasks: an actual level, that is, tasks which they can perform unassisted; and a potential developmental level, which denotes what students may be able to do with assistance. Vygotsky defined the ZPD as "the distance between the learner's actual developmental level as determined by independent problem-solving (unassisted performance) and the level of potential development as determined through problem-solving under adult guidance or more capable peers (assisted performance)." Vygotsky, 1978, p. 86.

In other words, enlightened by the IPA interpretive responses, the teacher now understands which tasks the students can *perform by themselves,* and *which tasks require assistance.* With this information, the teacher can set the stage for an enriching instructional interaction during the feedback loop.

Using assisting questions, and cognitive probes (Tharp & Gallimore, 1988), the teacher guides the students to become more aware of the various reading strategies that may be used to solve interpretive tasks. The feedback loop will be more beneficial and productive if the teacher provides cognitively challenging and co-constructive feedback rather than explicit feedback (Adair-Hauck and Donato, 1994). The following two protocols highlight the differences between explicit and responsive/co-constructive teacher feedback. The protocols refer to the French Intermediate IPA on "Your Health".

Explicit Teacher Feedback

(T) Most of you had difficulty with Section III, "Guessing Meaning from Context". We better go over these. Who knows the answer to Question 1, "en allumant"? It can be found in the first paragraph. Jeff?

(S1) "I didn't get that one".

(T) OK. Susan?

(S2) I think it means "opening".

(T) No, it doesn't mean "opening". "En ouvrant" means "while opening" that's in the sentence above. Trevor, you did well on this section. What's your answer.

(S3) "I put down 'while lighting".

(T) Correct. It comes from the verb – "allumer" which means "to light" or in this case, "turn on or light the lamps". OK. Let's go on to number 2. Annie?

(S4) I didn't get that one. Ok. Sam?

Responsive and Co-Constructive Feedback to Improve Student Performance

(T) Most of the class had difficulty with Section III – "Guessing Meaning from Context." This is a difficult section, and that is why it is considered to be a task that falls into the "exceeds expectations" category. But if you want to become better readers, we need to have strategies for guessing meaning from context. Let's try to figure out how to solve these "guessing meaning from context" questions so that you'll do better the next time.

(T) Look at question 1, "en allumant" which is in the first paragraph. How can we try to guess the meaning of that word? First, think to yourselves about some ways that you can make an educative guess about the meaning of this word. (give students some time to reflect on possible strategies).

(T) OK. Any suggestions on how we can guess the meaning of this word? Julie?

(S1) I looked at the picture right next to that paragraph. It's morning time. The woman is opening the curtain, she's letting in the sunlight.

(T) Yes. Good strategy. There's a picture to support your understanding and to help you understand the meaning of this paragraph.

(T) Other suggestions for ways to find the answer? Ray?

(S2) I think it's a verb. It looks like a verb.

(T) Good clue. Yes, it is a verb, and if it's a verb it's referring to what, Ray?

(S2) Oh, an action, a verb refers to some sort of action.

(T) Yes, what makes you think that it's a verb or action word, Ray?

(S2) It's preceded by the little word "en" just like "en ouvrant" which is in the same sentence. I know "en ouvant" means "while opening", but I'm not sure of "en allumant".

(T) We're on the right track. It's definitely a verb or an action word. There's still another reading strategy that can help us solve this question. What else can we do to try to guess the meaning of the new words, besides looking at the pictures and figuring out the part of speech? Jake?

(S3) I looked at the other words in the sentence: "en allumant les halogènes". I know that "halogènes" means "lights" or lamps in English—and it makes sense "to light", or "turn on the lamps", in the morning.

(T) Exactly. You looked at the other words in the sentence and guessed what would make sense from those contextual clues. We're starting to understand that there are multiple ways for trying to guess the meanings of these words. I'm curious too. Do any of you see a connection between a word in the subtitle and "en allumant"? Larry?

(S4) "Lumineuse" and "allumant"?

(T) Yes, that's it. Now what's the connection?

(S4) They both have the stem "lum".

(T) Good – and can anyone think of an English word with "lum" that we use frequently around the holidays.

(SS) A few students respond in unison "luminaries!".

(T) Great. You're catching on now. Now, let's try number 2. First, take a minute to reflect and see if you can find the meaning of the word: "tartiné". Share your predictions with a neighbor.

Commentary: The explicit feedback protocol exemplifies a didactic or "automatic" exchange with questions that mainly assess students' knowledge. With these types of questions, the students are given little opportunity to improve their performance from the feedback. On the other hand, the responsive and co-constructive feedback protocol represents joint problem-solving on the part of the teacher and learners. To do so, the teacher scaffolds the task by using both assisting as well as assessing questions (see definitions below). The teacher scaffolds the problem by holding the task difficulty constant, while simplifying the students' role by means of graduated assistance (Greenfield, 1984). This scaffolded assistance allows that learners to participate in activities that would be too difficult to perform without assistance from an expert or more capable peer.

As Vygotsky reminds us: "Teaching is effective only when it *awakens and rouses to life those functions which are in a stage of maturing, which lie in the zone of proximal development. Teaching must be aimed not so much at the ripe, but at the ripening functions.* (italics in original)" Vygotsky, 1986, p. 278.

(reprinted from the first *ACTFL Integrated Performance Assessment Manual* (Glisan at al., 2003), p. 12-15)

*** "assessing question: inquires to discover the student's ability to perform without assistance (e.g., to establish what the students may remember from yesterday's lesson)." Tharp and Gallimore, 1988, p. 59.

*** "assisting question: inquires in order to produce a cognitive operation that the learner can not or will not produce alone. The assistance provided by the question prompts the mental operation" Tharp and Gallimore, 1988, p. 60.

Appendix I
Sample Co-Constructive Feedback for "Does Not Meet Expectations"

Communication Standard 1.1 – Interpersonal Communication, Intermediate Level

T: So based on what we've just watched, where would you put yourself, um, starting at the top [of the rubric]?

> Assisting question to encourage student to self-assess

S: Well basically everything I said was memorized from the paper that I had written up about her for my biography.

T: Okay

S: For text type, again they're just kind of memorized phrases that I just saw. Like I kind of like just saw it quickly and just tried to remember what it was. Remembering like the wording of it.

> Student acknowledges text type limited to memorized phrases

T: Okay. And what could you do to prepare? To be able to talk more about her?

> Assisting question to encourage student to think of strategies to prepare for task

S: Well one thing I'm not really sure how to do is like… because I don't really know her…at all all. So, I…I haven't really seen any movies with her in them. So I don't even know who she is.

> Student notes his lack of knowledge

T: Uh huh.

S: And all I know is the information that I found out on the internet. So, I'm not really sure how I can like expand on who she is because I have no idea…like…I've never heard of her before.

> Again student notes his lack of content

T: Okay. So, what made you choose her?

> Assisting question on why student chose this famous person

S: What made? Well because I looked up…I just typed in "French celebrities" and a big list came up and I just picked her name from the list.

> Student states it was by chance

T: Okay. So, knowing that there are, for example, at (local video rental store) two films that you could rent what could you do to prep(pare)?

> Teacher providing "hints" about movies and assisting question on how student could prepare

S: Go watch them.

> Student is co-constructing strategies and plans

T: And as you're watching them, what will you be looking for?

> Assisting question to guide student "thinking" as he is watching the film

S: Personal qualities and traits and things like that I guess.

> Student co-constructing plan

T: Okay. And um…what as…so if you watch one or two of her movies, what could you then bring back this conversation?

> Assisting question on content of film

S: Um…the kind of actor she is. The kind of roles she plays.

> Student co-constructing plan

T: Okay. And what else? How could you…what about what is actually happening in the movie?

> Assisting question to help student think about plot of the film

S: Like what? What do you mean?

> Clarification question by student

T: Um…could you talk about the film as well? — **Teacher provides answer regarding plot of film**

S: Yeah. Yeah. Most likely. — **Student agrees**

T: How would you do that? — **Assisting question to encourage student**

S: I would just be like, "At this part, she was like this" or whatever. — **Student co-constructing plan**

T: Alright. So you could just narrate an interesting part of the film. — **Teacher assisting by expanding idea**

S: Yeah

T: Ah…coming down here (points to the Communication Strategies row of the rubric), did you, ah, did you ask any questions? — **Teacher focuses on Communication Strategies**

S: No, she basically like made sure that she was using really simple things so that I would understand her.

T: Okay. So, I…the other thing is I think you'll definitely have a different partner the next time that you do it.

S: Yeah so I'll have to ask more questions. — **Student acknowledging that he will have to ask more questions**

T: Right. So you'd have to ask more questions and depending on…So it would be interesting to see how it goes with someone who…is…and able to fill in a lot of gaps for you.

S: As opposed to a person who doesn't know how to do that much.

T: So your plan to prep[are] is what? — **Assessing question to encourage student to recap plan to succeed**

S: I'll go rent *The Da Vinci Code*. — **Student states how to start plan**

T: Okay. And there's also the film *Amélie*. — **Teacher co-constructing plan**

S: Mm hmm.

T: Okay? Um. And…that would be another good one to check out.

S: Okay.

T: Okay? And we'll give it another shot.

Appendix J
Transcript for Interpretive Listening Task "Hola, 911. Dígame ¿cuál es su emergencia?"

IPA on Providing Emergency Room Care (Spanish, Intermediate-High)

Created by Sarah Peceny and Eva Rodríguez-González, Department of Spanish and Portuguese, University of New Mexico

Note: This transcription of the audio is for instructor reference. Learners DO NOT see the transcript.

Hola, 911. Dígame ¿cuál es su emergencia?

MUJER: Hola ¿Es el 911? Necesito ayuda por favor. Tuvimos un accidente. Y mi novio está…. está sangrando por todas partes. ¡Creo que tiene una pierna rota!

TELEOPERADOR: Tranquila, señorita. Dígame, ¿cuál es su nombre, por favor?

MUJER: Sí, María González Serrano.

TELEOPERADOR: ¿Dónde se encuentra ahora mismo?

MUJER: Estamos en el medio de la carretera. Lo que pasa es que chocamos y la moto salió disparada. Mi novio está al otro lado. Yo tuve suerte… Creo que estoy bien, pero él se ve muy mal…

TELEOPERADOR: Por favor, tenga calma. Le enviaremos ayuda en unos minutos, pero necesito saber exactamente su localización. Dígame, ¿a dónde se dirigían ustedes en el momento del accidente? ¿Qué tipo de carretera es? ¿Qué hay a su alrededor? ¿Puede ver algún edificio cerca?

MUJER: La verdad, ¡no estoy segura! Solo hay una vía. No soy de acá, y no le puedo decir. Estábamos de vacaciones en la ciudad de Santo Domingo y hace más o menos una hora dejamos el hotel para ir a la playa. Lo único que veo por aquí es una casita blanca que tiene un puente de madera. Ay, ¡no sé qué decirle más! No conozco este lugar.

TELEOPERADOR: No se preocupe. Todo lo que me dice es muy útil. Creo que ya tengo una idea de dónde están. Es importante que esté tranquila en estos momentos. En unos minutos llegará la asistencia médica allá. Mientras tanto, ¿me puede decir qué pasó exactamente?

MUJER: Un coche nos adelantó y de repente frenó y, y sin darme cuenta, me encontré tirada en la hierba. Tengo un poquito de sangre, pero estoy bien. Mi novio está atrapado entre el auto y la moto y grita que le duele, pero no sé qué es. Por favor, ¡ayúdenos!

TELEOPERADOR: Sí, claro. Dígame, ¿su novio puede respirar? ¿Él está consciente?

MUJER: Sí, yo estoy aquí a su lado. Está respirando, pero dice que tiene mucho dolor.

TELEOPERADOR: ¿Hace cuánto tiempo que ocurrió el accidente?

MUJER: Hace unos minutos… ¡No sé! 4, 5 minutos.

TELEOPERADOR: ¿Y el otro auto? ¿Sabe si hay otras personas heridas allí?

MUJER: Bueno, solo está el conductor, y creo que él está bien.

TELEOPERADOR: Ok, no corte, por favor. Le voy a transferir la llamada a un doctor para que le pueda asistir mientras llega la ambulancia. Él le guiará para que usted pueda hacer los primeros auxilios.

MUJER: Sí, gracias. Mi novio no se puede mover y está sangrando mucho… ay Dios mío… ¿Le pongo algo en la pierna? ¿Qué hago? ¡Por favor!

TELEOPERADOR: Le ruego que mantenga la calma, señorita. Le comunico inmediatamente con el doctor. La ambulancia ya va en camino…

Permissions and Credits

The authors wish to thank the following persons and publishers for permission to use their articles or illustrations included in this publication.

Chapter 4

Page 31–32: G. Wiggins and J. McTighe (2005). *Understanding by design* (expanded 2nd ed.). Alexandria, VA: Association for Supervision and Curriculum Development (ASCD). Template adapted and reprinted by permission of ASCD.

Page 42: Antonio-Manuel Rodríguez-García. "¿Cómo sé si padezco 'nomofobia', miedo irracional a no tener el móvil (ni WhatsApp)?" *The Conversation*, October 4, 2021. Reprinted under Creative Commons license. Retrieved from https://theconversation.com/como-se-si-padezco-nomofobia-miedo-irracional-a-no-tener-el-movil-ni-whatsapp-168028

Chapter 6

Page 60, 63–64 Images from *WG-Gesucht* reproduced by permission of WG-Gesucht, Stuttgart, Germany.

Page 70: Image reproduced by permission of Akishima Kodomo Cooking. Retrieved from http://www.akishimapapa.net/shoku/index.html

Page 80: Beatriz del Carmen Quintana Velázquez. "Caso clínico Nº MQ/29/48/1258-001560." SalusPlay, July 8 2018. Image reproduced by permission of *SalusPlay*. Retrieved from https://www.salusplay.com/casos-clinicos-de-enfermeria/MQ_29_48_1258-001560

Page 92. Salam Al Mardi. "بطالة الشباب في الدول العربية". January 10, 2022. Text reproduced by permission of author.

Page 96. Díana Mateo. "Una carta abierta a mi comunidad Latinx." Image and text reproduced by permission of Díana Mateo & Benach and Collopy, Washington, DC. Retrieved from https://www.benachcollopy.com/2020/06/una-carta-abierta-a-mi-comunidad-latinx-de-diana-mateo/